THE ESSENTIAL
GERMAN
SHEPHERD
DOG

ROY AND CLARISSA ALLAN

RINGPRESS

RINGPRESS

Published by Ringpress Books Ltd,
Spirella House, Bridge Road,
Letchworth, Herts, SG6 4ET, United Kingdom.

Discounts available for bulk orders
Contact the Special Sales Manager at
the above address. Telephone (0462) 674177

Distributed to the Book Trade in the United Kingdom by
Bookpoint Ltd.
39 Milton Park, Abingdon, Oxon OX14 4TD
Telephone 0235 835001

First Published 1994
© 1994 ROY & CLARISSA ALLAN

ISBN 0 948955 13 9

Printed and bound in Singapore by Kyodo Printing Co.

CONTENTS

Search articles) Schutzhund; (Dumbbells; Bite-bars; Sleeves; Protective suiting; Whips; Hides); Obedience.

ACKNOWLEDGEMENTS

We are grateful to the Verein fur Deutsche Schäferhunde (SV) for permission to print archive material. We are indebted to those who loaned or took photographs, especially Mrs Stephanie Holbrook, who spent much time and effort taking photographs for the working side and on the Standard.

To our three handlers for establishing on that occasion a 'working scenario': Mesdames Ann Munks, Chris Gregory and Jill Wells with Indi, Zak and Polly – all our thanks.

Many photos were provided by Messrs Eric Stuttard, Jack Oliver and David Banyard – in fact the breed's most prominent dogs. Sadly, only a small number could be used, which in itself involved a painful task of selection in order to comply with the confines of space in this book.

Mr William E. Perry gave generously of his time helping us with his profound knowledge of GSD history and official records, especially Kör and Zuchtbücher. His advice was, and is, of inestimable value, and was greatly appreciated.

To those overseas correspondents who went to the trouble of sending us research material and photos of the GSD in their various countries, our deepest thanks. Some material arrived too late to be included. This was a pity, but the printing schedule could not be changed.

SOUTH AFRICA: We are especially grateful to Mrs Angela Ewart-Brookes for collating information and photos received from many sources in her country, then arranging everything in a logical and orderly fashion before despatch to us; Miss Carol Wilson provided us with valuable information on the SA working scene; lastly, we are indebted to Mr Mike Sullivan for updating us on the recent changes in the SA breed relationship with the international GSD community.

AUSTRALIA: Mr Louis Donald provided us with enough material to write a separate book on the Australian GSD. We hope he will understand and forgive us if he feels that we did not do justice to the theme. This was due to lack of space! But, in any case, thank you Louis.

NORWAY: Mrs Mimi Lønnum could not have been more helpful in obtaining for us much valuable information about the breed and working schedule in her country.

USA: The American GSD scene is a big subject, but we hope we achieved adequate coverage by including not only material from the GSD Club of America, in the person of Dr Carmen Batttaglia, President of GSDCA, who took a personal interest in the progress of this book. New and original material on Schutzhund in the USA, hitherto unpublished in any book on the breed, was given freely by the President of the United Schutzhund Clubs of America (USA) Mr Paul Meloy. Dr Morton Goldfarb, SV judging colleague, gave unstintingly of his views, which were at once penetrating and absolutely fair minded.

To all our overseas contributors, our profound thanks.

We owe a debt of gratitude to Dr Malcolm Willis and to Mr Eric Roberts for their expert contributions on Genetics and Protection Work respectively, without which the book would have been incomplete.

Last but not least, our grateful thanks to our secretary Mrs Barbara McManus, who managed to decipher our handwriting, tapes and typescript in order to get the book on to computer disks in time to meet the deadlines.

Clarissa and Roy Allan.

Chapter One

EARLY DAYS OF THE BREED

Nearly a hundred years after the breed's foundation, enthusiasts of the German Shepherd Dog can with good reason feel proud of an achievement, probably unmatched by any other breed: the largest contingent of operational dogs in the police, armed services and security firms; a sizeable representation in mountain rescue, drug detection and guide dogs for the blind; a large show contingent in most countries, not to mention an overwhelming presence in working trials and in the sport of Schutzhund. In addition, the German Shepherd Dog is still the most popular companion/guard dog, ministering to his family charges and protecting them from intruders, just as his ancestors did – in fact, still do – while guarding the flocks on the plains and hills of Germany from time immemorial.

It is fascinating to speculate on how this extraordinary success has been achieved, especially when many breeds of dog no longer perform the function for which they were originally created, simply because modern, urbanised society has meant the phasing out of many activities associated with certain breeds. How many Deerhounds hunt? Are Corgis still used with cattle? Do we still hear the baying of Bloodhounds, except perhaps in television or film drama or when they 'hunt the clean boot' at trials? Competition enters into the reckoning. The Dobermann and Rottweiler have been tried out by the police but they have never been likely to replace the German Shepherd, although these two breeds may have excelled respectively in certain skills such as tracking and protection work. Gundogs, particularly Springers Spaniels and Labrador Retrievers, have made inroads into drug detection, and guide dogs are mostly recruited from Labradors and Golden Retrievers, but by and large, the German Shepherd remains supreme as the all-round working dog. Was it just luck that the German Shepherd happened to be around when the need arose for certain tasks to be performed? Such a view would be mistaken, because the success of the German Shepherd depended not on luck but on careful planning and the creation of a structure to direct the breed and its future development.

REGIONAL SHEPHERD DOGS
If the German Shepherd as we know it is only about one hundred years old, then we must realise that its forbears, the regional shepherd dogs, go back centuries. Type and conformation varied according to the terrain and the movement patterns of the flocks for which the breed was responsible. In the hilly regions of South Germany, the need was for a dog with large bone and great strength in the hindquarters, as well as correct forehand angulation and musculature, essential to cope with movement up and down steep slopes, in order to control the sheep. However, on the plains of Central Germany, which featured fewer natural or made-made boundaries, a different type of dog was required, one capable of prolonged, tireless trotting over large areas. Such a dog had to be athletic, well-proportioned with balanced angulation. On these plains the concept and practice of using the shepherd dog as a 'living fence' was developed to contain the flocks and prevent wandering, to guard the sheep against wild animals such as the lynx

or wolf, and to see off sheep-stealers of the human variety. Local breeders, mostly farmers and shepherds, produced dogs suitable for local needs, but always the motive was improvement of function, rather than appearance.

By the nineteenth century, however, breeders began to look to other regions to enhance the virtues and correct the faults of their own shepherd dogs – thus, began a movement towards a national – a German – shepherd dog! This process gathered momentum as the century drew to a close. The qualities of central and southern shepherd dogs were amalgamated successfully. The Thuringian strains had improved ear carriage and coat colour, particularly through the introduction of wolf-grey, later to be regarded as important in the correction of colour-paling. The sturdiness and sheer strength of the shepherd dogs from Württemberg and Swabia made a valuable input into the gene pool of the racier breeding of Central Germany. The out-going temperament and 'joie de vivre' of the Thuringians received the added dimension of sobriety and steadfastness from the Swabians and Württembergers.

At this time dog shows were becoming popular, particularly among the wealthier classes, who had the leisure and resources to consider the dog as a companion and as a thing of beauty, rather than as an animal with a utilitarian function. It was inevitable that the shepherd dog should come to the notice of the fanciers, one of whom, Max Riechelmann, was soon, with the co-operation of Dachshund breeder Klaus Graf Hahn, to form a society whose aim was "to breed true to type" and to produce a dog "recognised as a German Sheepdog". On December 16th, 1891 the Phylax Society was formed. The significance of this era of the shepherd dog has often been overlooked, at most regarded as merely a hiccup in the long-term development of the breed, an era in which fanciers attempted to gain control and turn the shepherd's four-legged guardian of his flocks – a dog that had existed purely because of the function he performed – into a 'Luxushund', a glamorous show dog. Yet, bearing in mind the future development of the breed in other countries, particularly in Britain and America, the whole history of the breed might have been different, if the concept of the shepherd dog as show dog had gained support at such a crucial stage. The whole project of developing the national shepherd dog could have been strangled at birth. But in the motherland of the breed, there were forces at work to prevent this happening.

THE PHYLAX SOCIETY

In the beginning, the 'fancy' and its supporters enjoyed considerable show success, especially with a dog, owned by Riechelmann, called Phylax von Eulau, who gained many prizes. Phylax was hailed by members of the club which bore his name as a model shepherd dog. But when Phylax found himself in competition with genuine working dogs, especially from the Württemberg region, which were now beginning to be exhibited at dog shows, both laymen and experts alike could discern that the type of Phlax was not the way forward for the breed. The concept of cosmetic as opposed to functional beauty was therefore rejected by shepherd dog enthusiasts in Germany, just as in Great Britain today the 'curves and coat' of the traditional 'Alsatian' have, to some considerable extent, been replaced by the athletic, well-proportioned, working dog type of German Shepherd, indistinguishable from those seen in Germany and in most parts of the world.

The Phylax Society and their model dog of the same name now faced an uncertain future. The opinion of an eminent working dog judge, Herr Kull, was eagerly awaited. What would he think of Phylax? The critique was not one likely to enhance the reputation of this now famous but controversial dog. In fact, quite the reverse. Placing him 'down the line' after working dogs of the Württemberg type, Kull wrote of Phylax that he was "impressive, beautiful ...a dog who, with his wild expression, stiff movement and undomesticated demeanour would be ten times more suitable to a zoo than working use fully behind a flock of sheep."

Despite partisan support for either the central or the southern strain of shepherd dog, which was only to be expected from their adherents, the movement toward the creation of a national type of dog proceeded inexorably. At this point in the history of the breed, strong and responsible leadership was needed to take the new national shepherd dog, the German Shepherd Dog, into the twentieth century. With the inevitable decline of pastoral life. and the move towards the offices and factories in what was rapidly becoming one of the world's great industrial powers, a new role had to be found for the breed which would augment the traditional function of tending the flocks.

THE REIGN OF VON STEPHANITZ

Was it destiny that this leadership was provided by a former cavalry captain, Max von Stephanitz? Certainly, he seemed to possess all the attributes needed for the task which lay ahead: a penetrating mind, a sense of order and discipline, a deep knowledge of anatomy and movement acquired from his study of horses for use in the army, a serious grasp of the principles of breeding, a love of and feel for animals, an unerring insight into human foibles and weaknesses, and, after seeing and admiring shepherd dogs at work, the conviction that he had found his life's vocation. As a retired army officer, he had the leisure and resources to pursue his task without distraction. The formation on April 22nd, 1899 of 'Der Verein für Deutsche Schäferhunde' – the SV – brought into being what has become the largest breed club in the world, with a membership of more than 100,000. Von Stephanitz was elected President. Arthur Meyer, who had already proved himself a man with exceptional organisational ability in the establishment of the Dobermann and Dachshund breeds, was made Secretary.

The SV having been created as a formal structure to take the breed forward, what were the specific tasks which lay ahead and how should they be tackled? There can be no doubt that absolutely crucial decisions had to be taken, and taken quickly. The 'fanciers' had been seen off, but if von Stephanitz had been able to see a hundred or even fifty years into the future, he would have been even more convinced that the path he would set was the right one. He realised that he must fashion an administrative structure to influence the development of the breed. He also needed, at least in his own homeland, to convince all participants – breeders, users, or just plain enthusiasts – that the individual was less important than the achievements of the breed itself, and that co-operation rather than competition must be the keynote. He understood that with the new high profile, and the creation of what would be seen by many as a new 'national' shepherd dog, the dangers that threatened at the outset, must not be underestimated. With the decline of rural life, and the consequent phasing out of the tending function, new uses must be found for the German Shepherd Dog.

A conviction that the German Shepherd should continue as a working dog lay at the core of SV thinking. But first it was important to establish a 'blueprint' for the breed – a written Standard of points. The formality of breeding to fixed points of reference, as it were, was an entirely new concept in the breed, where matings had been carried out, mostly by farmers and shepherds, according to the 'ad hoc' needs of the moment, rather than as part of any grand design, the more so because of the lack of written records. Von Stephanitz visualised a Standard which would be sufficiently detailed as to give a clear 'word picture' of the dog he wanted breeders to aim for. This Standard, drawn up in 1899, has a degree of precision (e.g. angles of bones, proportions and overall measurements) which leaves little margin for individual interpretation.

Von Stephanitz now turned his attention to a system of records, firstly by the establishment of the Breed Register (Zuchtbuch) which would consist of details of all existing German Shepherds, together with proof of their origin. Two decades later he would launch the *Körbuch*, often referred to in the English-speaking world as the *Breed Survey Book*, a register of those dogs considered suitable to be bred from on the basis of their physical and mental characteristics. Von Stephanitz rejected the notion of a breed register based purely on show wins as exemplified by the British

Kennel Club Stud Book, and the American Register of Merit through winning progeny. He considered these to be misleading as a guide to breeding worth. In his masterwork, *The German Shepherd Dog in Word and Picture*, von Stephanitz wrote: "The demand that only exhibition qualifications should be considered would have placed the breed on too narrow a basis, and because this really depends on all kinds of contingencies, it accordingly would have given a quite false impression of the 'creme de la creme' of the race."

Von Stephanitz had created an organisation – the SV – for the development and administration of his beloved breed over which he exercised absolute authority, for he believed that the weakness of man's nature and the shortcomings of human endeavour must not be allowed to stand in the way of progress. The rapidly increasing membership of the SV anticipated an exciting future for the German Shepherd Dog, in which process they would all play a part. At the same time, they knew they must be prepared to accept strict rules, which, in fact, as the years went by, became more, rather than less, exacting.

THE LEGACY OF HORAND

The first entry in the new Breed Register, was a dog known as Hektor Linksrhein, acquired from the Sparwasser kennel by von Stephanitz, who renamed him under his own kennel prefix: Horand von Gafrath SZ 1. Later, von Stephanitz wrote of Horand:

"For the ... enthusiasts of that time Horand embodied the fulfilment of their fondest dreams; he was large, 60-61cm at the height of back – a very good medium size – with powerful bones, beautiful lines and a nobly-formed head; clean and sinewy in build, the whole dog was one livewire. His character corresponded to his exterior qualities: marvellous in his obedient faithfulness to his master; and above all, the straightforward nature of a gentleman with a boundless and irrepressible zest for living. Although untrained in his puppyhood, nevertheless obedient to the slightest nod when at his master's side; but when left to himself the maddest rascal, the wildest ruffian and an incorrigible promoter of strife. Never idle, always on the go; well-disposed to harmless people but no cringer, crazy about children, with a full capacity for loving. What could not have become of such a dog, if only we had had at that time military or police

Horand v. Gafrath and Mari v. Gafrath (sitting) as SZ1 and SZ2 the first registered German Shepherd Dogs.

service training! His faults were the consequences of his upbringing and never of his inheritance. He suffered from a suppressed, or better, a superfluity of unemployed energy: for he was delighted when someone gave him attention, and then he was the most tractable of dogs. Horand handed down these wonderful characteristics to his immediate descendants. These still survive today."

This observation on a dog which was to become the Adam of the breed, contains a profound truth which we overlook at our peril. When von Stephanitz wrote this critique of Horand, the new work for the German Shepherd Dog was already being undertaken, firstly in the police and later in the military. Von Stephanitz saw clearly that without employment and a strong bond of human companionship, the shepherd dog could turn into a delinquent and a nuisance to society. At the same time, he knew that only a certain proportion of these dogs could expect to take up a career in law enforcement or serve as part of the armed forces. The SV had to devise a system of training for all German Shepherds which would at once develop their manifold talents, and most importantly, bring the dogs under control in order to take their place in society. Today, in the motherland of the breed, all German Shepherds are required to undergo a character and endurance test, and then a course of training in obedience, agility, nosework (tracking) and protection work culminating in an exacting test known as the Schutzhund Prufung, before they can be bred from or entered in the adult classes at shows.

BUILDING THE BLOODLINES
Horand's most famous son was Hektor von Schwaben SZ 13. He was Sieger or German Grand Victor, in 1900 and 1901. His dam was the working bitch, Mores Plieningen, from Württemberg, SZ 159 HGH (Herdengebrauchshun) – active herding dog. Hektor sired the famous Beowulf out of Thekla von der Krone, a half-sister to Hektor, the dam-side being strongly bred on southern working lines. Thus, the process of utilising bloodlines based on Horand, strongly reinforced with good working stock, was to continue. The Beowulf grandson, Roland v. Starkenburg, Sieger 1906-7, was to exert wide influence on subsequent breeding, mainly through the 1909 Sieger Hettel Uckermark, but not without the introduction of undesirable faults. Over-size began to surface, probably as a result of the introduction of the substantial, strong-boned working ancestry from the south, much of it unknown. As well as size, another problem crept in through Hettel's son, Billo Riedekenburg. His dam, Flora Berkmeyer, was later criticised by von Stephanitz not only for compounding the size factor, but also for transmitting her own less-than-perfect front angulation: steep upper arm and shoulder. This gave rise to the advent of a tall, 'terrier-fronted' dog which was not the type visualised in the Standard, and which reached its nadir in the highly controversial Nores von der Kriminalpolizei, sire of the 1921 Sieger Harras von der Juch.

This unwelcome development in the German Shepherd underlined the need for the next great step in the implementation of the SV plan to influence the progress of the breed – the Körung, or Breed Survey. This was to be a process designed to breed from selected stock only, by which the principle of 'enhance the virtues, rectify the faults' would be the guiding factor. The first Breed survey was held in 1922. It took a long time – twenty years in fact – to introduce the Breed Survey. But to have instigated such a breeding selection programme system at all must be judged a remarkable feat, unmatched anywhere else in the world, even at the present time. To be fair, other countries outside the SV orbit have initiated Breed Surveys or assessments, but, by and large, these have had a more limited objective than those conducted under the SV system. It would not have been feasible to launch a Breed Survey any earlier due to lack of meaningful records, and the need for some knowledge of the characteristics of the various bloodlines in use. We also have to realise that at the outset, von Stephanitz and his associates had to launch the German Shepherd as the all-round working dog of the twentieth century. This was their main preoccupation up to, and during the First World War.

*Hektor v. Schwaben
SZ13 by Horand ex
Mores Plienigen, HGH:
United the central and
southern strains of the
German Shepherd Dog.*

*Sieger 1906/7 Roland v.
Starkenburg SZ 1537:
Line-bred on Horand,
he was to exert wide
influence in the breed.*

POLICE WORK

As early as 1901, the SV suggested to the police authorities that the German Shepherd might be considered for operational duties. The most obvious characteristic to exploit was the dog's guarding instinct, recognised from the way in which the regional shepherd dogs had for centuries protected the flocks from intrusion and attack. With the demise of the wolf and the lynx, at least in western and central Germany, the function of the shepherd dogs changed more to tending rather than guarding the sheep, the main objective being to confine the flock to pasture land and prevent it straying on to crops. Von Stephanitz was determined to keep alive the guarding instinct in the German Shepherd. This intrinsic quality, which the Germans called 'Kampftrieb' means not only the ability but also the *willingness* to protect. It should be noted at this juncture that the oft-used literal translation of Kampftrieb as 'fighting instinct' is injurious to the reputation of the breed, especially in these days of punitive anti-dog legislation. Such a translation gives a totally incorrect idea of the character of the dog. The German Shepherd is not, and never has been bred to fight either dogs or people! Efficiency trials were conducted in 1903, and the results were so satisfactory that police forces in many urban centres were persuaded to try out and eventually to adopt German Shepherds as an active part of the law-enforcement system. The Government established a centre for breeding and training police dogs at Grünheide near Berlin.

In the beginning, there was some reluctance on the part of senior policemen regarding the use of German Shepherd Dogs in detection and criminal investigation. This class of work demanded searching and tracking skills. However, it was soon discovered at Grünheide and other training centres which were being set up, that the German Shepherd had exceptional skills in the field of nosework. During the first decade of the new century, dogs from these schools graduated in ever-increasing numbers to operational duties, firstly in the civilian and later in the military police. The fame of these German Shepherds in service, performing so efficiently in pursuit of law-enforcement, soon spread to other countries around the world. Foreign police observers and trainers came to Germany, especially to Grünheide, where they learned at first-hand how the German Shepherd could be trained to track down and apprehend suspects. The noble and alert appearance of the dog inspired confidence and respect; the mere presence of a German Shepherd was in itself a deterrent factor recognised by the police in their ceaseless battle against crime in our society. The guidelines laid down in the Standard, when translated into the living flesh, were to produce a dog of compact construction i.e. slightly longer than high, not too large, athletic in build, strong and supple, and constructed so as to be able to trot over long distances without fatigue. But above all, the German Shepherd must possess boundless loyalty, courage and tractability in order to function properly as the good citizen's friend and protector. In this way, the foundations were laid for the police dog sections on an international scale which are today taken for granted as an integral part of law-enforcement.

MILITARY SERVICE

At the outbreak of the First World War, the quality and skills of the German Shepherd Dog which had been fully demonstrated in police service, were recognised by the military. As well as exceptional scenting ability, the erect ears of the dog gave acute hearing which was invaluable at sentry posts to give warning of enemy attacks. Another characteristic exploited on the battlefield, was the dog's love of his master. After specialised training, this instinct could be employed to send messages back to trench and dug-out – the nearest thing to home in that terrible conflict. Thus, the despatch-dog became an integral part of the communications network, the efficiency of which is essential to front-line operations. The tracking and searching skills of the German Shepherd Dog, developed and utilised by the police in criminal detection, now began to be adapted to seek out wounded soldiers on the battlefield, many of whom were buried in collapsed trenchworks or concealed from the human eye in copse or woodland. These wonderful dogs daily risked enemy fire in their endeavours to save human lives. In the Second World War the same skills were harnessed during the Blitz on British cities, where Shepherds of the Crumstone prefix were successfully employed to seek out air-raid victims buried under debris. Nowadays, German Shepherds operate in rescue organisations, performing the dangerous work of finding people lost or injured on mountains or on ski-slopes after an avalanche.

THE SPREAD OF THE GERMAN SHEPHERD

As the German Shepherd became established in the motherland of the breed, its fame spread to other countries, especially the United States, though no dog of importance arrived there until after the formation of the German Shepherd Dog Club of America in 1913. Apollo von Hunenstein became US Grand Victor in 1919, though he actually set foot on American soil some five years previously. In fact, it was not until after the First World War that the breed really caught on overseas. This was doubtless due to the returning soldiers and the stories they told of the wondrous feats of German Shepherds under fire. Later, the public imagination was stirred and directed toward an appreciation of the qualities of the German Shepherd by the exploits of *Rin Tin Tin* and *Strongheart*, as champions of good against evil, and right against wrong, on the moving-picture screens of the world. But a shadow was cast over the euphoria surrounding the arrival of this new wonder dog, especially in Britain, where anti-German feeling was running high after the terrible war years. This hatred extended to a condemnation of German art, music – and even her dogs! Thus returning British army officers, convinced of the bravery and usefulness of the German Shepherd, were faced with a dilemma. How were they to introduce a German breed of dog to the British public at such an unpropitious time in the relationship between the two countries? The answer lay in the employment of a piece of geographical sleight of hand, placing in the British national consciousness the notion that the breed originated in Alsace, a region over-run successively by French and German forces since the war of 1871. It was an ingenious idea, bringing the dog out of a sort of no man's land. The term did not deny the German connection in any absolute sense, but concentrated on a name – Alsace – which, being French in flavour, was eminently more acceptable. It fitted in with notions of entente cordiale and admiration for French culture affected by the British upper classes, who had the leisure and resources to devote to breeding and importing, and who would create the administration to enable the breed to prosper and develop in Great Britain.

The name 'Alsatian' was coined, no doubt serving its purpose in the eyes of early devotees such as Lord Brabazon of Tara, Colonel James Baldwin and Air Commodore Cecil Wright, but forming, as it did, an anti-German stance in the breed in Great Britain. This had far-reaching consequences in later years, especially as these gentlemen, along with other enthusiasts of the day such as F.N. Pickett, were to occupy positions of power and authority in the canine establishment and the Kennel Club. Before the war, German Shepherd imports, and they were few, were lumped together under the heading 'foreign sheep dogs' by the Kennel Club. Now was the time for the new devotees to apply for a separate register and the formation of a new club for the breed, which was launched as the 'Alsatian Wolf Dog'. Why the title 'Wolf Dog' was added is beyond belief. Presumably, those responsible thought the dog looked like a wolf, or maybe they wished to convey the notion that the dog was some kind of hound, bred to hunt wolves in the forests of Alsace. Apart from the fact that wolves had long become extinct in western Europe, the title 'Wolf Dog' was not only absurd, but, more importantly, fuelled a campaign of vilification by detractors who claimed, with some justification where irresponsible breeding was involved, that the breed was savage and unreliable. Long after the title 'Wolf Dog' was dropped (in 1924), the alleged wolf ancestry was cited by the press and other media of the day as responsible for the breed's undesirable characteristics, when the true cause was the abuse of freedoms by ignorant and irresponsible breeders. In 1924 the club for the 'Alsatian Wolf Dog' was merged with the 'Alsatian League' to form the Alsatian League and Club of Great Britain, now known as the German Shepherd Dog League of Great Britain.

THE BREED SURVEY

The war over, von Stephanitz turned his attention to establishing the Körung or Breed Survey. What specifically is a Körung? The word Körung comes from the word 'Kiesen', meaning 'to choose or select'. The more correct translation would appear to be 'Breed Selection' rather than 'Breed Survey', which merely denotes a process of looking over. Nevertheless, as the term Breed Survey seems to have become firmly established as the equivalent of Körung, we will use it throughout this book. At the outset, von Stephanitz was concerned lest individual breeders should romp along doing their own thing, and using dogs which took their fancy, without thinking of the consequences. With the concentration on lines which contained much Nores von der Kriminalpolizei, there was a danger that genetic faults could be fixed and, by the 1920s, evidence of this fixation became only too apparent. Von Stephanitz took control of the situation, and on January 29th 1922, the first Körung took place at Reutlingen. The results were published in the first *Körbuch* or *Breed Survey Book*, issued in 1922. The following is an extract of a review of this publication, compiled from official SV sources:

"The first *Körbuch* of the SV foreshadows extraordinarily important progress for the breed and for its furtherance in general. The comparative figures of the *Körbuch* are also instructive because they furnish us with such a complete survey as we have had up to now ... The *Körbuch* in question contains measurements of the height at wither, of the depth of chest, of the contour of the chest, of the general body length, and of the weight of the body ... It is only the motto of our breeding 'To breed a German Shepherd Dog is to breed a working dog' that is to be considered, and that is why we should put special value on the correct ratio between height at wither and length of body. The use and work of the German Shepherd Dog require endurance in trotting. For this purpose a rather rectangular and not a square formation is required ... According to the correct figures concerning 239 dogs, all males (in the survey) in measurements and in weights, the 'normal' German Shepherd male should, in order to satisfy the requirements of the present time, be produced bodily as follows:

Body length: approx 71cm
Wither height: approx 64.5cm
Excess of length over height: approx 6.5cm
Depth of chest: approx 28cm
Chest contour: approx 75cm
Weight: approx 27.5kg...."

BREEDING CONTROLS

As the years went by, so control over the direction of the breed was firmly established. Today, specially appointed experts known as Körmeister supervise the taking of measurements and weight, and make an assessment of the dog against the Standard in respect of temperament, conformation and functional ability. Dogs recommended for breeding are admitted into Class 1; those suitable for breeding go into Class 2. The essential prerequisites for admission into Class 1 or Class 2 of the survey are: possession of suitable hips (A Stamp); working test for obedience, agility, nosework and protection (Schutzhund Prüfung), and a test for endurance (Ausdauer Prüfung). The introduction of the Begleithund Prüfung (BH Test) as a prerequisite to the Schutzhund 1, was the SV's response to the anti-dog lobby, which in recent years has influenced the media to promote the dog as an enemy of society rather than as man's best friend. Thus, the BH Test could be described as test of character, temperament and control in a modern urban environment – in fact, it is a searching evaluation of the German Shepherd as a good canine citizen. This test , which may be taken at one year of age is seen by the SV as the starting point for the career of any German Shepherd, whatever form it may take.

Breeding recommendations are given as well as warnings. Dogs not classified in the Körung, the results of which are published annually in the *Körbuch*, are not used for breeding, and are discarded as far as the SV system is concerned. Dogs must have reached the age of two years to be eligible for the Körung. Successful dogs are described as angekört in Korkclasse 1 (recommended) or Korkclasse 2 (suitable). Of course, scientific developments dictated certain modifications in the requirements for approved breeding material. For instance, the advent of X-ray techniques for the screening of hip joints, has helped in the fight against hip dysplasia, prevalent in many large breeds of dog. In the late sixties, the SV introduced a scheme by which dogs with hips considered suitable for breeding would be given an endorsement on their pedigrees. This was known as the A Zuerkannt or 'the A Stamp'. It should be noted that there are three grades of 'A' Stamp: A Normal

Sieger 1920 Erich v. Grafenwerth PH: Sire of the 1925 Sieger Klodo v. Boxberg.

ABOVE: Sieger 1909 Hettel Uckermark SZ 3897: The Roland son, whose correct size and harmonious build was recognisable in the descendants of Utz and Klodo.

LEFT: Horst v. Boll PH: Combinations of Horst/Hettel tended to compound the size problem.

– Normal Hips, A fast Normal – Near Normal Hips and A Noch Zugelassen – Still Acceptable Hips. It is worth mentioning that under the SV system, only pedigree certificates issued by the administrative headquarters in Augsburg, are considered to be authentic. Breeders' pedigrees have no role to play in the motherland of the breed.

The comprehensive list of qualifications required by each dog for classification in today's Körung is, of course, a far cry from the situation which prevailed in those early days. The existence of faults such as over-size, poor angulation and incorrect proportions was the raison d'etre of the Körung, and at the first survey, von Stephanitz had to contend with a number of dogs whose pedigrees were incomplete because of unknown ancestry. Some dogs had protection qualifications (Schutzhund), others were working police dogs. Only a few herding dogs were present. If nothing else, it demonstrated that the German Shepherd was moving away from its original herding function, and was taking its place as the new working dog of the twentieth century.

Over half the animals presented for the early Körung events had no qualifications at all. The task which lay ahead for the SV was twofold: to build up and extend the breeding base, and, at the same time, to ensure that genetic faults were, if possible, eliminated or at least controlled. It was also of the greatest importance that dogs considered of value to the breed, whether actual or potential, should be recognised and promoted. The SV resolved that dogs of special merit must be brought into the breeding process. Dogs of little or no value to the breed had to be down-graded in such a way as to leave the public in no doubt about the hazards of breeding from such animals.

In those early days the recognition and promotion of desirable bloodlines rested very much on the shoulders of von Stephanitz and his immediate associates. Of course, he was aided by his band of Körmeister (Breed Masters) who, as we have seen, gave their opinions as to stock presented for evaluation at the Körung. But with the rising tide of interest, a means had to be found to educate the public in what was desirable and undesirable in the German Shepherd, and later the SV adapted the dog show for this purpose. Meanwhile, von Stephanitz occupied himself with the task of restoring the breed to the correct, middle-sized working build from which it had departed since Horand.

From the Breed Survey of 1922 he observed that something like a third of the dogs assessed were over-size and that these were predominantly of the Kriminalpolizei breeding. The Roland son, Sieger 1909 Hettel Uckermark, though within the height standard, and of balanced harmonious build, had not been wisely used by breeders, despite warnings from the authorities. A change of direction came about with the crowning of the 1925 Sieger Klodo vom Boxberg, a dog well under medium-size, of good depth and proportions, and possessing the balanced working build visualised in the Standard. Klodo's sire, the 1920 Sieger Erich von Grafenwerth, was inbred on Hettel but carried the blood of Flora, from whom he presumably inherited his rather 'terrier-type' forehand construction, with steep shoulder and upper arm coupled with high wither. His dam was Elfe vom Boxburg, who also had lines to Hettel. Von Stephanitz wished to consign the leggy, over-size, steep-fronted dogs to the history books, or at least he wanted them off the scene. The 1924 Sieger Donar v. Overstolzen (67cm at the withers) arrived in Britain where he found many admirers. On June 27th 1928, Donar gained his English Championship. His owner, F.N. Pickett, was a man of considerable influence in the canine establishment. He did his best to undermine moves to return to the Standard – especially in regard to height – at the same time affecting support for the notions of von Stephanitz. We shall near more of how Pickett plotted and influenced others to take Britain out of the German Shepherd mainstream.

A RETURN TO THE STANDARD
The promotion of Klodo vom Boxberg as 1925 Sieger – a dog very different in type from his immediate predecessors – was to have a great effect on the development of the breed. It is a fair assumption that the line-breeding of Klodo, based on Hettel, was successful in producing the qualities needed for a return to the Standard. Klodo had a profound influence over a whole range of qualities considered to be intrinsic parts of the German Shepherd ideal. Through his sons, Curt Herzog Hedan, Donar Zuchtgut and the 1929 Sieger Utz vom Haus Schütting, improvements appeared respectively in size and character, working ability and conformation. While Curt and Donar did much to improve the mental aspects of the breed, it fell to Utz to determine the make and shape of the German Shepherd for generations to come. In the opinion of von Stephanitz, Utz was: "the purest form of shepherd dog build, powerful without too much weight". Only just within the height standard (61cm), he was to produce dogs of the desired middle-size, with greater depth and length of body. At the same time, the long bones of the forehand and of the hindquarters were better angulated, which tended to produce a longer striding, and therefore more economical shepherd gait. Utz had a profound influence on the shape of the breed, not only in Germany but

*Sieger 1925 Klodo v.
Boxberg: Sire of Utz.*

*Sieger 1929 Utz v. Haus
Schütting Z.Pr: 'Father' of
the modern German
Shepherd Dog.*

also in Britain and America, where influential progeny were exported. Utz himself went to America. Whatever the subsequent evaluation of this dog – and there were critics of Utz and his progeny in Germany and in the rest of the world – there can be no doubt that he is worthy to be called the father of the modern German Shepherd. Seven years after the crowning of Utz, Von Stephanitz died, his life's work completed. He was the driving force behind the creation of the most versatile and widely-used of all working dogs. He had lived to fight off those who attempted to undermine his concepts. In no way would he tolerate the fancier's show dog, which looked pretty in the ring but was pretty useless the rest of the time. The SV was a structure designed to keep the German Shepherd on course for development and improvement. Perhaps the greatest achievement of the Rittmeister was his ability to convey to his colleagues and to the membership of what is now the greatest one-breed club in the world – the SV – that the Breed as a whole is far more important than the individuals, both dogs and people, within it.

Chapter Two

KLODO/UTZ AND THE AFTERMATH

At the time of von Stephanitz' death, almost all the breeding stock approved at Körungs was on the line of Klodo vom Boxberg, mainly through Utz. About 75 per cent of angekört females were of the same breeding. Thus, the Klodo/Utz type, which von Stephanitz had proclaimed as the correct type of German Shepherd, became firmly established. But what is perceived as a radical movement will often create a backlash.

THE BREED DEBATE

Certain prominent people, especially Dr Sachs of 'von Hain' and Tobias Ott of the famous Blasienberg Kennel, were anxious to restore the correct working temperament, which they feared was being undermined by these trends. These two men were important and influential members of the SV, both judges and Körmeister (Breed Masters). Ott became National Breed Warden, while Sachs was chairman of the powerful working dog committee of the German Kennel Club. Sachs, in particular, introduced the concepts of 'altbluter' and 'altblutlinie' (the old bloodlines) and pressed for their use. But to have returned unreservedly to the old herding lines would, in the official view, have upset the development and stabilisation of type, as exemplified by Klodo and Utz. There would have been a danger of a return to the tall, square dogs which von Stephanitz had condemned as not in accordance with the Standard. Therefore, the success of this movement was limited by the system, in particular the assessments conducted by the main body of Breed masters. Yet if Sachs, Ott, and their supporters had not stood out for what they believed to be right, there would have been no Arno v. Haus Gersie, Axel Deininghauserheide, and Volker v. Zollgrenzschutzhaus. After the Second World War, these dogs, and many others, were to play an important part in the development of the German Shepherd Dog, particularly with regard to temperament and character.

THE PURPOSE OF DOG SHOWS

The dog-show, previously a competition to find the most beautiful animal in the eyes of the judge, had been developed to become an integral part of breed improvement. Throughout the years,under the SV system, emphasis at dog-shows has been placed on the word 'Zucht' (breed). On the other hand, in countries where Anglo-Saxon traditions prevail, the judges' decisions rest entirely on how the animal looks and performs on the day. There is no time or opportunity for a thorough test of temperament and character. No positive identification of the dog is allowed, which means that working qualifications, hip-status, or in the case of adult males, breeding track-record, have no role to play in the award of top qualifications, such as Championship titles. It is not difficult to appreciate that, under these criteria, many top animals could completely fail, on one or more of these points, to the extent of rendering them useless for breeding. Yet, outside the SV system, breeders often include top-winning breed animals in plans to mate their bitches. Furthermore, every attempt is made in the Anglo-Saxon tradition to highlight the winners: in classes, in the

Group and in the supreme award of Best in Show. A judge will tell the ring steward: "Finished with the rest", a practice which has given rise to the sardonic comment that the remainder of the entry, in fact the majority, has been 'thrown out with the rubbish.'

This system, which is mandatory and binding on the judge at British Kennel Club shows, clearly does little to inform the public or to instruct exhibitors, especially novices, some of whom may never learn about the faults and virtues of their dogs. They become depressed and despondent and, eventually, give up. At such shows, speed is of the essence, and there is no tradition on the part of the judges, especially all-round judges, to give critiques on the animals exhibited, except on the first two placings for the canine press. A red card and/or rosette is on offer for every class winner, but such awards give no indication of the quality of the competition. An exhibitor may proudly display a houseful of red cards and rosettes, but the dogs awarded them may be indifferent specimens in breed terms. They may not even be particularly good in the conformation department. The only absolute award is the British Kennel Club Challenge Certificate, which should be conferred when the dog is "of such outstanding merit as to be worthy of the title of Champion". But even the value of this award may vary considerably, giving rise, at least in British GSD circles, to the opinion that any Challenge Certificate is only as good as the judge who awarded it. A large number of GSD enthusiasts in the British Isles disagree with, and actively rebel against, shows run on the lines described above.

THE SV SHOW SYSTEM

We must now examine how the SV dog show differs from the British Kennel Club version, and how it functions alongside the Körung as an instrument of breed improvement. Readers may be wondering at this stage why a chapter on the breed in Germany, immediately following the reign of von Stephanitz, should contain such a detailed account of the SV breed show system and how it differs from the Anglo-Saxon concept, especially as practised in Great Britain. Our purpose is twofold: firstly to show how the SV type of show educates and informs both its membership and the public; secondly, to explain how the difference between the two traditions has contributed towards a split in the breed in Great Britain, between those who follow the Kennel Club system, and those who are convinced that the SV method of staging a show is the correct way.

At SV shows, the basic principle is openness and consistency. Judges must pass a series of examinations before being allowed to officiate in the ring. The keynote is close adherence to the Standard. When faults creep in to such an extent as to be a problem, judges must act to penalise them. At all shows, whether large or small, dogs in the class are placed in order of merit from first to last. In this way, onlookers, especially novices, learn to appreciate the finer points of animals at the top of the class, as well as their faults, since no dog is perfect. At the same time, they come to understand the reasons why other dogs finish lower down the line-up. This process of evaluation is facilitated by the award of grades to each dog, from 'Very Good', through 'Good' and 'Sufficient', to 'Faulty'. The grade of 'Excellent' is reserved for animals of two years and over, in deserving cases. (It is of interest that the 'V', or Excellent, grade was awarded to 'Jugend' — 12-18 months — and 'Junghund' — 18 months-2 years — classes until 1958). For example, when the judges have been instructed to penalise size, if this is believed by the authorities to be a real problem, then the fact will be reflected in the line-up. The desired medium-size dogs will be placed at the forefront of the class, followed by the top-size dogs, who may still receive the 'Very Good' qualification, or 'Excellent' if it is an adult class. As a further clarification of the placings, it is normal at SV shows for verbal critiques to be given by the judge, usually over the loudspeaker, so that everyone can hear. The dogs at the bottom of the class may have serious faults of construction or temperament. Any such deficiencies will be included in the critique.

Making the faults of any dog public in this way is generally considered repugnant in Anglo-

Saxon canine circles. Why should the world be told about bad dogs when people only want to hear about good ones? Anyway, the argument goes, breeders only want their good dogs to be seen in public, in other words, at shows. Their bad dogs, if they have any, should be hidden from view. Generally, good breeders only show good dogs. But what happens to the less good ones? And what about novice breeders who want to have their stock evaluated in the show-ring? They have to start somewhere, and if the judges constantly dismiss their dogs from the ring without any sort of constructive criticism, how can they be expected to learn? Owners of 'Tail-end Charlies' at SV shows cannot be expected to like being last in the class, but if they are sensible they realise that the system is there to help them. There is no disgrace in having faults in one's dogs. Appreciation of the quality of stock, good, bad or indifferent, in the home kennel is the first step towards progress in any breeding programme.

Another important aspect of the SV system is the way in which the grade or qualification awarded to each dog in the class can completely alter the perspective of the exhibitor. To be last in a class is less galling if the class is of high quality. Recently, an SV judge awarded the grade of 'Very Good' to every dog in a class of Juniors. All the exhibitors went away as pleased as Punch, clutching their grading cards. The actual position of their dogs in the class was of little significance.

QUALITY CONTROL

It is an indisputable fact that, under the SV system, a German Shepherd cannot rise to the top unless it has acceptable hips (the A Stamp), has passed the endurance test (AD Prüfung), is classified in the Breed Survey (angekört), and has obtained approved working qualifications (usually the Schutzhund Prüfung). Furthermore, there is no way that an adult dog can be classified 'Excellent Select' at the yearly Sieger Show, unless it has produced, or is likely to produce, stock of the highest quality. Potential 'Excellent' and 'Select' winners at the Sieger Show also have to undergo a courage test. Failure means demotion to the lowest grades. Some years ago, a male exhibited at the Sieger Show failed its courage test. The dog had been classified as 'Excellent Select' the previous year, but was downgraded because he failed to meet the Standard on the key issue of temperament. Within hours, news of the tragic fall from grace of this high-profile dog had flashed round the world, as a consequence devaluing existing progeny and putting an end to any future use of the unfortunate dog. The bloodline has now virtually disappeared from our pedigrees.

It would be a mistake to assume that all these stringent controls were brought in at the same time. On the contrary, it was a gradual process over the years. For instance, the courage test at the Sieger Show was not introduced until 1967, during the presidency of Dr Werner Funk. In the thirties, although mechanisms for control of the breed were not anywhere near as stringent as those of today, views which ran counter to SV policy (such as those of Dr Sachs, Tobias Ott and others) were staunchly opposed by the combined forces of Körmeister, judges and breed wardens, all of whom were acting on the instructions of the SV Executive. Moreover, the system had a deeply committed ally in the person of Dr Funk himself, long before he became president of the SV. Dr Funk had bred Utz, and his 'vom Haus Schütting' affix was to become indelibly linked with the rise of the German Shepherd in the world order. Despite constant pressure from the 'old guard', Dr. Funk refused to countenance any radical outcrossing to bring in new, or old, blood, on the grounds that this would upset uniformity of type.

We should contrast this outlook — a veritable identification of interests to produce a common objective — with those countries in which freedom prevails, notably Britain and America. In those countries, type can differ even down to the level of individual kennels, although there are strong indications that a growing body of British and American breed opinion is in favour of adopting the SV approach, albeit in a modified form to suit the differences in national character.

Donna zum Reurer
Sch.H: Dam of Utz.

HEREDITARY FAULTS

It would be wrong to assume that the Germany's old guard had no grounds for their criticisms which were, as we have seen, mainly in respect of working temperament and character. Any concentration of breeding on a few related lines will cause faults, many of them recessive, to surface sooner or later. The price paid for the establishment of a uniform type of German Shepherd, consistent with the Standard and the model for succeeding generations, would be justified if serious attempts were made to eliminate, or at least minimise, those faults in the descendants.

What were the faults which emerged from the Klodo/Utz line? There is no doubt that there were dental problems. Utz himself had two missing pre-molars. This fault was passed on, and remains to this day in the genetic pool (viz. the modern British Alsatian). Utz's dam was Donna zum Reurer, who was colour-paled. It must be assumed that she played her part in bequeathing this problem to subsequent generations. The white GSD, still bred in some kennels in Great Britain and North America, though banned by the Standard (and its American version), is the end of the colour-paling process, not to be confused, of course, with albinism. The British Kennel Club version of the Standard is ambivalent on the question of the white, preferring to let judges treat it as a show fault. In practice, no decent judge would give the white GSD a second glance. So, in spite of the way the KC Standard is worded, it is a rarity to see a white exhibited at a British dog show.

Non-entirety in the male (one or more testes not descended into the scrotum) was not considered a bar against breeding in the early days. Falko vom Indetal was non-entire. He was the grandsire of Utz on the maternal side, i.e. through Donna zum Reurer, Utz' dam. Donna's litter brother, Drusus, was also non-entire. Non-entirety, usually referred to as orchidism, was transmitted on the Utz line. Other problems in the line were a tendency towards over-long bodies, too much depth of body, short front legs, and perhaps, most important of all in the working dog, alleged faults in temperament.

TEMPERAMENT AND TYPE

Any question of the genetic transmission of temperament and character faults is fraught with problems — not least because environmental factors weigh so heavily. The Körung report on Utz certainly gave no indication that he had anything other than a good character. Therefore, allegations about temperament failings in the Klodo/Utz line can only be conjectural. Clearly there

Viki v. Bern Z.Pr:
The Utz daughter
so influential in
early US pedigrees.

Kurt v. Herzog
Hedan: A son of
Klodo, who had a
very good influence
on subsequent
generations,
especially with
regard to
temperament and
character.

is a genetic component in any assessment of temperament and character; the rest is environmental. But how do the factors weigh against each other? That the SV should have accorded top honours to animals with serious faults may come as some surprise to the present-day GSD enthusiast, who is used to an SV system which gives short shrift to dogs with incorrect dentition, non-entirety, poor temperament and severe colour-paling. Yet we have to remember that these were the formative days of the breed. There was an ongoing battle to establish type and sometimes backward steps had to be taken in order to go forward.

Other faults, of a recessive nature, only surfaced with the passage of time. The SV authorities, therefore, had to keep a watchful eye on developments and take steps to ensure that things did not get out of hand. The 1935 Sieger Jalk vom Pagensgrub, himself with incomplete dentition, passed on faults of orchidism. Because of this, the authorities warned against further use of this dog. A warning was also issued against the use of Harras von Glockenbrink, to whom von Stephanitz had given the 'V' or 'Excellent' rating at the Hanover Show. Von Stephanitz was later to regret the award in the light of faults passed on by this dog. Harras was tail-male descended (i.e. through the sire line), not from Utz, but from Erich v. Grafenwerth, Utz' grandsire.

Yet we can see how the situation can get out of control when warnings go unheeded, outside the SV orbit. For instance, the son of Harras, Alex v. Ebersnacken, had a warning issued against his further use in the homeland, as he had produced orchidism, colour-paling, faults of dentition and temperament. His breeding lies behind Pfeffer von Bern, one of the three most important modern foundation sires in the United States. Pfeffer was sired by Dachs von Bern, out of Clara von Bern. Dachs was sired by Alex v. Ebersnacken, and his dam was the highly regarded Viki von Bern, a daughter of Utz. Clara von Bern was a grand-daughter of Utz through her sire-line. Pfeffer was a truly great dog, with a superb build and an excellent character. He had rich colouring and great nobility of expression. He was an excellent mover. Pfeffer returned in 1937 to Germany, where he won the Sieger title. Pfeffer was to pass on his fine qualities to his progeny, many of whom were themselves excellent producers. But, because Pfeffer was inbred on Utz, faults of the line were also transmitted.

The influence of other important sires, based on the Klodo/Utz type, in the United States will be discussed in a chapter on the breed in that country. We shall also examine how the Klodo/Utz type was established in Great Britain, and how the legacy of von Stephanitz was eventually frittered away to produce what is known today as the British Alsatian, even though the title of the breed in Britain is now the German Shepherd Dog, as it is everywhere else. The GSD Breed Council, the GSD League and the British Association for GSD are all trying to promote, despite Establishment opposition, the correct international type of dog. Meanwhile the thirties drew to a close with the advent of the Second World War. It was also the end of an era, with type established but threatened in Britain and America by the fashions of the show ring and the cult of individuality which rested in the prestige of individual kennels.

Chapter Three

THE BRITISH ALSATIAN

The early development of the breed in Britain must be seen against the conflict between national attitudes and the earnest desire on the part of some dedicated breeders to take the breed forward, as far as possible, in parallel with the motherland.

THE FRENCH CONNECTION

To sustain the 'French connection theory' some of the UK's early imports came from the Ponthieu kennels. Lord Brabazon of Tara's first acquisition was Deal Ponthieu. Colonel Baldwin bought Lad of Picardy, Cilla of Picardy and Tosca of Picardy from the Terraqueuse kennel of M Tourtille. In 1920, the breed had been awarded Challenge Certificates by the Kennel Club. One of the champions made up in that year was Felix of Fairway, bred by Lord Brabazon of Tara. Felix was sired by Deal Ponthieu out of Ginette de Terraqueuse. It is worth mentioning that all these French bred dogs went quickly back to German lines.

GERMAN IMPORTS

In 1921 German dogs "started to come in with a rush", as F.N.Pickett put it, one senses with some regret because he points out that prior to that date, "British fanciers had taken a liking to the dog, and as yet the Germans had hardly appeared upon the scene". The fact was realised that if the breeding base were to be extended, the only place to get the dogs was from Germany.

Pickett tried to deny the origin of the imports, and in this he was aided and abetted by the Kennel Club. For instance, you might suppose that Caro of Welham was bred by Pickett himself, until, upon closer scrutiny of the records, we discover that his true name was Caro v. Blasienberg, and the breeder was Tobias Ott. Pickett considers that Caro displaced the famous Ch. Allahson of If in the race for top awards, obtaining his title on May 21st 1924. Fortunately, the practice of allowing the anglicising of German names in official Kennel Club records has now been discontinued.

Thus began the build-up in Great Britain of the type which, by 1922, von Stephanitz had identified as the one he wanted to get rid of – tall, square, leggy and terrier-fronted. Representatives of these were: Ch. Lady Flora (correct name Gelma v.d. Flandersbach) who, through her dam, was descended from Flora Berkemeyer, Ch. Alf v. Tollensetal, Ch. Erichsohn v. Starkenmark, Ch. Kuno v. Brunnenhof, Ch. Teut v. Haff, and Ella v. Leipzigerhof. All these were sired by the 1920 Sieger Erich v. Grafenwerth. The influential Southmore kennel boasted that their lines contained pure Uckermark, Riedekenburg and Kriminalpolizei blood. Allah v. Rolandsbogen was owned by this kennel, and he was the sire of the widely-used Allahson of If, who in turn sired the famous Ch. Cillahson of Picardy, bred by Col. Baldwin. Cillahson's dam was Cilla of Picardy, one of the bitches purchased from the Terraqueuse kennel in France. Allahson's dam was Diana of If (Dierma v. Humboldtspark).

It was upon these dogs, and many others of similar type, that the breed was founded in the British Isles. It was Pickett's opinion that "later importation of new crosses from Germany was to weaken rather than strengthen the breed". No doubt he was referring to the Klodo/Utz breeding. Pickett, when writing at a later date about the breed in Germany, contended that, far from having advocated a return to the Standard, (i.e. the Standard for the working German Shepherd), von Stephanitz had actually resisted such a trend.

"The first World War had weakened the finances of the Society (the SV) and it strengthened the element of revolt against the old man's benevolent despotism... Other voices made themselves heard, and he was forced, by sheer necessity, to agree to a change in the methods and Standard to be used in selecting Grand Champions, and a cry arose for smaller, working dogs. The old nobler, bigger Grand Champions were sold out of the country, and little dogs which were just within the Standard, and some even sub-standard, were given honours."

By the time Pickett wrote these words and others equally scandalous, von Stephanitz was already dead and could not defend himself.

THE WORKING TRADITION

Thus, Pickett was able to underwrite his support for the older, bigger dogs, by claiming they were being championed by von Stephanitz himself, whereas quite the opposite was the case. Yet, unlike Tobias Ott and Dr Sachs, Pickett and his associates did not necessarily admire these early dogs for their character and working ability. So far as is known, these early British enthusiasts of the breed were more interested in showing their dogs than working them, with notable exceptions such as Mesdames Workman, Griffin, Barrington and their friends. Also, with the commencement of Working Trials organised by the Associated Sheep, Police and Army Dog Society (ASPADS) in 1924, a number of enthusiasts devoted themselves to developing the working side of the breed, for instance: Mr and Mrs Rex Walker and Major Beddoes. Captain Gurney and Lady Kitty Ritson visited the German police school at Grunheide and brought back much valuable information on German training methods. Interest in the working side culminated in the establishment, by Colonel Baldwin, of the RAF Police Dog School at Gloucester during the Second World War. The breed and the working fraternity went their separate ways for the most part, which may account for the fact that, to this day, the breed community shows very little interest in the working aspect of the German Shepherd Dog.

In fact, Pickett made much of the German Shepherd's unsuitability to work with flocks in the British Isles, claiming that the practice of biting sheep in order to control them was abhorrent, and that native British breeds, such as the Border Collie and Working Sheepdog, were much more suitable for the task. This is another example of Pickett's distortion of the truth. In fact, no claim was made by the Germans or anyone else, that the German Shepherd should come into Britain in order to replace native Sheepdogs. In the first place, their function is quite different. The sheepdogs in Britain work mainly as the 'long arm' of the farmer. Their main duty is to keep control of the flock and to see that it does not stray during the journey from one place to another, as required by the farmer, who remains in direct control of the dogs, commanding them by voice or whistle. The situation in Germany is quite different. Sheep are pastured between arable crops, and it is the duty of the Shepherd Dog to keep the flock on the pasture and away from the crop. Pasture is usually separated from the crops by a furrow. These dogs operate on their own initiative, taking decisions as necessary to control the sheep. Von Stephanitz describes the operation of the German Shepherd as a herding dog in the following way:

"When warding off in front of the crop, the dog must never make unnecessary exertions; he walks up and down the furrow before the pasturing flock when the occasion demands it, and stands from time to time to convince himself that all is in order behind his back. He will drive off single pilferers by a short run, and the obstinate ones are punished by a short firm bite. If the sheep should advance toward the crop in a body, he must throw himself on them without hesitation. If the dog does not know how to assert his authority over the sheep, the greedy flock will immediately press forward more and more eagerly, and finally force a weaker dog to stand back, or will even trample him under their feet if he dares to stand fast... The bite of the haunches is the only bite by which he can hold the sheep fast and administer a punishment which will be felt afterwards, without doing any serious harm (to the sheep)".

As we saw in Chapter One, the German Shepherd Dog was launched as a police and service dog in the motherland, although it was, and still is, used for tending sheep on the plains and hills of Germany.

NEW INFLUENCES

The Klodo/Utz influence, so strong in Germany as we have seen, was not apparent on the British scene until the arrival of Voss v. Bern. This was because the trend set by Pickett tended to be followed by others. Miss Workman imported Armin Ernaslieb in 1927. Nearly top-sized, he was line-bred to Horst von Boll. His great-grandmother on the dam's side was from unknown parentage, and the dam of Armin was a great grand-daughter of Nores von der Kriminal Polizei.

The breeding behind this popular and influential dog of his day was, in the opinion of some commentators, questionable to say the least. But this assessment of Armin's ancestry does not, in our opinion, stand up to closer examination. Apart from the Kriminal Polizei element, there were warnings out on Horst von Boll, which came from von Stephanitz himself. Armin had been mated with daughters of Caro of Welham and Allahson of If, which gave lines back to Hettel Uckermark through Alex Westfalenheim (sire of Erich Grafenwerth) and Greif von der Peterstirn, the latter a Billo Riedekenburg son, against whom allegations have been made that he produced bad temperament.

While there were indications that Greif might have produced some animals with weak temperaments, he was not, in fact, warned against at his Körung, as some would have us believe. The influence of Hettel Uckermark must be generally considered good, but von Stephanitz had grave reservations about combinations involving Horst von Boll. However, it must be made clear that the 'grave reservations' about combinations involving Hettel and Horst von Boll are purely with respect to height. In the 1932 revision of *'The German Shepherd Dog in Word and Picture'*, von Stephanitz wrote:

"Quite often, Hettel is being blamed for a considerable increase in size in the breed. This is not justified, in the first place because the low-to-ground dog with his good conformation for work and power of heredity cannot be made responsible for that... breastless and flat, but at the same time also high-legged and square, 'beauty' of a period which fortunately has meanwhile passed; where the real responsibility for such a transformation lies has been explained earlier. I myself have measured Hettel at an exhibition in Berlin on January 29/30th, 1910. His height was 64 cm., that is to say fully within the limits. It was... the mass of bones which made the impression of excessive height; these bones were transmitted to him by his mother Gretel Uckermark, who, on her part, got them from the maternal Schatten-line, going back to Swabian sheepdogs.

"At that time, for this reason, I warned about using Hettel blood together with Horst blood. Unfortunately, this warning has not been heeded enough, and the combination of both did not create harmonious results. Their blood seems to have been little true to type, although Horst von Boll on his father's side and through Munko von Boll, Beowulf and Hektor leads back to the Horand strain as well. The maternal strain going back to Swabian service dogs, through Hella von Boll, seems to have had a stronger power of heredity which can be seen very clearly in combinations of Hettel and Horst blood... in that Swabian service dog of old, the blood of the bigger and heavier old German dogs, the hunting dogs, predominated.

"I measured Horst at the same exhibition in Berlin (1910), his height at that time, when he was only nine months old, was already 68 cm... Later on he became still bigger and heavier. At that time, as yet, we unfortunately had no breed survey, and besides we knew too little about the dangers which were about to threaten our breed from the mass influx of such damaging blood."

There is evidence for believing that often too much has been read into so-called warnings on certain dogs. Schäller was one writer on bloodlines who, in 1932, stated that comments made in the Körung report did not amount to general warnings. Modern Körbucher also advise against the further use of various dogs without the named animals turning into 'warning' dogs.

Armin won ten Challenge Certificates, which proves that he was admired by judges of the day. His famous son, Ch. Adalo of Ceara, became a widely-used sire of the period, producing more winning progeny than virtually any other dog of the time, including the outstanding Champion Roland of Coulmony, who won thirty Challenge Certificates and twenty Reserve CCs. Yet, in the run-up to the appearance of Voss von Bern in the British Isles, breeding decisions were being made which provided signposts to the type-change, which would by the thirties and forties become established in the UK, mainly through the contributions of the influential Brittas kennel.

Picardy-bred dogs were at the forefront in the early thirties. Allei of Picardy, a son of Allahson of If, was mated to the Utz daughter, Beda von Anderton. From this litter – the J litter – emerged the three famous champions, Janitor, Jade and Jocose. When Dr Werner Funk judged in England in 1933 (his first judging trip to the British Isles), he expressed concern about the influence of Armin and Adalo, especially if there was a concentration of genetic line-breeding. His main criticism was temperament and dentition, as well as the strong suggestion that type should be brought more into line with Germany's prevailing trends of robustness and toughness, correct proportions rather than leggy elegance, strong masculinity with correct angulation, instead of curves and beauty.

Yet, as we have seen, the opinion of Dr Funk, to which he was fully entitled, did not necessarily accord with the opinions of others about Armin and Adalo, especially on the question of temperament. Armin himself was a dog of good character and tended to produce the same in his progeny. A clearer signpost was the Adalo daughter Irish Champion Fee (Bell), dam of the Utz grandson Int. Ch. Gerolf of Brittas, the foundation of many 'families' of German Shepherds in Great Britain. Some importations of the time, such as the Klodo daughter Dieta von Zuchtgut (bred by von Stephanitz at the official SV breeding kennel) left no surviving progeny. Sylvia v. d. Schreckenstein, daughter of the influential Klodo son, Alf v. Webbelsmannslust, was imported to be campaigned in the show ring and bred from by Thelma Gray of the Rozavel kennel. Sylvia obtained her title but produced nothing of note, even when mated to leading sires of the day.

VOSS AND THE BRITTAS LEGACY

When Mrs Gwen Barrington imported Voss von Bern, she did so as a result of consultations with Herta von Stephanitz, daughter of the Rittmeister, with whom she was very friendly. As a member of the SV, Mrs Barrington also had access to all the up-to-date information on breeding trends. She did more than any other breeder to establish the Klodo-Utz type in the UK. Voss was undoubtedly a dog with a good genetic background and much potential, which was later realised in the list of high-quality dogs which subsequently came from the Brittas kennel.

Voss's sister, Vikki, was one of those bitches who reinforces the dictum that the breed needs great-producing broods, as well as top-quality sires. Would the German Shepherd have got where it is today without Liane von der Wienerau, Wilma von der Kisselschlucht, Flora vom Königsbruch and, more recently, Palme vom Wildersteigerland?

Vikki's daughter, Traute von Bern, was made Siegerin in 1937. We have seen that Vikki was also grand-dam of Pfeffer von Bern, of paramount influence in the United States, and himself Sieger in the same year. Gockel von Bern, Vikki's son, was tail-male descended from Utz through Wigand v. Blasienberg and Baron v. d. Deutschen Werken. Mated to the colour-paled Illa v. Oppeln-Ost,

Ingo vom Piastendamm: Sire of Ingosohn of Errol and grandsire of Ch. Avon Prince.

Gockel produced Ingo vom Piastendamm, a dog which was to have enormous influence – not necessarily for the good – on the breeding of German Shepherds in Great Britain, as we shall see later.

Voss came to Britain with a working degree in what would now be termed Schutzhund. He had acquired the ZPr and the HGH, which is the qualification for active herding dogs. Most, but not all, German imports came with one or other of the working qualifications – ZPr, Sch.H, or PH. These three tests in that order of difficulty were changed by the German Kennel Club on January 1st 1938, to their modern equivalents, as follows:

ZPr. (Zuchtprüfung bestanden) became Sch H1
Sch.H (Schutzhund) became Sch.H2
PH (Polizeihund) became Sch.H3

Each test contained the three phases: Obedience (including Agility); nosework (tracking); and protection work.

It is noteworthy that the Champion progeny of these imports are not listed as having any German working qualifications. It must be assumed that the importers, anxious though they were to build up the breed in the UK, had no intention of importing the working system of the German Kennel Club as part of the tradition of the breed. This may have been due, in part, to the existence of British Kennel Club Working Trials, but was more probably due to a strong objection to any working-system of German origin. A few dogs who became Champions did obtain British working trials qualifications, but these must be considered only a very small percentage of the total list of Champions. Therefore, we can only conclude that German Shepherd enthusiasts were, for the most part, not interested in working their dogs. If this judgement is correct for the period under review, it remains correct for Britain in the nineties. The arrival of Schutzhund on these shores may, in the long term, change this attitude.

The Brittas kennel, with its progressive view of the German Shepherd Dog, was not among the kennels in the British Isles who denied the purpose for which the breed had been created – as a general-purpose working dog. Voss, in due course, obtained his British working trial qualifications PD and TD, and, for a brief period under the inspired direction of its owner Mrs Barrington, the Brittas kennel brought the breed of German Shepherd into the mainstream in Britain. That it did not remain on track was due mainly due to the Second World War.

Ironically, it was not opponents of the type of Utz and Klodo who created a backlash to the Brittas movement. Britain had no equivalent of Tobias Ott or Dr Sachs, who were concerned mainly with restoration of the working qualities of the old Shepherd bloodlines, or altblutlinie. The seeds of decline were planted by false prophets, one in particular as we shall see later, and by the influence of the 'fancy', which reduced the breed, or at least that part with the highest profile, to the status of a show-dog, a fate from which the breed in Germany had been decisively rescued. A further irony is that the Brittas legacy, with its series of great dogs – Int. Ch. Gerolf of Brittas and Int. Ch. Vagabond of Brittas to name just two of the most illustrious – and the bloodlines upon which they were based, became the fountainhead of the show-dog output from the new post-war German Shepherd breeders. Eventually, all that remained were the faults of the Klodo/Utz era. The virtues had been lost on the way.

BAD PUBLICITY

Problems, in the pre-war period, arose from the popularity of the breed, which attracted as many enemies as friends and supporters. Nor was this entirely due to unjustified onslaughts by the Press, based on the public view of a dog that looked like a wolf. Indeed, as we have seen, it bore the name of 'Alsatian Wolf Dog' until 1924, and was thus linked with an animal historically regarded as a vile, menacing, ferocious beast, worthy only to be driven to extinction. It is only now that this has almost been achieved, that wildlife experts and conservationists have re-evaluated the wolf and discovered that man – the greatest predator of all – has made a tragic mistake.

Many of the attacks upon the breed were based on incorrect reports that Alsatians had savaged humans and, upon investigation, usually carried out by the Alsatian League and Club, it was often found that the dog concerned was not an Alsatian at all. Nevertheless, it must be admitted that there were cases involving pure-bred Alsatians. It is worth reflecting on the dangers involved in importing and using – perhaps over-using – bloodlines upon which warnings had been issued. This is serious enough, and presumably breeders who used these lines did so knowing they were taking risks. On the other hand, some breeders, being outside the orbit of the SV, did not have their ear to the ground about the incidence of faults in certain lines. If experienced breeders can make serious errors in their breeding policies, what hope is there for people who breed dogs without regard for the material they are using?

We have already seen that breeding in the Anglo Saxon world is based on freedom of choice in the context of individual kennels. Also, the Kennel Clubs of Britain and America tend, with their award systems, to encourage competition rather than co-operation in the breeding of dogs. Such a system could be said to promote secrecy, especially concerning breeding faults, some of which may be genetic in origin. In such a climate, small wonder that dog breeders tend to keep the faults of their breeding to themselves. Secrecy about breeding is comparable to the mystique surrounding judging decisions. In this private world, breeder is pitted against breeder and exhibitor against exhibitor. What suffers is the breed itself.

Nowadays, at last, things are changing. In recent years, breeders have been forced by necessity to become more open, as is witnessed by the various screening programmes for hips, eyes, and so on. Yet, no authority in the UK, least of all the Kennel Club, will act to make registration of stock conditional upon good hip status and freedom from other hereditary faults, which could be detected by screening.

IRRESPONSIBLE BREEDERS

In the thirties, no such schemes existed to help with breeding decisions. When it became clear that the Alsatian, or German Shepherd, was a highly-marketable product attracting quick profits, the puppy-farmers moved in. Litter after litter was produced, with scant regard for temperament and constitution. In some cases, dogs of mixed-breeding were sold as 'Alsatians'. The established breeders of the period were kept on track by the sanctions of show ring performance, bearing in mind that many shows were judged by visiting specialists from Germany and other countries. But it must be realised that there was another category involved in the breeding of the German Shepherd,whose practitioners were not so much unscrupulous as ignorant.

Anyone in the UK can set up as a breeder of dogs, and anyone with a dog and a bitch can breed a litter. The only sanction is the law of the land, which imposes penalties for nuisance and unacceptable behaviour. These penalties are very stringent today, under the provisions of the Dangerous Dogs Act, but such legislation is directed at the owner. A breeder who produces the dog that goes around attacking people escapes scot-free. Some cases are caused by the dog's lack of socialisation and training, as well as by environmental influences. But we are convinced that a hereditary component exists, and if this is denied or ignored, the whole concept of selected breeding is undermined.

The Breeding of Dogs Act of 1973, an attempt to control puppy-farming, has failed. Puppy-farms are often spick-and-span, which impresses the inspectors, who are more concerned with nuts and bolts and bricks and mortar than with the quality of stock, the assessment of which is beyond their expertise, in any case. Thus, even today, the general public has no protection against bad breeding in the UK, beyond the advice given by genuine lovers of the German Shepherd, by the study of good books about the breed, and by membership of a GSD Breed Society. Those who miss the signposts to better breeding can, and often do, fall victim to ignorant and unscrupulous operators. If this still happens in the nineties, imagine the situation in Britain sixty years ago.

THE BREED IN DECLINE
From the highpoint of 1926, when 8,056 Alsatians were registered with the Kennel Club, numbers fell steadily, to only 2,057 in 1939. In 1936, the official title of the breed in the UK was changed to Alsatian (German Shepherd Dog). This was doubtless due to pressure from Germany, where it was

Ch. Avon Prince of Alumvale: A great show dog and forerunner of the post-war British Alsatian type.

argued that if the English Kennel Club expected the Germans to send over their judges, then it was only fair to give some recognition to the breed's country of origin in the official title for use in Great Britain.

Pickett considered that the change of name, plus what he called "the alteration of the Standard" was largely responsible for the decline in registrations. In fact, there had been no change in the Standard, merely a return to the correct middle-size dog. But Pickett and his fellow exhibitors found themselves out on a limb because most of their dogs were oversize. Thus he wrote after the war:

"The effect of the alteration of the Standard had been very largely to destroy the popularity of the Alsatian. Kennel Club registrations had fallen to a hopeless degree, and it looks as though the breed was on a fair way to extinction."

Our own view is that, whatever objections some people may have had to the addition of 'German Shepherd Dog' to the official title of the breed, they could, and overwhelmingly did, continue to use the name 'Alsatian'. It was not until an AGM of the Kennel Club in the mid-Seventies that the name was reversed on a proposal from the floor by Breed Geneticist, Dr Malcolm Willis. The breed became 'German Shepherd Dog (Alsatian)', and the word 'Alsatian' began to be phased out. As for the size factor, only some exhibitors were affected because their dogs were too big.

By far the most likely cause of decline in popularity and numbers was due to the abuse of freedoms by bad breeders. This brought the German Shepherd into such disrepute that even today, some people cannot trust this noble and intelligent breed. This is a sad consequence of some instances of indifferently-bred and badly-behaved German Shepherds giving the whole breed a bad name.

Chapter Four

THE POST-WAR YEARS

GERMANY – PROGRESS AND DEVELOPMENT
The impact of the Second World War on the GSD in Germany was severe and, though many good dogs, such as Faust vom Busecker Schloss, were lost, there was still enough valuable stock to enable a new start to be made. Sieger shows were suspended during the period 1938-1954. The Auslesegruppe system (Select group) was to take its place. During the war two shows of this type were held, in 1941 and 1942, and, after the war, two were held in 1946, in the British and American zones respectively. Alf v. Nordfelsen was the first Sieger of the post-war period, gaining his title in 1955. It is of interest that the Sieger title was again abolished between 1974-1977 in order to persuade breeders not to concentrate on the Sieger for stud purposes, but to make use of other Select (VA) dogs. In 1978 the title of Sieger was once more revived, it is believed by popular demand, when Canto V. Arminius was crowned. Descendants of Ingo vom Piastendamm may have been incorrectly used in British breeding programmes, but the reverse was true in Germany. This line, through Rolf vom Osnabrückerland and similar breeding, produced an excellent type which excelled in front angulation, in head and in powerful, correct movement. There was, however, considerable in-breeding, which took place in the Osnabrückerland and Preussenblut kennels, resulting in slightly too much length in the back and perhaps less-than-perfect rear angulation. There was also a tendency towards colour paling. By and large, however, Rolf and the 'R' litter Osnabrückerland produced just what was needed at this stage of the development of the breed in Germany, which was very much a milestone for later breeding.

POST-WAR BREEDING
We must not overlook the importance of Rolf's sire, Lex Preussenblut, in helping to re-establish the breed after the war. Lex was line-bred on Utz through Ingo vom Piastendamm, and any subsequent colour paling in the Rolf line probably stemmed from Ingo's dam, Illa von Oppeln-Ost. However, Lex also had lines back to Klodo v. Boxberg, without Utz, through Kurt von Herzog Hedan and Bodo von Brahmenau. Kurt's descendants were generally good on temperament and strengthening of colour. But long coats came through, and a tendency to long backs and short front legs. Lex's son, Danko vom Menkenmoor, was exported to Britain and was to fix the latter characteristic into British bloodlines with far-reaching effect. But the virtues of Lex and his progeny were well utilised in Germany, especially correct forequarter angulation and good heads, which became fixed characteristics in the Preussenblut/Osnabrückerland line-breeding.

It is noteworthy that parallel bloodlines were developing in Germany, some of which came from the 'old' breeding – pre-Klodo v. Boxberg, which would play their part at a later stage in producing the excellence that today is taken for granted in the German Shepherd Dog. One of these was Nestor vom Wiegerfelsen, the sire of Immo vom Hasenfang. One of his sons, Axel von der Deininghauserheide, sired the 1955 Sieger Alf vom Nordfelsen. Mutz von der Pelztierfarm, one of the three pillars of the breed in the modern era, is descended from this great-producing dog.

Rolf v. Osnabrückerland: Represented a 'milestone' of post-war GSD breeding.

Axel v.d. Deininghauser heide: Influential ancestor of modern breeding lines mainly through Mutz v.d. Pelztierfarm.

Mutz has been instrumental, not only in the production of several quality dogs with high Vs and VAs, but is especially significant for his influence on today's top-producing stock, such as Nick von der Wienerau, who appears on the pedigrees of Double Sieger Uran vom Wildsteigerland and Double Sieger Quando von Arminius. The other two great-producing dogs, Canto von der Wienerau and Quanto von der Wienerau, also pillars of the modern era, stemmed direct from Rolf by two separate routes. Canto was tail-male descended from the Rolf son Alf Walddorf-Emst and Quando from the Rolf son Arko Delog.

INFLUENTIAL LINES

We must emphasise that it is not our intention to go into great detail about individual dogs and their descriptions. This has been done adequately and, indeed, assiduously by other writers and, for those who can read German, the reports of each of the dogs shown at the Sieger Shows appear in the December issue of the *SV Zeitung* each year. Our purpose has been to trace the development of the breed and to highlight significant dogs and breeding which have, in our opinion, advanced the German Shepherd Dog. The central principle has been, firstly, that the dog should be bred to be an efficient and enduring working Shepherd, and secondly, that the type should be maintained and hopefully improved. The great popularity of the 'R' litter Osnabrückerland, due to the excellence of the type produced, resulted in something of a bottleneck. It then became the task of the German authorities to find alternative but complementary lines to carry the breed forward on the principle of 'enhance the virtues, correct the faults'.

We have followed the practice of tracing bloodlines through tail-male descent. The main reason for this is the abundance of information about the descent of various German Shepherd lines through males, and a paucity through females. It will doubtless be appreciated that, even if this were not the case, the male exerts far more influence than the female, simply because of the wide usage of males across the spectrum of the breed. However, certain females have exerted an enormous influence on the breed. One example is, of course, Palme vom Wildsteigerland, whose name will be well-known wherever German Shepherds are bred and exhibited.

One practice that has been widespread is the transfer of bitches, known to be good producers, from one kennel to another. Although the male is still in a pre-eminent position to influence the direction of the breed, the female must be given full and complete recognition. This outlook accords very much with our own view that the strength of a kennel lies in its bitches. We believe that there are enough good dogs around to mate our bitches to, but without the necessary quality in the bitches themselves, there is no chance of achieving anything more than mediocrity.

The task of the authorities was to retain the virtues of the 'R' litter Osnabrückerland but to prevent the faults, to which we have already referred, gaining ascendancy. At the peak of the Rolf period, something like sixty per cent of the surveyed stock was line-bred on the 'R' litter. Attempts were made to seek other lines which would combine with Rolf. One example was Hein von Richterbach, who was tail-male descended to the Utz son, Hussan vom Haus Schütting, via Billo vom Oberviehland, out of Rosel, litter sister to Rolf. However, this line did not continue in favour because of faults in the progeny, such as unevenness in type, though there were individual examples of outstanding merit. Cryptorchidism and dental problems were also noted. His grandson through Cäsar von der Malmannsheide, Hein's son, was influential in Britain. The grandson was Cent zu den Fünf Giebeln who, mated to the Avon Prince daughter, Hella of Charavigne, produced Champion Ludwig of Charavigne and Lorenz of Charavigne.

Ludwig was a very popular sire and was used over a wide range of bitches, most of whom were descendants of Avon Prince. The one thing most people found very attractive was the colour, a red coloration, but this was not really a strengthening process, if anything the reverse. Avon Prince was often held to account for the faults produced by Ludwig and litter brother Lorenz, but there is no doubt that Cent must take his share of the blame. It must be admitted that the type from Lorenz was superior to that of Ludwig, reflecting more of the German influence.

THE IMPORTANCE OF TEMPERAMENT

Another very important dog, Vello zu den Sieben Faulen, sprang from the Rolf son, Donner zu den Sieben Faulen, through Yasko Tiede and Lex vom Drei Kinder Haus. Vello was a large dog with an excellent temperament, a quality he seems to have produced. He is reported as not having been successful in the Breed Survey, but it is unclear whether he was entered and failed, or whether he did not present himself. Vello produced the 'B' litter von Lierberg, Bernd and Bodo. Bodo was made Sieger in 1967 but was exported to America shortly afterwards, and so was lost to the scene in Germany. Bernd was VA3, and though Dr Funk seemed to have some reservation about Bernd's size as he did about Bodo's (he would have preferred them both a bit smaller) the thing that assured their position in the Auslesegruppe was their excellent performance in the courage test, introduced for the first time that year.

We should take care not to read too much into the SV's 1967 decision to bring in this test of courage. We must bear in mind that a test of courage forms part of the Körung and is an integral part of the Working Degrees all dogs must have if they are to compete in the adult classes of the Sieger Shows. The Working Test is the Schutzhund Prüfung. It would appear that the SV wished to make a public statement to all onlookers at the Sieger Show that temperament was uppermost in their minds. They wished to make it clear that the dogs which were being awarded the highest grades were also dogs that were not to be doubted on the matter of their temperament, in particular their courage and ability to stand up to pressure. Indeed, those of us in the ring at the time when it was decided to give Bodo the title and to confirm which dogs had been given the VA rating, heard Dr Rummel announce that "this is the year when temperament is paramount."

The test of courage was a complete surprise, at least to those outside the orbit of the SV. It did create a great impression, and if it was the wish of the SV to use it as a public relations exercise, it did succeed in broadcasting to the world that however close to the Standard a dog might be in bodily construction and ability to perform, unless it had the necessary character and temperament, it could not properly be called a German Shepherd. Indeed, although Dr Rummel was not, as yet, to take over the Presidency, on that occasion and many times afterwards, he repeatedly made the point that the temperament aspect must be given absolute prominence. The message was that however good the German Shepherd might be in its appearance, the correct mental characteristics must be 'Ausgeprägt' – present to a very marked degree.

It is true to say that the 'B' litter von Lierberg became noted for its contribution to the working German Shepherd scene. This litter has received high praise around Europe and elsewhere in the world, and it has been customary to give the credit for this to the sire of Bodo, Vello zu den Sieben Faulen. It must not be overlooked that the dam of Bodo and Bernd, Betty von Eningsfeld, was a daughter of the Leistungs-Sieger (Working Trials Sieger) Arko v. Riedersknapp.

It is noteworthy that at the same show Dr Funk had earmarked a number of high-ranking dogs for the VA Group but, because of their less than desired performance in the courage test, they found themselves outside the Select Group. These dogs were Abo z. Aspenweg, Gundo von Preussentor, and Condor von Kupferhof. The sires of these three dogs were Quido von Haus Schütting (a son of the 1964 Sieger Zibu v. Haus Schütting), Mutz a. d. Kückstrasse, who was exported to England, and Cäsar v. d. Malmannsheide. The courage test for adult dogs and bitches at the Sieger Show has remained ever since, and it is welcomed with loud cheers as the dogs show their paces when placed under pressure during the test.

However, during recent years, certain criticism has arisen because some of the dogs have not, when 'taking the sleeve', come off on one command. In some extreme cases they have actually had to be pulled off. Consequently, for the first time in 1993, it is now a requirement that dogs cannot be classified in the Select Group if they fail to come off the 'sleeve' on a single command. This has been dictated by the need to respect the general public perception of the dog and to emphasise the need for control as well as courage. It could be said that the watchword for the 1990s is 'Courage without control is no courage at all'.

WORKING BLOODLINES

We have already mentioned that two of the three sons of Klodo vom Boxberg were important for their ability to produce good temperaments and working qualities. These were Donar v. Zuchtgut and Kurt v. Herzog Hedan. A dog who was to prove a very useful out-cross to the Rolf breeding was Klodo aus der Eremitenklause, descended from Kurt through Arras v. Adam Riesenzwinger. A grandson of Klodo, Hero vom Lauerhof became the VA2 and Reserve Sieger in 1972 and 1973. Hero had a double pre-molar 1 in the upper jaw on the right and on the left, and though this was not mentioned in Dr Rummel's report on him the first year, it certainly appeared in the report the second year. Nowadays, this fault will not prevent a dog from becoming classified as V, but it will block entry into the VA Group. Klodo's chief importance for England is in the three sons who were exported to the UK: Ch.and Irish Ch. Condor vom Schiefen Giebel, Ferdl v. d. Eschbacherklippen, and Ilk v. d. Eschbacherklippen. Condor played an important part in the breeding of the Dunmonaidh German Shepherds. Ilk, of course, wielded tremendous influence as the grandsire of Ch. Rossfort Premonition.

Mike vom Bungalow and his son, Eros vom Busecker Schloss, were directly descended from Donar v. Zuchtgut. Eros and Mike have continued to exert a wide influence on the pedigrees of dogs primarily concerned with success in competitive Schutzhund competitions, such as the Bundessieger Prüfung and WUSV Working Trials. In fact, close study of the monthly editions of the *SV Zeitung* will reveal that a very large proportion of those dogs advertised at stud as primarily of interest to working as opposed to show enthusiasts, contain Mike and Eros on their pedigrees. These dogs are so advertised because of the enormous respect that Working people have for everything that these dogs stand for.

Another very important dog from the vom Busecker Schloss kennel was Valet vom Busecker Schloss, a son of the 1957 Sieger Arno vom Haus Gersie, ex a daughter of Lido Friedlichen Heim. A half-brother to Eros by Ebbo v. Astenor Moor out of Seffe Busecker Schloss, Rocco v. Busecker Schloss made V6 at the 1974 Sieger Show, and V2 at the 1975 Sieger Show. Rocco was inbred 4:5 on Alf vom Nordfelsen, the 1955 Sieger and Lido Friedlichen Heim 4:5.

We saw Rocco and Seffe on a visit to Busecker Schloss kennels in 1974. Rocco was what you might call a hard dog and Seffe was about seven or eight years of age, and presumably at the end of her career as a breeding bitch. But it was wonderful to see these animals with their strong temperaments and terrific presence. In the eyes of some breeders, not only in Germany but also elsewhere, including the United Kingdom, Herr Hahn has not always followed fashion with regard to the shape of the German Shepherd, which has admittedly, over the years, become more uniform and more angulated in the hindquarters. Herr Hahn has always believed that the German Shepherd is a functional dog, and that its function is work. He has never veered away from this doctrine, which is why the bloodlines of the famous Busecker Schloss dogs remain revered and popular with all who regard the German Shepherd as a working dog.

The end of the 1960s saw the gradual withdrawal from leadership of the SV on the part of Dr Funk, and the greater prominence of Dr Rummel in the decision-making process. Some said that at the 1967 Sieger Show Dr Funk had wanted to put Quax v. Haus Beck VA2 into the first position instead of Bodo. That is a matter for conjecture, but what certainly is true is that Dr Funk wrote in his notes that if Quax had been older (he was born on February 28th 1965), this son of the 1964 Sieger Zibu v. Haus Schütting would have been placed first, assuming there were enough progeny present to justify his being characterised as a good producer. At the 1966 Sieger Show, the title was given to Basko v. d. Kahlerheide, also a son of Zibu. This was a very impressive dog with an excellent topline, perhaps a fraction on the long side. He did not stay in Germany long after he obtained his title and was exported to the United States. Basko was a good dog, however, and although his blood was little used in Great Britain, it was incorporated, through his son Letton Barolf of Brittas, into Shootersway breeding with good results. Zibu was also the sire of the 1968 Sieger Dido von der Werther Königsallee.

BRITAIN – ALSATIAN VERSUS GSD

Imagine taking an overseas visitor, with an eye for a good Shepherd, on a trip round the UK shows to any of the events run by member clubs of the GSD Breed Council, the GSD League or BAGSD (the British Association for German Shepherd Dogs). If you followed such an excursion with an outing to the GSD (Alsatian) Club of the UK and their satellites, your visitor would be struck by the type difference, almost to the extent that you appear to be looking at two different breeds. Indeed, there has been an attempt to persuade the Kennel Club to split the register into Alsatians and German Shepherds. Fortunately, the would-be petitioners could not find the necessary majority within the ranks of their own club – the GSD (Alsatian) Club of the UK.

THE CASE AGAINST TWO BREEDS

Had the movement to split the register proceeded, it is extremely unlikely that the Kennel Club would have given its approval, if only because it would be extremely difficult to establish proper criteria for any division of the breed. If this had been the view of the Kennel Club, should the matter have been put before them, then we, as breeders, would have been in complete agreement. In strict terms, the concept of two separate types is erroneous in the case of the German Shepherd, for the simple reason that, given a strict and clear Standard of points, dogs vary only in the degree to which they adhere to, or depart from, that Standard. In other words, the concept of two types, not to mention two breeds, is entirely bogus. There are only good dogs and bad dogs, with degrees of goodness and badness in between these two extremes. Others think it all comes down to the question of interpretation.

Whether you think that the Alsatian is a British version of the German Shepherd, or is merely a bad version of the same breed, does not alter the fact that in Great Britain the German Shepherd did depart from the mainstream in the years following the Second World War. There are various reasons for this phenomenon. Admittedly, post-war British breeders were cut off from influence from the motherland, as a result of the war and its aftermath. At the same time the state of mind of the breed's enthusiasts was particularly favourable to the Anglicisation of this native German breed. This was partly due to the circumstances in which the dog was brought to these islands in the first place, but even more important was the inherent tendency of British, and, for that matter, American dogdom to change a foreign breed of dog to suit the tastes of the 'fancy'.

One example of this is the Cocker Spaniel, which went to the USA and was subjected to so many changes that when it came back to these shores, it was another breed altogether – the American Cocker. The British Alsatian was thus nurtured in a favourable climate of opinion, which, at the same time, was reinforced by necessity. Realistically, the Germans would have been unable to supply new blood in any appreciable quantity, simply because they could not prejudice the build-up of their own breeding base, which had been undermined as a result of the war.

POST-WAR BREEDING TRENDS

The two dogs of importance that did arrive in Great Britain during this period were, ironically enough, destined to compound, rather than correct, the faults inherent in the blood of Utz and Klodo. The arrival of Ingosohn of Errol during, and Danko vom Menkenmoor after the war served to consolidate the defects of their immediate forbears, and their common ancestry of Ingo vom Piastendamm and Utz. In our opinion, the advice of false prophets was also heeded and took its toll. Ingosohn was born on a ship in the North Sea, and there can be no doubt that the incorporation of this dog into the breeding plans of numerous British fanciers, chiefly through his grandson, Ch. Avon Prince of Alumvale, heralded the post-war era of the breed.

The chief GSD prophet of the forties and fifties was Joseph Schwabacher, a fugitive from the Nazis, who had managed to escape to Britain. He succeeded in re-establishing his Secretainerie line in the British Isles. Ingosohn was by Ingo vom Piastendamm out of one of his own bitches, Franze Secretainerie. According to the breed authority, the late Nem Elliott, Schwabacher promoted Ingosohn far and wide, mating the dog to many bitches, not all, by any means, suitable. Elliott wrote:

"The country was flooded with Ingosohn stock, much of it bad... Ingosohn had a number of undesirable recessives such as orchidism, whites, colour paling and long coats, and he transmitted these to a considerable extent." Ingosohn refered to other faults "... round ribs with lack of brisket... flat croups, high-set tails, weak pasterns, soft backs and a definite tendency to bone weakness."

Breed geneticist, Dr Malcolm Willis, supports the view of Nem Elliott, stating that Ingosohn was "a dangerous dog for the breed." In considering the importance of Ingosohn, through the popularity of his grandson, Avon Prince, let us first consider the characteristics of the Klodo/Utz line, both good and bad, and the breeding behind Ingosohn. So long as Ingo vom Piastendamm was recognised as the purveyor of the best qualities of the Klodo/Utz line, he was sure to remain, as he did, on the main stem of breeding in Germany. In fact, the other lines from Utz on the German breeding pale into insignificance compared with those from Ingo.

After all, the pillars of today's breeding of the German Shepherd, Double Sieger Uran vom Wildsteigerland and Double Sieger Quando von Arminius, descend from Utz through Ingo. Ingo was an important link between Klodo/Utz through Rolf v. Osnabrückerland to what are regarded as the best of today's German Shepherds in the motherland. This seems difficult to accept in the light of the effect of the same dog, Ingo, on the British scene – apparently the complete opposite of the German legacy.

It became fashionable to combine the blood of Avon Prince with that of Danko, a son of the dominant German sire, Lex Preussenblut, who was related to Utz and Ingo by direct tail-male descent. Why were the descendants of these two dogs mated with each other? The answer was because they produced winners in the show ring. As long as judges heaped honours on great show dogs like Avon Prince, and on their progeny year after year, with the same winning formula scoring again and again, breeders continued to produce what the fanciers wanted. The glamorous show winner made the running, until by the early sixties, a point of no return might have been reached had it not been for a small group of dedicated breeders and enthusiasts. They were worried about the direction in which the breed in Great Britain was heading, and resolved to do something about it.

LOOKING BACK ON SOME GREAT SHEPHERDS

It would be wrong to assume that there were no great, or even good, dogs during this post-war period. When we started exhibiting in 1959, we can remember the thrill of seeing the famous Ch. and Irish Ch. Asoka Cherusker at Crufts, even though he was beaten on the day by Ch. Demetrius of Kentwood. Both of these dogs had much in common breeding-wise. Demetrius was a son of Ch. Quince of Southavon out of Ch. Perdita of Kentwood, and was thus line-bred on Gottfried of Coulathorne. Cherusker was tail-male descended via Ch. Crusader of Evesyde, Quince, Ch. Romana Peppino, and Mario Romana from Gottfried. The fountainhead of this line was the all-black Dulo v. Minsweert, whose greatest claim to fame was that he produced Ch. Dante of Charavigne, one of whose sons was Gottfried.

Dulo, through Dante, did improve angulation in the German Shepherd, but he seems not to have contributed firmness of temperament. Nem Elliot, nevertheless, considered this line, especially through Gottfried, whose qualities of firmness, good proportions and smooth action, was a corrective for the faults of Danko and Avon Prince – "low-set fronts, lack of withers, long level backs or overbuilt rumps ". Perhaps, because this line did not excel in heads, with their lack of black-mask, and because of the glamour and curves of the Avon Prince/Danko progeny, Nem Elliott's advice went largely unheeded.

The other most interesting feature of Cherusker, who captivated a generation, was the dam-line of Crusader, Cherusker's sire. Here was the first important occasion when the new post-war German 'greats', in this case Rolf vom Osnabrückerland, was introduced to British breeding. His son, Ch. Axel v. Lübbeckerland, was imported into Britain, but not generally admired by the fancy. Had this assessment of Axel been otherwise, Rolf might have made more of an impact at the time than he did. Certainly, the type of Cherusker was not that of Avon Prince or of Ingosohn of Errol, well represented on the side of his dam, Vikkas Alda av Hvitsand. We must not overlook the fact that Alda herself had lines back to Ch. Dulo v. Minsweert through Tara, Dora and Ch. Karaste Karenina, all of the Vikkas av Hvitsand, and in the case of the last-named, the Hvitsand affix. We must bear in mind the solid background of Brittas forbears, particularly through the maternal grandparents.

It is not our intention to make lists of dogs which were around at the time, and to give critiques on them. These dogs have been well described and assessed by other authors. Our purpose is to chart the course of the breed, in this case in Great Britain, and in particular, try to show how the split in the breed has come about. It is a unique situation with nothing like it anywhere in the world, except perhaps in the United States, where the United Schutzhund Clubs of America have imported German dogs, mainly from kennels specialising in high performance working dogs, and established a highly successful breeding base from there

As well as Cherusker, there were many other fine dogs to be seen in the show rings when we started in the breed. Clearly, any list will be subjective, but we believe all of the dogs mentioned below exhibited good proportions and type and correct movement, and while these examples of the breed may differ from the best of those seen today in our rings, the differences will be marginal rather than essential. We include some of our own breeding, and feel that, if they were good animals, they should not be left off the list of most-admired Shepherds of yesterday, just because we bred them. Some of these dogs were in our midst before the new wave of German imports became established, virtually replacing the 'old' British lines. The point must be re-emphasised, however, that all so-called 'Alsatians' are a German breed, as indeed are all German Shepherds. Every dog can be traced to Horand, the Adam of the breed.

Ch. and Irish Ch. Gorsefield Granit will always have a place in our memory. This fine sable, a great dog in every way, was half-brother to Cherusker, being by the same sire. He inspired Herr Alfred Hahn, of the famous Busecker Schloss kennel, to write a rave report for the SV magazine, after he had judged him in the UK.

We also admired Ch. and Irish Champion Kondor of Brittas, who seemed to be neglected as a sire. This may have been because by that time Mrs Barrington had moved to Ireland, which was then a bit far to go for a stud. However, through his son El Halcon, he produced the very good Ch. Turnstyle Chalice, and Mrs Barrington's own Ch. Charmione of Brittas. Kondor had a liberal sprinkling of 'R' litter Osnabrückerland, plus the 'old' German line from Hettel Uckermark through Axel Deininghauserheide, noted for his working qualities and incorporated into post-war German breeding. Wider use of Kondor could have had a salutary effect on the bottleneck caused by the over-use of Avon Prince/Danko combinations.

Other Shepherds that have lived in our memories since we saw them for the first time at a show include Ch. Churlswood Tosca of Brinton, a very beautiful bitch, grand-daughter of Cherusker through the very good Cherusker son, Ch. Archer of Brinton. Another fine dog was Ch. Makabusi Otto, a very good-moving masculine dog of very good pigmentation, who used to do well under foreign as well as British judges. When he was shown under Dr Funk at the BAA Championship Show, he did not get a higher placing because Dr Funk had some reservations about his temperament, although it is obvious that he liked him very much and referred to him as a very correct type. Otto was a grandson of Avon Prince, but his maternal grandfather was Ch. Cito v.d. Meerwacht, a dog that came into this country with a Schutzhund II Degree and then proceeded to acquire his Working Trials qualifications, CD, UD, and PD. A third dog of very good type was Ch. Cherrods Fine Fella, who was line-bred on Crusader 2:3. He was sable in colour and particularly noteworthy for his very good wither placement and slope of top-line, as well as his strong masculine outlook and excellent proportions.

In bitches, Ch. Athena of Hatherton dominated the rings, seemingly for an endless period of time. Most of us used to be fearful of the presence of this excellent bitch, as she was virtually unbeatable, gaining twenty-five CCs. As a matter of fact, it was one of our own bitches, Ch. Shootersway Hermione, who dislodged Athena from her pedestal when she won the CC at Bolton. It was on the same occasion that the imported Impuls aus Germany got his one and only CC. The ringside crowd did not take to the dog, and in fact, he was never shown again. The situation is best summed up by Percy Elliot, who imported the dog:

"In 1970 I brought into this country an outstandingly good young male in Impuls aus Germany by Caro v. Schaafgarten, who was Reserve Sieger in 1968, ex-Ute v. Schloss Ahaus, a daughter of the 1963 Sieger Ajax v. Haus Dexel. Impuls came nearer to the ideal than any dog that I had seen to date. A superb dog of this breed, but as was the case with other imported dogs up to this time, he was not readily appreciated. Today, breeders would be in raptures were a dog of this class available."

We were very proud of Hermione, who won the bitch CC at Crufts in 1973, and felt she was a worthy daughter of her dam, Ch. Shootersway Persephone, Best of Breed at Crufts in 1968. Perhaps Persephone's greatest achievement in the show ring was at the 1966 Championship Show of the BAA at Birmingham, when she went Best in Show under Dr Christolph Rummel and obtained the coveted SV Gold Medal. She repeated the performance the following year under Herr Franz Woker, who was then the National Breed Warden for the SV. Persephone had in 1964 obtained the Silver Medal under Dr Funk when she won the Junior and the Special Yearling Class. Although Persephone was line-bred on Avon Prince 3:4, she did not reflect the type of Avon Prince but more that of her German ancestors, Rolf vom Osnabrückerland and Axel von der Deininghauserheide. She was, in fact, also line-bred on Lex Preussenblut, having a considerable amount of the blood of the Lex son, Danko vom Menkenmoor who, of course, became a Champion in Great Britain not long after the end of the war. Persephone was by Ch. Atstan Impresario, grandson of Avon Prince through his son of Ch. Celebrity of Jackfield, out of our foundation bitch, Shootersway Lucretia of Stranmillis. Nem Elliott wrote in *Modern Bloodlines in the Alsatian*: "Impresario's greatest claim to fame will undoubtedly rest on his daughter, the extremely good Ch. Shootersway Persephone, a strong, well-balanced bitch of excellent sound movement, in whom her sire can be discerned but immeasurably improved, an indication of all that is worth having in his interesting breeding without his own limitations."

The Atstan Impresario son, Dromcot Quadra of Charoan, mated to Druidswood Yasmin, a daughter of Ch. and Irish Ch. Gorsefield Granit, produced the influential sire Ch. and Irish Ch. Druidswood Consort. Quadra's maternal grandsire was Lorenz of Charavigne, one of the two sons of Cent zu den Fünf Giebeln, who was generally considered to produce the more Germanic type, more the type of his father Cäsar v. d. Malmannsheide than his litter brother Ludwig. It is also interesting that Yasmin's maternal grandfather on the same side, that is to say through Druidswood Marynka, was Ch. Makabusi Otto.

Consort produced some excellent progeny including Ch. Shedowcast Condor, Ch. Delridge Indigo and our own Ch. Shootersway Xanthos of Colgay. Of all these fine Champions, perhaps Xanthos, a dark sable, most closely resembled Consort and not only in appearance. If we could have wished for anything to be different in Xanthos, it would have been more verve in movement. We well remember the occasion when a show, judged by Herr Hahn, ended in a contest between the two Consort sons, Ch. Delridge Indigo and Ch. Shootersway Xanthos. In the end, Herr Hahn gave the CC to Indigo and the Reserve to Xanthos and he was quite right to do so, because on that occasion Indigo displayed that extra something which decided the issue.

THE PROGRESSIVE MOVEMENT

Before considering the great Champion Rossfort Premonition and the part he played in the GSD scene during the seventies and beyond, we should look at the rise of the progressive movement in Great Britain and its attempts to improve the breed and correct faults which had a grip on the German Shepherd in Britain. The watershed came at the 1961 Championship Show at Birmingham, judged by Sven Hyden from Sweden. The judge set a simple temperament test in which he went down the dogs in the classes, shaking a plastic mac to watch the dogs' reactions. Assembled before him was the cream of the fancy in Great Britain – top-winning dogs, CC winners and Champions. At the end of the show the judge gave his opinions of the dogs he had seen on the day. He described them as, for the most part, untypical specimens, particularly in the realms of temperament and character. This was a shattering blow and can only be described as a day of infamy for the breed in Great Britain.

The more thoughtful breeders and exhibitors present will never forget the shame we experienced upon being told what was the awful truth – that something must be done about the breed in Great Britain. The Challenge Certificate in dogs went to Ch. Celebrity of Jackfield and the Reserve to his son, Vikkas Lariat av Hvitsand. We were pleased that our own Shootersway Benedict, a son of Ch. Jaguar of Stranmillis out of a litter-sister to Ch. Letton Tregisky Eloquence, stood up to the temperament test and was awarded two Firsts. The same dog, in fact our first show dog, had won two Firsts, also at Birmingham, the previous year under Dr Funk, who had described him as very typical of the Utz type – in other words very strongly bred on Brittas lines. Brittas was, of course, a kennel based on the Klodo/Utz type.

Leading lights in the movement to improve the breeding in Great Britain were the Elliotts, and through their writings, particularly *The Complete Alsatian and Modern Bloodlines in the Alsatian*. By means of numerous articles in canine and breed journals, not to mention their imports, they gradually made the breed fraternity realise a solution to the problems existed. It was the importation of new blood in an attempt to bring the breed more into line with Germany itself.

GERMAN IMPORTS

From the early sixties, imports started to arrive. Naturally, there had been imports before that time but, significantly, the first high-profile import was the 1962 Sieger Mutz a. d. Kückstrasse, who was by the 1958 Sieger Condor v. Hohenstamm. Mutz does not seem to have been very popular with the GSD community at the time. He sired over fifty litters, and although many people admired the dog's wonderful character and terrific movement, it was in only a few kennels that he seems to have had much of an influence. Two examples are the Jugoland kennels and our own, Shootersway, where Mutz appears on the pedigree of Ch. Shootersway Hermione. Probably the best son of Mutz was Gustav of Jugoland out of a double Cent grand-daughter Ch. Atstan Lulubelle. Another son of Mutz, Derby v. d. Schlinklergrenze, sired two very nice bitches in Ch. Karenville Ophelia and Ch. Zia of Marlish.

The influence of Vello zu den Sieben Faulen has already been discussed with reference to the breed in Germany. A couple of Vello sons, Roon zu den Sieben Faulen and Billo v. Saynbach, appeared in the UK. Billo was not used very much, though he won a CC. Roon lived with his owner in London and, tragically, died in a road accident not long after he came into the country. Roon was to appear on the pedigree of Ch. Rossfort Premonition through his daughter Rike of Houseromulus.

The Elliotts brought in a dog called Dux v. Braunschweigerland, a grandson of Cäsar v. d. Malmannsheide out of a daughter of Rolf v. Osnabrückerland, Bärbel v. Braunschweigerland. Dux's greatest contribution to the breed was perhaps the fact that he appeared on the pedigree of Ch. Delridge Erhard through Vikkas Bartok a. v. Hvitsand and his son, Vegrin Erhard, out of

Delridge Camilla, a grand-daughter on the sire's side of Gustav of Jugoland, and on the dam's side through Delridge Delsa, the Klodo son, Ilk v. d. Eschbacher Klippen. Delridge Erhard proved a very good sire. He was a dog of very correct type and produced a large number of excellent progeny.

We have already mentioned Ilk, who was also imported by the Elliotts. His greatest claim to fame was the fact that he appeared on the pedigree of Ch. Rossfort Premonition. Premonition has often been described as the ideal combination of the best in British and German breeding of the time. Out of a Brinton bitch, Vondaun Belissima of Brinton, Premonition was by Lex of Glanford who was a Lincolnshire police dog. It is a matter for conjecture how much time he spent on the beat, but he was certainly used widely at stud and the Police Force was happy to accept a puppy instead of a stud fee. Lex of Glanford was by Ilk out of Rike of Houseromulus (mentioned above) who was a daughter of Roon zu den Sieben Faulen. Premonition was widely used in the breed and the general effect was to improve type, particularly toplines, and to contribute greatly to good movement. Top-winning progeny included Ch. Dermark Kari, Ch. Jacnel Philados, Ch. Letton Premium, Ch.and Ir. Ch. Charmione of Brittas, and Ch. Emmevale Natasha. Premonition combined very well with Consort, evident in the lovely bitch, Ch. Labrasca Chica, and the excellent Ch. Shedowcast Condor. The Premonition verve in movement seemed to be a very strong contributing factor to the quality and type produced by Consort.

Two other Klodo sons came into this country, Ferdl v.d. Eschbacher Klippen and Condor v. Schiefen Giebel, who became a Champion in Great Britain and Ireland. Ferdl sired a very good daughter in Ch. Turnstyle Chalice. Condor produced very well in the Dunmonaidh kennel, the most famous offspring were Ch. Peregrine of Dunmonaidh and Ch. Rolf of Dunmonaidh. He also produced a dog which gained one CC, Timbervale Secret Alien, as well as Dunmonaidh Faber of Markinch who got a Reserve CC, and Ch. Hargret Rivercroft Nylon.

High-quality stock resulted from the mating in Germany of the 1967 Sieger Bodo v. Lierberg to a daughter of the Leistungs Sieger Arko v. Riedersknapp. At the end of the sixties the Elliots brought in two sons of Bodo. One was Joll v. Bemholt who became a Champion in Great Britain, and the other was Verus v.d. Ulmer Felswand, who was out of Dina v. Lahnblick, a daughter of the great Valet vom Busecker Schloss. From Joll came Vikkas Tanfield Caro, who has produced some very good progeny including three Champions – Labrasco Dulce, Medlock Cai, and Druidswood Sapphire – and also some very good working stock. Ch. Vornhill Vigilante, a superb type of Shepherd, was a grandson of Verus through Spanish Ch. Vikkas Scipio av Hvitsand, out of Ayeshazk of Jugoland.

There were, of course, other imports who made their contribution, such as Tadellos Hein v. Königsbruch, famous for being the sire of Canto v. d. Weinerau. He was used quite widely in the Irish kennels of Dr Basil Crofts-Greene (the Violethill kennels) and in the Iolanda kennels with very good results, not forgetting the home kennel of his devoted owner, Valerie Egger. Zanto zu den Stöcken produced a very good son out of a Premonition daughter in Emmevale Zarrof, who was exported to Australia although he eventually returned to this country. Donar v. Fiemereck produced the excellent Ch. Jonimay Devil Dick, WT Ch. Jonimay Drusus, Ch. Langfaulds Amos and Ch. Silberwalds Ischka. Donar also appeared in the pedigrees of other leading dogs such as Nero of Shootersway, who is featured on the jacket of this book.

Elan v. Michelstädter Rathaus produced to a Premonition daughter an absolutely outstanding sable dog in Dunmonaidh Junker, who had a scintillating career 'Down Under'. A very good sable, Orsoff v. Busecker Schloss, came to this country but did not appeal to the show crowd, although he did produce one breed Champion in Ch. Tanfield Delphi. The Working fraternity, however, thought differently and Orloff's most famous son is Working Trials Ch. Vonfisk Argo. Orsoff was a grandson of the famous Valet vom Busecker Schloss. Round about this period other dogs were imported into Britain, such as Barry v. Status Quo, a grandson of Quanto v. d. Wienerau. Another is Kay v. Surenheider See, a grandson of Canto v. d. Wienerau, through Sieger Canto v. Arminius.

CHANGE OF TYPE

It was quite clear that the gradual absorption of these new bloodlines from Germany was producing an improvement of type, at least in the eyes of people who were bringing the dogs in and using them in their breeding programmes. Equally, there was a large number of people in Great Britain who had no wish to change the status quo, since they were quite happy with things as they were. Indeed, many of them were rather concerned in case the introduction of new bloodlines should bring faults, including hereditary faults, into the existing bloodlines. Many of these breeders were long-established and very experienced, who were familiar with the faults and virtues of the particular native bloodlines they were dealing with. They were not keen to take a chance on what new bloodlines might bring. There was also a deep suspicion about what could be described as the upsetting of long-established traditions, the way the breed was organised and shown in the UK, plus, perhaps, a nagging fear that closer ties with the motherland could introduce alien practices as well as a different type of dog.

A REVISED STANDARD

Matters came to a head during the seventies when the Kennel Club decided that Breed Standards for registered dogs should be revised. To the progressive community, here was a wonderful opportunity which could not possibly be missed. It proved to be the one outstanding occasion when the whole of the breed, some fifty or so GSD clubs, actively participated. At last it might be possible to get the Kennel Club to accept the original Standard, the one drawn up by von Stephanitz. Suffice it to say that the breed clubs were able to get their full version accepted, although it differs slightly from the version recommended by the FCI and the WUSV. This Standard, also known as the League/BAGSD version, has now been in use by British breed clubs for over a decade.A very much shortened version, based on this, has been adopted by the British Kennel Club and was published in 1986 as one of the breeds which form part of the Kennel Club Working Group of dogs.

There is no doubt that a very strong faction in Great Britain was in sympathy with the movement on the part of the SV to promote a worldwide upgrading and standardisation of the German Shepherd in respect of judging, breeding, and exhibiting. The World Union of German Shepherd Dog Clubs (the WUSV), which was formed in the early seventies, was represented in Great Britain by BAGSD, and later the German Shepherd Dog League. Their mission was to promote the aims of the WUSV in their own country, within the framework of existing canine government i.e. the Kennel Club.

A NEW NATIONAL CLUB

It was at about this time that the Alsatianists decided they must act. The first thing they did was to set up a new national club for the breed. Although the notion of a third club with a national membership was rejected by the breed clubs, the Kennel Club decided to recognise this new club, which was known as the GSD (Alsatian) Club of the UK. The first major task of the new club was to oppose the introduction of a German version in the review of Standards, by attempting to introduce one of their own. Its members were defeated by a common front formed by the rest of the breed clubs and, on a democratic decision, it had to abide by what the majority wished.

THE SITUATION TODAY

What were the aims of the Alsatianists? Their intention was to preserve the British Alsatian as

Ch. Rosehurst Chris: Born in quarantine, sired by Uran, and is proving to be an influential sire.

Ch. Jonal Basko: One of the many top-winning Cito progeny.

Ch. Cito v. Königsbruch: The Nick v. d.Wienerau son who did much to improve proportions and toplines in the breed.

developed in the forties and fifties, the period when German influence was, of necessity, at a low ebb. Some among the Alsatianist ranks claim that, because the breed has been in this country for something like seventy years, it has become a British breed by adoption and owes nothing to any outside influences. This belief is the bedrock of the conflict that has developed between the two factions of the breed in Great Britain. In the early days there was much unpleasantness with a propaganda war being waged in the canine press and at shows. This situation has now more or less settled down, and the passage of time has brought a tacit agreement to co-exist as peacefully as possible. Alsatianists go their way, and the German Shepherd enthusiasts carry on with their pursuits. But the differences in outlook are now extremely fundamental, and the pro-SV faction prefer to run their shows more or less on the same lines as shows are run in Germany, on the continent, and in most other countries.

The merging of imports with native bloodlines has been an on-going situation, but there is now some evidence to suggest that much of the old bloodline base on the progressive side has now been virtually replaced by the same bloodlines as in Germany, namely Canto, Quanto and Mutz, and their more recent descendants such as combinations of Quando and Uran. Imports have risen dramatically during the last fifteen years, and it is now quite standard practice to send bitches to be mated to top German dogs and to bring them back to this country in whelp. Perhaps the two best-known examples are the two Uran sons, Ch. Bedwins Pirol and Ch. Rosehurst Chris. They are not only excellent specimens in themselves, but have also produced extremely well. In the meantime, there is some evidence, on the Alsatian side of the breed, that some adherents have adopted a more progressive approach and are using German bloodlines to a limited degree.

Of the German imports during the last ten years, the dog who has had possibly the greatest influence is Ch. Cito vom Königsbruch, who was brought into England as a highly-rated but relatively young dog and very quickly established a reputation as an excellent sire. He has produced a very good type, with very clean toplines, good proportions, good movement, and he very much reflects the type of his sire Nick v. d. Wienerau. Up to 1990 he had produced seventeen Champions, which must be a pretty good indication of his worth, bearing in mind, of course, that the progeny of Cito have been shown in best competition under overseas as well as British judges.

It has not been within the scope of this book to give more than a brief survey of the development of the breed in Britain. We have not set out to give an account of every import and every prominent dog, and any owners of top dogs who feel that they have been left out, we hope will accept our apologies in advance. We have not mentioned many excellent animals who have attained top honours, and there have been some extremely good imports, particularly in recent times – many of whom attained top qualifications in Germany – and will, no doubt, play their part in the development of the breed in Britain.

THE FUTURE
Now comes the question which seems to occupy the minds of most members of the breed at present – where are we all heading in this country? The split between the two factions is most unfortunate because the breed really needs to be able to go forward on a common front with full autonomy and every shade of opinion represented. Frequent attempts have been made to establish a forum for the whole of the breed, especially when it comes to dealings with the Kennel Club, which exercises absolute power over the world of registered dogs in great Britain.

Hopes for a forum have been partly realised by the formation of the German Shepherd Dog Breed Council, consisting of about forty clubs, but the Alsatianists do not wish to become part of this. Also, the two main breed clubs – the British Association for German Shepherd Dog clubs and the GSD League Council of Great Britain – both one-time members of the Breed Council, have no apparent intention of rejoining. This is a pity. It is trite to say that 'united we stand, divided we fall', but it is nevertheless true. The German Shepherd Dog League has always had the reputation, deservedly so, of having the breed at heart, and throughout the years they have done a lot to further the cause of the German Shepherd. However, many German Shepherd enthusiasts think the initiative has now passed to the Breed Council and that the future of the breed lies in its hands.

Ch. Cello v. Ashera: Imported into Britain and producing well.

Ch. and Irish Ch. Chanask Edison.

Ch. Vorhanden Aphrodite.

Both these dogs are well-known Champions of the nineties of very correct type.

A new element on the British scene is the advent of Schutzhund, which is under the sole control of the British Schutzhund Association. This organisation is currently concerned with establishing its membership and branch formation, its judges, and the helpers and trainers, so necessary for a working organisation to prosper. In this they are being helped by many experts from the GSA Ireland and from overseas, as well as those from within the ranks of our own working fraternity. The BSA would like to establish a good relationship with the two WUSV clubs, League and

BAGSD, and with the Kennel Club. Up to the present time, there is no evidence that the Kennel Club will accept Schutzhund in Great Britain, although the KC is not apparently against Protection Work, otherwise they would not hold approved PD Trials,nor run their own annual TD and PD Championships.

One very encouraging development has been the attitude of the Association of Chief Police Officers in Great Britain, which has definitely come out on the side of the BSA in terms of its organisation and the responsibility of its officers and National Council. Police chiefs are also of the opinion that the method of training protection work in the Schutzhund system in no way promotes aggression in the German Shepherd, or in any other breed of dog.

We would like to sum up this review of the breed in Great Britain by expressing the hope that divisions in the breed will ultimately be healed. This seems unlikely at the moment, but people may grow to accept that the concept of a breed of dog with its Standard of points and traditions which have been developed over the years in judging, breeding, and exhibiting should transcend national barriers. Just because a dog crosses national borders, it does not mean that the receiving country has the right to change the breed and its traditions to suit its own purpose. The German Shepherd Dog, through its international organisation the WUSV, is very fortunate to have very strong factors binding together member clubs throughout the world.

The German Shepherd was developed as a working dog, and although several kennels in Great Britain believe in the dual-purpose ideal – Coolree, Dunmonaidh, Rothick and Shootersway among them – the majority of British breed kennels still do not seem interested in the working aspect of the German Shepherd, which is a loss to the breed. Shepherds should be trained for some form of working qualification acceptable to all breed clubs in this country. We will go further and say that it should ultimately form part of and become an indispensable prerequisite to top awards. At the same time, there should be some sort of temperament testing to prevent shy and aggressive dogs from being declared Champions. We should also like to see this aspect of the German Shepherd taken seriously by breed people. We should also welcome the same conditions i.e. working qualifications and courage testing apply in the otherwise excellent National Breed Survey, organised and conducted by the GSD Breed Council of Great Britain.

GERMANY – TOWARDS THE IDEAL
THE ERA OF DR RUMMEL

Dr Rummel arrived on the scene at the dawn of a new era for the German Shepherd Dog, not that any particularly radical changes took place during the period he was in control. But he was in charge when the breed became largely standardised on a worldwide basis. The World Union, which had started off purely as a Group of European Clubs (the EUSV) in the late sixties, was thrown open to the rest of the world in 1974 and became the World Union of German Shepherd Dog Clubs (the WUSV). Dr Rummel was a superb ambassador for the German Shepherd Dog, visiting many countries, and during this time the GSD, although it did not change in its essential qualities, seemed to become more attuned to the requirements of the enthusiasts in various countries.

In the early days, the dogs had lacked a little angulation in the hindquarters and length in the croup, but it was noticeable that they were now becoming more angulated. The backs changed very slightly from being just straight to becoming straight with a long croup, joined to create a slight curve. This subtle change in the breed took many years to become consolidated, but it is very noticeable that the Shepherds you see today in Germany and most other countries, are much more harmonious. This balancing of curves without exaggeration is noteworthy.

The trend did, in fact, create problems on the way, and there were some examples of what are known as roached backs and drop-away croups. This gave rise to criticism, particularly from

British traditionalists – the Alsatian fraternity – who attacked and ridiculed what they referred to as "roached-back whippets" because a few imports, particularly the earlier ones, looked light-framed and lacking in substance in contrast to the rather heavy Alsatians. This did provide serious grounds for criticism, certainly in the beginning, but the quality of later imports rendered this criticism completely unjustified. Today, no-one could claim that the German Shepherds arriving in Britain or any other country, from Germany, are lacking in substance. Most have correct substance and bone.

A perusal of the FCI/WUSV Standard, or the World Union Standard for the breed, which is used by the majority of countries, makes it quite clear that the roached back is a serious fault and should be penalised by judges, just as a 'dippy' back is a serious fault. The original Standard in use in Great Britain prior to 1986 was approved by the British Kennel Club in 1950. No mention was made of the 'croup', but the relevant area of the anatomy was described as follows: the rump (should be) rather long and sloping." Read 'croup' for 'rump' and there is no real difference, except that no angle is mentioned. Croup made its appearance in the Revised British Standard, and it is firmly fixed in the minds of present-day breeders and exhibitors on the German side of the breed, that the croup should be long and gently sloping at an angle of 23 degrees. The back, therefore, is not, as some people suppose, the area covered from a point behind the ears down to the tail. It is the area between the withers and the loins, which is relatively short. So that the occasions when you would see a definite roach in the back would be very rare indeed and would be roughly similar to a hump on the back of a camel. Most people who refer to roached backs, are using incorrect terminology. What they are really seeing is a back joined by a correct long croup. It is important for the future well-being of the breed that these problems of terminology and interpretation are resolved.

PILLARS OF THE BREED

The three dogs previously hailed as 'pillars of the breed' in the modern era – Canto von der Wienerau, Quanto von der Wienerau, and Mutz von der Pelztierfarm – rose to prominence during the early years of Dr Rummel's Presidency. Dr Funk judged the Gebrauchshundklasse for males for the last time in 1969, and the report on his placings and the dogs he had chosen was compiled in co-operation with Dr Rummel. The progeny groups were judged by Herr Schneeloch.

In 1969 and 1970 Heiko vom Oranien Nassau was made Sieger. Descended from Rolf via Alf v. Convent, Lardo v. d. Spargelhalle and Alf v. Walddorf Emst, Heiko cannot claim to have been a particularly popular dog either with breeders or onlookers. Nevertheless, Heiko was a middle-sized dog of good substance and proportions with good angulation of the forehand and of the hindquarters, good chest development, firmness in hocks, and well-muscled thighs. He was what could be described as a 'dry', firm dog, especially in the back and in the elbows, but his performance was characterised by a spectacular out-reaching gait, showing great thrust and forward reach. In the opinion of Dr Rummel, he was a tireless, trotting dog with a quiet, steady temperament.

However, progeny of Heiko which appeared in 1971 and 1972 did not impress the authorities. While the stock on the day showed good construction in general, it appears to have lacked correct croups. The undoubted hind-thrust shown by Heiko himself was not evident in his progeny. Furthermore, he seems to have produced a type which could not be described as uniform. The following year it was noted that his progeny had good substance and were extremely good and energetic movers, but they were not of even height and, in some cases showed excessive length of body. In the circumstances, it is not surprising that Heiko vom Oranien Nassau had little future in the canine hierarchy which was about to take over. Although he was Double Sieger he must be regarded as a transitional dog.

*Canto v.d.
Wienerau.*

*Mutz v.d.
Pelztierfarm.*

*Quanto v.d.
Wienerau.*

Ch. Amulrees Heiko: Obtained the breed record with 47 CCs.

Before we consider the influence of the big three, Canto, Quanto and Mutz, we must remember that there was a fourth dog who initially attracted a great deal of attention among the authorities. This was the 1972 Sieger Marko vom Cellerland. He had made VA9 in 1970, VA4 in 1971, and Sieger in 1972, but was demoted slightly in 1973 by only attaining the position of VA4. He was by Kondor v. Golmkauer Krug, an HGH dog, that is to say, a dog on the herding side, out of Cilla vom Hunenfeuer. Marko had a progeny Group in 1972, the year he became Sieger. He was placed in the top Group together with Mutz von der Pelztierfarm, Quanto von der Wienerau and Crok v. Busecker Schloss.

Albert Schneeloch, who judged the progeny groups, remarked that the offspring of all these four dogs were alert, energetic and willing movers. They were strong, had good croups, good ear and tail carriage and were well pigmented. Dr Ernst Beck wrote up the progeny results in 1973, the year when the first Group was occupied by Mutz, Canto and Quanto which was, of course, an historic decision. Dr Rummel had downgraded Marko in 1973 and, although his general criticism of the dog did not differ, the deciding factor was that Marko did not have the condition on the day to warrant a repeat of the previous year's placing. This tended to show up in the gaiting round where he exhibited some lack of firmness which cost him the placing. Dr Beck thought that Marko's progeny lacked uniformity and had failings in croups and forequarter angulation.

In the following year, 1974, Marko progeny were again in the second Group. This time the judges were Dr Rummel and Albert Schneeloch, and they seemed to have had a better opinion of Marko's Group. There were 59 progeny, the most in the whole of the competition and they were all, according to the judges, very uniform in type, slightly over-middle size and with very good firm backs, good heads, dark eyes, very good angulation of the forehand, croups that could be a little longer, and very good gait. Dr Rummel and Herr Schneeloch praised the uniform coloration throughout the Group. In 1975, Marko's progeny were back in the first Group, together with Quanto and Canto. The same applied in 1976. It is worth noting that the first year Herr Hermann Martin appeared in the role of adjudicator of bitches was 1975.

Whatever opinions the authorities held about Marko and his progeny, he was responsible for producing two very good VA dogs in Eros vom Hambachtal and Kai vom Silberbrand, who was exported to America. There are those in Germany today, particularly at grass-roots level, who still believe that Marko had a lot to offer, especially in terms of temperament and pigment, even though he is no longer counted as one of the 'pillars of the breed', an assessment many thought he fully deserved.

CANTO VON DER WIENERAU

Before consideration of the role of the giants of modern German breeding, we need to comment on the breeding of Canto. He was sired by Hein v. Königsbruch, who through Fix zu den Sieben Faulen and Asslan Maiweg, was descended from the Rolf son, Alf Walddorf-Emst. However, many commentators believe Canto's success lay not through his sire, having regard for what else was produced by Hein, but rather through his dam, Liane von der Wienerau. Liane was litter-sister to Lido von der Wienerau and one of the great 'L' litter, which had such a far-reaching influence in the Wienerau kennel, and perhaps in the breed in general. Lido's sire was Jalk vom Fohlenbrunnen, whose father was Vello zu den Sieben Faulen. Jalk was a very well-constructed dog of excellent substance and appearance, very suggestive of the Shepherds we see in the rings today; considerable harmony of lines, with no exaggeration. There is a colour paling factor which allegedly comes from Jalk, but wherever this comes from, the fact is that the progeny of Jalk were noted as showing colour paling to some degree.

QUANTO VON DER WIENERAU AND MUTZ VON DER PELZTIERFARM

Quanto, by Condor Zollgrenzschutzhaus, was descended through Condor vom Schnapp and Condor v Hohenstamm, from the Rolf son, Arko Delog. Mutz's progeny group first appeared in 1970 with Albert Schneeloch as the judge. Mutz was described as producing very good bodily proportions in his progeny, strong, powerful, with very good firmness in the back and good lay of croup, good forehand angulation, of good colour and a free-moving, ground-covering gait.

Dr Rummel took over the assessment of progeny in 1971 and both Quanto and Mutz were in the first group. He described Quanto as having a group of thirty animals which were powerful, of good size and colour, with very good forehand and excellent sex characteristics. He would like to have seen more length in the croups. He described Mutz progeny as having a very even type, excellent sex characteristics, very good movement, good croups, and satisfactory pigment. He thought the dogs were better than the bitches.

ASSESSMENT OF PROGENY

The following year in 1973, when Dr Beck placed Mutz, Canto and Quanto in the first group and Marko in the second, he had a great deal to say about the qualities being produced by the top three. Mutz only had fifteen animals in the Group, Canto had twenty-six and Quanto twenty-four.

He thought Mutz's progeny outstanding as to uniformity and the proportions length to height, and he said that they exhibited a quality of firmness with excellent bone. He considered the group very typical of the father, with progeny who were robust and had great exuberance and outgoing qualities. The group from Canto had the largest number, and they reminded Dr Beck very much of Jalk vom Fohlenbrunnen so far as type was concerned. The other characteristics of the progeny were excellent proportions, which he thought was an inheritance from the Axel line, bearing in mind that Canto was line-bred on Axel von der Deininghauserheide 5:5., 5:5. Many of the dogs were described as having "much harmony." In the area of firmness the progeny of Canto were not quite as outstanding as those of the Mutz group, but there was excellent angulation of the hindquarters although some of the angulation was bordering on being somewhat over-done.

Flora v. Konigsbruch Sch H1: Canto daughter and great g/granddaughter of Joll v. Bemholt and Klodo a.d. Eremitenklause who has had such a profound influence on the breed.

Nick v.d. Wieneran Sch H3: Sire of Palme v. Wildsteigerland and grandsire of Double Sieger Uran and Quando.

The Quanto group was a different type from Canto. Dr Beck contrasted the type of Quanto to that of Canto and likened Quanto to his father, Condor Zollgrenzschutzhaus. The twenty-four progeny exhibited had, as well as very good type, very good colour and sex characteristics.There were occasional faults in croups, but only minimal instances of Quanto's own fault, weakness in pasterns. These lines have combined well, producing excellent quality stock during the last twenty years.

In the last ten years, during the presidency of Herr Hermann Martin, the scene has been dominated by Double Sieger Uran vom Wildsteigerland and Double Sieger Quando von Arminius. Both are tail-male descended from Quanto von der Wienerau – Quando though Xaver v. Arminius to the Quanto son, Lasso Di Val Sole, and Uran through Irk von Arminius, Pirol von Arminius and

Quando v. Arminius: With his half-brother Uran, the most important sire in the modern German breeding system with worldwide influence.

Sieger 1992 Zamb v.d. Wienerau Sch H3: Continuing the Quando line, sire of 1992 Siegerin Vanta v.d. Wienerau also Junghund SG2 and SG3.

Youth Vice Sieger and VA Mark v. Haus Beck Sch.H3: Son of VA Fedor v. Arminius ex Quina, litter sister to Quando; consistent top producer of mainly medium-size progeny of excellent type.

Cliff vom Haus Beck, who was a son of Quanto. Both Uran and Quando have the same dam, Palme vom Wildsteigerland, who is descended via Nick von der Wienerau through Johnny Rheinhalle, to Mutz von der Pelztierfarm. The dam of Nick von der Wienerau is the excellent breeding bitch Flora vom Königsbruch, who is by Canto. Palme's mother was the VA bitch Fina v. Badsee, who was a Canto great-grand-daughter through Asslan v. Klämmle.

The fact that Uran and Quando are half-brothers may worry some people, but such is the faith of the authorities in GSD breeding in Germany at present, that these lines have been continued and there is no very great movement to bring in outcrosses.

THE NINETIES
A number of the leading German sires of the nineties are combinations of Uran and Quando, and if the desire of the authorities has been to establish a completely uniform type, as was evident at the 1993 Sieger Show, they have certainly succeeded. The dogs were without exaggeration, with good toplines and, on the whole, good croups, good withers and correct fore-reach and hind-thrust, plus

Yago v. Wildsteigerland VA: Typical representative of the type of his sire Sieger Eiko v. Kirschental. Another classic Uran/'Q' litter Arminius combination.

Cello v.d. Romerau Sch H3, FH: Leading sire of VA and top V progeny by Natz v. Hasenborn ex Quana, litter sister to Quando. Picture of Cello taken as young dog (graded SG2).

Jeck v. Noricum Sch H3, FH Sieger 1993: sired the Quando son Odin v. Tannenmeise.

good sex characteristics. The very dark colours of yesterday do not seem to abound, nor do the very long-striding animals that one can remember from the past, but the formula for the best all-round German Shepherd, in both construction and performance, certainly seems to have been found, and no doubt the authorities wish to maintain this.

THE FUTURE

The SV system has identified problems and has always done something about it. At the beginning, the shape and construction of the breed needed improvement and steps were taken accordingly when they realised that the conformation of the dog was incorrect. In 1967 a public statement was made about the need for character and temperament. We have to assume that the tremendous emphasis placed on the excellence of construction and performance of the German Shepherd in the nineties will continue to be matched by its mental qualities and working character. This, after all, is the formula which was developed by Von Stephanitz and has been the guiding principle of the SV ever since.

Chapter Five

TO EVER FURTHER SHORES

THE BRITISH INFLUENCE

We have seen how the GSD left Germany and came to Britain and America. The breed then began to spread to other countries around the world, some belonging to the British Empire or Commonwealth. For many years, these countries and their kennel clubs, particularly South Africa, Australia, and New Zealand, were very influenced by the scene in Great Britain. A strong link existed between their kennel clubs and the Kennel Club in London, to whom they looked for a lead.

Many other countries also looked to Britain for their imports, including the British West Indies, as they then were, Singapore, Malaysia, and India to mention just a few. The British Alsatian could be seen in abundance in many of these countries. Germany was not a great exporter of her national breed until the formation of the World Union of German Shepherd Dog Clubs (WUSV) in 1974. Even then, momentum for an increase in German exports did not really gather until the late seventies and early eighties. The case of Australia is a special one, in view of the long period during which no German Shepherd was officially allowed into the country. Indeed, many of the first imports after the ban had been lifted in the early seventies, were from England, although they could scarcely be described as the typical English Alsatian, as we shall see later.

BRITISH INFLUENCE WANES

In South Africa, the tide of support turned away from the Alsatian towards the German Shepherd, whether direct from Germany itself or from Britain at the end of the 1970s. One German import, Into v. Adeligen Holze, arrived in South Africa and was judged during 1977 by several judges from Great Britain – including Roy – and received top honours. This made a profound impact on the national scene and started a trend towards a more Germanic type and, by the same token, hastened the decline of the old English Alsatian in that country. The same thing happened in Zimbabwe, Kenya and other parts of Southern Africa.

In the period from the mid-seventies and throughout the eighties, many of the overseas German Shepherd Dog Clubs in these regions – Australia, South Africa, Zimbabwe, Kenya, the West Indies and to a lesser extent the Far East – invited UK judges to officiate at German Shepherd events. It was noticeable that the way in which those judges assessed the entry, made the placings, and wrote the critiques, was along the lines of the German model. Eventually, only judges who adopted this practice were invited.

Some countries differed from others only in a marginal sense, but by the end of the eighties, the corps of British judges had largely been replaced by those direct from Germany. Certain countries were prepared to continue receiving judges from Great Britain who had the SV Overseas Licence, but by the start of the nineties it was rare for British GSD judges to be invited to judge for breed clubs abroad. Of course, a large number of all breed shows are still judged by British all-rounders. However, the breed societies in various overseas countries stuck to the specialists, and gradually trained their own corps of breed judges. Even so, an overseas judge will always be an attraction in every country. They are presumed not to know the scene, the dogs, the handlers, or the owners, and by and large they draw good entries, as indeed they should.

Europe, to a greater or lesser extent, has followed the German model. There is much inter-relation and exchange of bloodlines and the use of German sires is now even more widespread than it was before. However, there are slightly different scenarios in Norway and Sweden, both of whom have always had close canine links with Great Britain.

NORWAY

The Norsk Schäferhund Klub was founded in Oslo in March 1922, and has about 4,500 members. It aims to co-operate closely with other GSD clubs in the Nordic countries and in Germany, and it works in tandem with the Norsk Kennel Club (the Norwegian Kennel Club, which is a member of the FCI). The main purpose of the Norsk Schäferhund Klub is to keep a watch on the breeding and training of German Shepherds, to further the cause of the working dog and maintain its usefulness by engaging in tracking, searching and other disciplines. The club arranges Breed Surveys (Korungs) for breed and working dogs, with a separate Korung for each. Dogs owned or bred by members must be registered with the Kennel Club.

The Schäferhund Klub arranges shows and competitions for working dogs (Trials). There is also a programme for encouraging the participation of youth, instruction on how to bring up dogs, and an education programme for judges and instructors. The club has about 29 local branches with their own officers and committee. At the annual meeting representatives from each of the branches, one per 100 members, discuss and debate policy and elect a national General Council. Members of the General Council are elected for a period of two years. There is a separate council for working and one for breeding, and an editorial staff for the club's handbook which is called *Schäferhunden*. This is published six times a year with a total of 500-600 pages.

Branches arrange their own shows which are recognised by the Kennel Club. There are courses in training dogs and competitions for working dogs, youth shows are run and the branches are also responsible for the administration and organisation of Breed Surveys (Korungs). It should be noted that Breed Selection and Working Dog Selection are separate events. Temperament and character tests are also considered an important part of the programme, as well as an analysis of the dog's performance. These two tests are registered with the Kennel Club and the dog is accredited merit status when the tests have been successfully completed. No dog can obtain the title of a Selection Dog (i.e. selected for breed or selected for work) unless it has passed the character test, including a gun test.

BREED SELECTION

The selection for suitability in breed, Breed Survey or Korung is divided into two grades or classes.

Class I: Consists of a very good type, that is to say First Prize in an Open Class in a show. The dog must have passed a character test, be a Selected Working Dog grade I and be considered free of hip dysplasia. The dog is written up in terms of its conformation, measurements and general description.

Class II: Dogs are dogs of good type, who must be Second Prize in an Open Class, with grade I hips, which is equivalent to the German 'A' Stamp Noch Zugelassen. The dog must have passed a character test. In Class II you find dogs of high quality who would normally be worthy of inclusion in Class I. Perhaps the dog has not had the opportunity, or lacks the ability to go through the Working Tests Selection Grade I. Dental irregularities such as premolar 2 or missing incisors also indicate that a dog should be retained in Class II, as do other minor faults. Whatever grade of working dog test, even Grade III, the dog has passed, it will not obtain a classification higher than Class II if these other faults are present.

WORKING DOGS SELECTION

Working Dogs Selection has three grades of difficulties, I, II and III. To enter the Norwegian Winners Show, organised by the main committee of the club, the dog must have obtained Selection Working Dog Grade I. In Norway, interest in working dogs is very keen. There are many competitions and three classes, C, B and A. The General Council (Hovedstyret) organises the two most important events in the year – the Norwegian Winners Show and the Norwegian Championship for Working Dogs. Results of these events are not registered with, or accredited by, the Kennel Club as they are entirely run by the club itself. The Norwegian Winners Show is divided into age classes, similar to Germany, and the grades are the same as in Germany, including a Selection class VA. There are no gun tests as in Germany, but German judges officiate. There is no requirement for the Schutzhund Test as, with the exception of the police and armed services, owners are not allowed to become involved in Protection Work. The show lasts three days.

The first day features the Youth Show, which is not part of the official classification, and divided into four classes, aged from four-12 months. Kennel groups and progeny parades are also part of the show. On the second day, the official part of the show commences. Classes are fully described in the catalogue and, on the third day, the progeny and kennel groups are given full range. There are no prior qualifications to exhibit in classes for 12-18 months. In the 18-24 months class, the dog must have been X-rayed and possess the status of at least Grade I, equivalent to Noch Zugelassen. In the case of adult classes, that is to say dogs over 24 months, there must be a Working Dog Selection Grade I, and hips Grade I. In 1992, 600 dogs were competing, including the youth dog section. Judges were Herr Hermann Martin and Herr Hans Peter Rieker, who awarded eight VAs, four to males and four to females. Both VA I exhibits were Norwegian-bred, and both VA II were of German breeding.

The Winners Show is only open to members. Many foreign guests attend and a lot of German handlers take part. The dogs, however, must have Norwegian owners. Critiques are published in the publications of Urban Pettersson of Sweden, and a good selection of the best dogs appear in *Schäferhunden*, which is translated into Swedish. In 1990, the results were also given in German.

There is no doubt that the breed in Norway remains true to the tradition of the WUSV, with a very strong commitment to the notion that the German Shepherd is a working dog. Although Norway has no place for the protection aspect of the working schedule, there is heavy emphasis on the other activities of tracking and obedience. Furthermore, the type of dog being bred and exhibited in Norway is either based on modern German bloodlines or consists of imports from Germany, which are subsequently drawn into the breeding programme whenever possible. There seems to be a very good relationship between the ruling body, the Kennel Club in Norway, and the German Shepherd breed. Consequently, the breed is prospering and exhibiting a high level of achievement, as is evidenced by visiting judges and the awards they give.

UNITED STATES OF AMERICA

In the chapter on Klodo/Utz and the aftermath, we mentioned three important dogs who virtually became the foundation of German Shepherds in the United States. They were Pfeffer von Bern, Odin vom Busecker Schloss, and Clodulf von Pelztierhof. They were dominant stud forces and employed in intense in-breeding and line-breeding programmes. Pfeffer von Bern was sired by Dachs v. Bern, out of Clara v. Bern. Pfeffer was, therefore, line-bred on Utz, and was fortunate enough to become the property of the Hoheluft kennels, where excellent use was made of this superb dog, producing such greats as Nox, Noble, Nora of Ruthland, Lady of Ruthland, Vetter of

Dornwald, and Ajax and Amigo von Hoheluft. Pfeffer was certainly a great producer.

THREE IMPORTANT SIRES

The Pfeffer line was of paramount influence in establishing a uniformly superb type. But, in the opinion of the commentators of the day, not only the qualities but also the faults were passed on, coming down from Alex v. Ebersnacken, Utz himself, Odin von Stolzenfels, Ferdl v.d. Secretainerie and Dachs von Bern. The faults which occasionally cropped up, generally through Pfeffer's children or grandchildren, were missing dentition, faulty temperaments, over-long bodies and loins, and also orchidism.

Odin was Pfeffer's half-brother. His dam was Gerda v. Busecker Schloss, a bitch who received the top rating in Germany. When Dr Sachs judged Odin in Germany in 1936 he described him as: "fully developed (he was two and a half years old), very good bodily construction, and a far-reaching gait. He appears to me to be of a 'dry' type of herding dog but somewhat over-heavy in condition and, therefore, does not show the necessary energy or endurance in the long gaiting session required of a herding dog. One pre-molar missing."

Like his half-brother Pfeffer, Odin was dominant in passing on his qualities to his progeny rather than his faults, and he was used extensively for line-breeding, almost invariably establishing his excellent type and construction in his offspring. Clodulf von Pelztierhof was used extensively on the West Coast of America. He was a grey sable, like Odin, and he was a rather substantial dog, tending to heaviness in bone, rather deep with a tremendous forechest. Clodulf was tail-male descended via Alf Webbelmannslust to Klodo v. Boxberg.

These then were the three important sires upon which the breed was based in the United States and, generally speaking, they were a force for good, establishing uniformity of type – the type of Klodo/Utz. Of course, many other very important dogs were imported into or resident in the United States for a period of time, including Klodo v. Boxberg, and Utz himself, but it was through their imported descendants rather than through home-bred animals that the influence of these two dogs was perpetuated.

THE AMERICAN GSD

The progress of the breed in the United States, subsequent to the period we have been discussing and after the Second World War, was dominated by a single dog, Ch. Lance of Fran-Jo. GSD enthusiasts who have visited the United States, especially to their National Specialty Show, find it quite striking that the dogs on show do seem to be different in type from Shepherds in Germany and in most other countries. We took this question up with the German Shepherd Dog Club of America, asking for some insight as to how the breed developed from the Klodo/Utz type to its present-day standing. The President of the German Shepherd Dog Club of America, Dr Carmen Battaglia, states:

"The influence of Lance of Fran-Jo in the breed in America is unmistakable. His style and outline have become popular, particularly with respect to the high wither and rear angulation. The fact that the US Breed Standard calls for a slightly longer dog contributes to its popularity. The German Shepherd Dog in the United States is slightly longer-bodied than in other countries, and generally has a higher wither and longer upper arm. When taken together as a package, the longer upper arm provides the opportunity for a longer stride, if there is good drive from the rear. This makes movement efficient and very appealing to the eye. The observer sees ground-covering dogs that take fewer steps than those with shorter backs and upper arms and with less rear angulation."

Clearly, American breeders believe that their slight departure from the World Union Standard, produces a superior dog with superior performance. This confident attitude differs very sharply from the attitude of British 'Alsatianists' who have never, as far as we know, publicly justified their departure from the WUSV concept of the breed. The Americans like a slightly longer dog with more hind angulation, a longer upper arm, and a higher wither, because they claim that this produces a more efficient German Shepherd with a longer striding, more powerful gait. The Alsatianists seem to prefer a longer dog, but one with short front legs, a rather heavy, deep dog, not characterised by a great deal of firmness. It is not our intention to pass judgement on whether these deviations from the WUSV concept are right (with regard to the American GSD or the British Alsatian). This is a matter for the individual German Shepherd fancier to decide. However, a large number of active breeders in America follow the European, indeed the WUSV, line on breeding and performance, particularly those who compete in the sport of Schutzhund.

CH. LANCE OF FRAN-JO

In 1957, Troll v. Richterbach came to the United States and was awarded the title of Grand Victor, a title given at the annual Speciality Show organised by the German Shepherd Dog Club of America. Troll was sired by Axel v. d. Deininghauserheide, and his dam, Lende v. Richterbach, was a daughter of the famous Rosel v. Osnabrückerland, litter-sister to Rolf. Troll was mated to Frigga of Silverlane who was by the grey Ch. Cito v. d. Hermannschleuse. Frigga was the grand-daughter of the Pfeffer son, Ch. Dex of Parrylin. The mating between Troll and Frigga produced the 'F' litter of Arbeywood, six of whom – Fashion, Falko, Ferd, Field Marshal, Fels and Fortune – obtained titles. It was Fortune who was mated to Elsa of Grunen Tal, a daughter of Ch. Riker von Liebestraum. Riker was by the Hein son, Bill v. Kleistweg, and Elsa was a double great grand-daughter of Hein. The result of the Fortune/Elsa mating was Lance of Fran-Jo.

Lance started his show career at a puppy match with 100 entries. He was only slightly over four months of age, and he won. By eleven months, he was winning consistently at matches and just when everything was going well, he was stricken with panosteitis, which is often referred to as a disease of the long bones. The outward manifestation of this condition was that Lance was limping badly, and at one point his owners, the Fords, considered euthanasia. However, Lance started to improve and, by the time he was fully mature, he was remarkably handsome, a well-balanced, superbly-moving animal. He moved with a very long, smooth, powerful gait and the Shepherd fancy spoke in terms of him as starting a new era in the breed.

Lance's contribution to the American German Shepherd scene can only be described as fantastic. He produced more US and Canadian Grand Victors and Grand Victrices than any other sire in the breed's history. A Grand Victor himself, he produced a list of sixty Champions. Lance attained his

GV Troll v. Richterbach, sire of the 'F' litter Arbeywood.Fortune mated to Elsa of Grunen Tal produced Lance.

GV Ch. Lance of Fran-Jo: The dog that started a new era in the US.

Ch. Ekolan's Paladen: A Lance grandson.

Ch. Covey-Tucker Hill's Manhattan: In-bred on Lance 3:3.

title in the capable hands of top handler James Moses, and never looked back after his early bout of ill-health. Lance was mated to daughters and grand-daughters of the imported Bernd v. Kallengarten, a son of Watzer v. Bad Melle, whose sire was Axel v. d. Deininghauserheide. Bernd was out of a Rolf daughter, and Bernd's son, Yoncalla's Mr America, sired the 1966 and 1968 Grand Victor, Ch. Yoncalla's Mike.

Close in-breeding on Bernd produced the outstanding breeding bitch Coberts Melissa, whose matings to Lance and his grandson, Ch. Ekolan's Paladin, were particularly successful. Melissa's first litter to Lance produced the top-winning Ch. Lakeside's Gilligans Island. Lance, mated to another Bernd daughter, produced the 1970 Grand Victor, Ch. Mannix of Fran-Jo. He was rather more influential for the type of Bernd, with very good forehand angulation. Mannix himself was mated to a Lance daughter with close in-breeding and gave the 1973 Grand Victor, Ch. Scorpio of Shiloh Gardens. Scorpio sired the 1977 Grand Victor, Ch. Langenan's Watson. Select Ch. Haag and Haag's Dapper Dan was also a very typical Lance son.

Troll also produced the top-winning Grand Victor, Ulk v. Wikingerblut, who was imported from Germany. But the Troll line continued through Lance rather than through Ulk because it was the Lance-type that people wanted. Two very influential brothers, Doppel Tay's Hammer and Hawkeye, were line-bred on Lance 3:2.

IN-BREEDING

It is obvious that the breeding of German Shepherds in America has been characterised by a degree of in-breeding which has not been seen elsewhere. The interesting thing is that many top German dogs have been imported into America over the years, such as Sieger Bodo v. Lierberg, Youth Sieger Asslan v. Klämmle, Vax v. d. Wienerau, Kai vom Silberbrand, Basko v.d. Kahlerheide and many others. But it appears that American breeders have not been very influenced overall by these imports. They have been of interest only to the kennels more attuned to producing a European-type dog. Furthermore, it would appear that the three main pillars of the breed – Canto, Quanto, and Mutz – who have had such a profound and far-reaching influence on the breed elsewhere in the world, have not been absorbed into modern American breeding. Combinations of Lance and Bernd are as popular as ever, and if the Americans wanted to get away from their very angulated dogs, with long upper arms and high withers, they would find it difficult to adapt type to bring it into line with the rest of the world. From what we can gather, American breeders are quite happy with what they have got and have no real wish to change.

THE WORKING GSD

In this respect, American show breeders differ markedly from their colleagues in the United Schutzhund Clubs of America, who do not appear to be getting their working dogs from Lance/Bernd lines. With regard to the GSD Club of America's attitude towards the working German Shepherd, the German Shepherd Dog Club of America has issued the following statement for inclusion in this book:

"The working dog in the United States is defined as those that either perform in WUSV Trial work, or in the police, military or Seeing Eye dog scheme. This broad category has a great deal of support. The AKC prohibits 'bite work' in any form at the moment. This policy could change, and we have requested that it be reconsidered, given legislation in Europe and our discussions with President Hermann Martin and the WUSV. More than 15,000 participate in WUSV Trials in the US."

As for the relationship between the German Shepherd Dog Club of America and the United Schutzhund Clubs of America, GSDCA state:

"The WDA/GSDCA is a liaison of the GSDCA, and represents the United States as the official representative at the WUSV Trial with a right to vote on all matters. The *USA* organisation (the Schutzhund movement) is not connected to the AKC, and operates separately from both the GSDCA and the AKC. Generally, there are good relations between the United Schutzhund Clubs of America and the GSDCA, but you must remember that these are competitors in Trial Work, and therefore they differ about certain things, as you would expect competitors to do."

On the question of duplication of programmes between the United Schutzhund Clubs of America and the GSD Club of America, the GSDCA states: "The GSDCA is a Breed Club with over forty committees, an operational budget of 600,000 dollars, and with programmes that include conformation, obedience, working and herding. We have 120 regional clubs and host 240

Speciality Shows and nine regional Futurities and Maturities each year. Because of our affiliation with the AKC and the hundreds of all-Breed Shows and events, the GSDCA has a different purpose. The United Schutzhund Clubs of America is primarily interested in the working dog, and focuses on Trial Work."

THE SCHUTZHUND MOVEMENT

The first traces of a European-style GSD Schutzhund movement in the United States was a relatively small training club in the San Francisco area of California. It was started by a handful of people interested in Search and Rescue and police-type work, plus a few German nationals who had a working knowledge of the sport of Schutzhund. The year was 1959 and the group was known as the Peninsula Police K9 Corps, which later evolved into the Peninsula K9 Corps, today still a full member club of the United Schutzhund Clubs of America. By the mid-1960s, the first Working Trials observing international Schutzhund rules were conducted in the United States. There was still no national organisation as there is today. There were five or six local clubs scattered around, in California, Wisconsin, Northern Illinois, St Louis, Missouri and Texas.

In those early years, only Schutzhund trials were conducted. Those who witnessed the start of the movement maintain that training and performance was unpolished, and enthusiasts had very little true knowledge of how to train their dogs to competition level. However, what the early American Schutzhund pioneers lacked in knowledge of the competition aspect of the sport, they made up for in enthusiasm and a determination to be successful, and to bring the training of the working dog far beyond the level of Obedience training and showing previously seen. Furthermore, there was the conviction that at long last the GSD in America was being trained in the German Shepherd tradition, as practised by the rest of the world and Germany in particular.

In the early sixties it was common practice for enthusiasts to travel for days by car merely to attend another small club's activities in training and Schutzhund Trials. Gradually the movement spread, and many people who had been interested in the AKC Training Schedule and Breed Shows came to the conclusion that what was on offer was something better and more rewarding for the German Shepherd. Gradually, clubs were formed in various parts of the United States but there was still no national organisation or regulatory body to control and co-ordinate the activities of individual clubs. By the seventies it became apparent that the sport was growing, and the first meetings were held of what was to become the United Schutzhund Clubs of America. In 1976, an inaugural meeting was held in Texas and the United Schutzhund Clubs of America was formed.

At the very beginning this club, which was to become the overall governing body for the sport in America, was sanctioned by the German Shepherd Dog Club of America, at that time the only national German Shepherd Dog Club in the United States. Even though *USA*, as it came to be called, was formed as a breed club, the American Kennel Club, the umbrella organisation for canine interests, did not object to the existence of Schutzhund, which was under the aegis of the GSD Club of America. Apparently, nobody in the United States considered that *USA* was a national German Shepherd Dog Club, and for a couple of years everything went smoothly. In fact, the SV received a letter stating that *USA* was the recognised representative for Schutzhund of the GSDCA and asking permission to compete in the WUSV Championships, at that time known as the Europa Meisterschaft. In due course, and in the knowledge that *USA* was part of the GSDCA, indeed its working arm, members began competing in WUSV Championships. During this time, full records were maintained, the training of judges was developed, and control and administration formalised.

THE SPLIT

After much deliberation, *USA* decided on a complete split away from the American Kennel Club, as members wanted to avoid control exercised by an outside body which could possibly modify or influence their aims and aspirations. It was, and still is, considered a brave move on the part of a fledgling organisation. Some years later, for reasons that have not been established, the American Kennel Club advised the GSDCA that they must divorce themselves from all Schutzhund activity. As the GSDCA is under the direct control of the AKC, there was no real choice but to obey this instruction.

At the same time, there were personality conflicts between the GSDCA leadership and the then president of *USA*. Escalating disagreements resulted in the GSDCA attempting to withdraw their approval for *USA* to be America's working dog representative in international competitions. However, *USA* had proved its worthiness time and time again to the SV and the WUSV, and the SV President at the time, Dr Christolph Rummel, advised the AKC and the GSDCA that *USA* would continue to be recognised by the WUSV. The WUSV additionally confirmed its intention to provide not only working dog judges but Körmeister too, so that dogs competing in Schutzhund trials would have the opportunity to be assessed by SV experts as to their worth as breed specimens.

By the beginning of the eighties, the time was considered ripe for a separate bid by *USA* to join the GSD world community, and application was accordingly made for WUSV membership. The petition was vetoed by the GSDCA, but guest membership was granted, and full membership obtained after three years.

WORKING BLOODLINES

During the early years of working dog clubs in America, certain handlers and trainers stood out from the rest. At the same time, it became apparent that certain breeding lines had also assumed a predominant position in the working field. It is the considered opinion of *USA* officers and trainers that German Shepherds from imported bloodlines were far superior and much more trainable than dogs bred in the United States from American lines. The reason for this was thought to be the controlled breeding systems, and the emphasis on breeding working dogs in various other countries, in particular Germany. It was felt that efforts of the breed in America had been primarily directed at the production of dogs pre-eminent chiefly for their conformation. But even the standard of conformation was not comparable to the standard considered normal in international competition.

USA noted that the mental stability of imported dogs and bloodlines was considerably superior to dogs bred in the United States, whose breeders over the last seventy-five years, in the opinion of the working dog people, had paid insufficient attention to the temperament and character of the German Shepherd Dog. To take the argument even further, it is the opinion of the *USA* adherents that conformation is more than just visual appearance and cosmetic aspects. They consider it involves the basic balance and structure of the dog and its ability to carry out all the various requirements of a working breed.

On the subject of constructional fitness, statistics show that less than one per cent of GSDs born in America were ever submitted for hip-certification under the OFA scheme. Therefore, the working dog enthusiasts, realising that the European GSD was more suitable for their needs, began to import top bloodlines and working lines. This policy appears to have borne fruit. The integration and use of these bloodlines by *USA* members and the breeding programmes based on these imported lines, was truly vindicated by the results of the 1992 World Championship-winning American team. Three of the dogs were American born and bred.

During the 1950s and 1960s, very few advertisements appeared in the canine publications featuring dogs with Schutzhund titles and imported bloodlines. Nowadays, it is extremely rare to pick up a magazine on the subject of German Shepherd Dogs, and other breeds too, which do not carry many advertisements for the sale of dogs with Schutzhund titles. These same animals are used by many well-known kennels in the United States. The situation is similar in Canada. In American breed circles, and also at the meetings of the World Union of German Shepherd Dog Clubs (WUSV), the considered view has been that the salvation of the GSD in the US has been due to the United Schutzhund Clubs of America. Statistics are available which indicate that in less than fifteen years *USA* has overtaken the membership of the GSDCA, even though the latter has been in existence for more than sixty years longer.

REGISTRATION

Gradually, *USA* expanded the scope of operations to include its own breed register, which eventually developed into a dual register with the SV. This means that Shepherds are registered with both *USA* and the SV and carry registration numbers from both organisations. For a number of years, breed surveys (Körungs) have been held, and conformation shows are now based on absolutely strict adherence to the SV system, with the exception that classes are provided for American Kennel Club registered dogs. It is considered that such classes will contain animals for exhibition who would not be considered capable of meeting the requirements of European-style shows.

The purpose of this was to give as many American GSD fanciers as possible the opportunity to make a comparison between the two types. This is regarded as educational, and there is a strong conviction that this is a very important way to proceed. Dogs born in America and registered through *USA* do in fact appear in the Zuchtbuch (Breed Book of the SV), and the breed surveys conducted in America by *USA* appear in the Körbuch. This is a facility and privilege granted only to dogs owned by members of *USA*, whose main objective has always been to consider ways of producing German Shepherd Dogs as close as possible to the Standard, with special emphasis on correct temperament, construction and working ability. This is, of course, an ambitious aim, but it has been a driving factor in the success of the movement. *USA's* endeavours have not gone unnoticed among outsiders and this has drawn many into the fold. Major factors in the success of the organisation have been support from and acceptance by the SV and the WUSV. *USA* also controls and regulates its own affairs, and is not answerable to any higher body in the United States.

USA SUCCESS

What is the secret of the *USA's* success? There are many ingredients: the development of a national publication as a common link for all members; a diligent and painstaking attention to detail; the maintenance and integrity of the record-keeping system; a programme for training and examining national judges; an integrated structure from national level down through the regions and to local grass-roots membership. Certainly, the movement has grown and everything works satisfactorily. It has reached the point that the organisation now has a full-time office with permanent staff, a great change from the original undertaking which operated out of a member's home. It is quite phenomenal that the organisation has been built up to its present high profile and standing in such a short space of time.

WORKING DOG FEDERATION

Over recent years, as *USA* continued to grow and prosper, it became obvious that there was a need for an overall body to provide an avenue for open dialogue between the various organisations and breed clubs involved in the sport of Schutzhund and European-style conformation shows. Such dialogue would give more assurance of uniformity in judging and interpretation of rules and decisions reached at an international level. It would also create a united front which would help to resolve many problems. *USA* therefore started to develop the basic idea for an American Working Dog Federation, closely patterned on the German VDH system (German Kennel Club). After discussions with various breed clubs, the American Working Dog Federation has become a reality and is extremely popular in the United States. The Federation currently has as its member clubs The United Schutzhund Club of America representing the German Shepherd Dog; The United States Rottweiler Club; The North American Working Bouvier Association; The United Dobermann Club; The Working Schnauzer Federation; and the United Belgian Shepherd Association. Applications are in hand from more breed clubs. A dialogue has also developed with DVG America (a working all-breeds association with strong links, as the title suggests, with the German all-breeds working dog association) who are also interested in membership of the American Working Dog Federation.

The acceptance and progress of the American Working Dog Federation exceeded expectations by far, and was totally without precedent. The Federation has applied for membership of the FCI, and *USA* and the Federation have both enjoyed very favourable growth and an ever-increasing level of involvement by their memberships over the years.

This has been important overall and beneficial to various clubs and the breeds they represent. The success of the United Schutzhund Clubs of America, as well as the other breed clubs comprising the America Working Dog Federation, can be attributed to many things. Above all, the dog-owning public has been provided with something it definitely needed – a sound, stable, working German Shepherd Dog. It has been proved that a superior breed of dog can be provided. A greater degree of flexibility has been demonstrated than existing breed clubs were prepared to offer. *USA* is progressive and recognised worldwide, adhering strictly to international rules and regulations.

Information about the United Schutzhund Clubs of America has come from their official administrative offices, and was approved by USA President, Paul Meloy.

AUSTRALIA
GERMAN SHEPHERD BAN
The period of discrimination against the German Shepherd, during which none of the breed was officially allowed into the country, ran from 1929 to 1972. The period before the ban was imposed covered the years in which Australia, like many members of the British Empire and Commonwealth, was very much under the influence of Britain and, in particular, the British Canine Establishment. Those were also the years when dogs seen in the show rings of Great Britain were being bred from. Many were exported to Australia and formed the basis of the breed 'Down Under.'

The late Dr Spira, international all-round judge and a great authority on the Australian canine scene, considered that, looking back on the era, it seemed clear that the Australian Government's anti-GSD stance stemmed primarily from antagonism engendered in World War One. Anti-German attitudes were the same as those which encouraged British enthusiasts of the breed to alter the name to Alsatian. Indeed, the dog was also popularly known in Australia as the Alsatian during this particular period. The breed was also known by the unfortunate title of Alsatian Wolf Dog, as in Britain, but some Australian kennels and clubs preferred to use the correct title of German Shepherd Dog, or simply Shepherd Dog.

EARLY IMPORTS
Big-name British breeders and the stock they produced could also be seen in the rings of Australia. Picardy, the kennel name of Colonel Baldwin, was very much to the fore, as were its typical dogs, such as Undaunted of Picardy, a son of Ch. Cillahson of Picardy. Some eighty-eight Shepherds

were imported into Australia during the pre-ban period, including a couple of illegal imports. Two dogs, one known as Little Caesar, who had been a US Army War Dog, and another called Captain Le Rummond, who was a son of Maris v. Haus Schütting, were thrown overboard in Newcastle harbour. They were forced to swim ashore to avoid being destroyed, as the GSD ban had been imposed while they were in transit. The other two illegal dogs, Blitz Steinbusch and Adda v. Herbertshof, arrived in 1929, and were somehow smuggled ashore without being apprehended.

Other dogs imported during the pre-ban period were Pinkerton Rhoda, formerly Crumstone Rhoda, who arrived in June 1925, the year she won the Challenge Certificate at Crufts. Flash of Fallowdale, by English Champion Teut v. Haff, also arrived in 1925. Arras v. Schachengrund, whose sire was Rolf v. Heide, was one of the early imports of 1926 and is found in the pedigrees of many Shepherds from Victoria and Queensland. Another 1926 import was Shelagh of Glengyle, formerly Shelagh of Wolfslair – the change of kennel name being due to the disadvantage of identifying the Shepherd with the Wolf. Shelagh was sired by Ch. Kuno v. Brunnenhof. Eric of Rylens, siredby Ch. Erichsohn v. Starkenmark, also arrived. The latter two dogs were grandchildren of the 1920 Sieger Erich v. Grafenwerth, and it will be recognised that Kuno v. Brunnenhof and Ch. Erichsohn v. Starkenmark were important dogs in building up the breed in England after 1918. Erich v. Grafenwerth's son, Ch. Teut v Haff, was also an important foundation sire of the British Alsatian.

Cilla of Mattesdon, whose sire was Ch. Erichsohn v. Starkenmark, was from a very influential English kennel of the time. Ace of Picardy was sired by Caro v. Blasienberg but, of course, better known in England as Caro of Welham. Bertha of Versailles was a daughter of Ch. Allahson of If. Gerda of Ceara was sired by Caro v. Blasienberg, or, if you prefer, Caro of Welham. Ceara was an extremely important and successful kennel, probably best-known for Ch. Adalo of Ceara.

We do not intend to go through the whole list of pre-1929 imports into Australia. The details so far given should indicate that early Australian breeding was pretty well identical to the breeding of Shepherds in Great Britain, right down to the famous prefixes of British Shepherd/Alsatian circles. Possibly the most famous import of the period was Claus v. Eulengarten SchH, PD. He arrived in Melbourne on February 22nd 1929 and was considered to be: "the only dog in the world to hold the British Challenge Certificate, as well as the British and German Police Certificates." We are not sure what is meant by a 'German Police Certificate', but Claus did possess what was originally known as the Schutzhund qualification, renamed as Schutzhund II in 1938. Claus was a foundation dog in most early pedigrees in the state of the Victoria.

PREJUDICE

We have already outlined Dr Spira's beliefs on Australia's anti-Alsatian and anti-German mood. However, the specific reason given by those who succeeded in imposing the forty- three year ban, was that the breed had wolf blood in its veins. They contended that the dog was therefore a sheep killer, and if it was crossed with a Dingo, it would be even more dangerous. Again, we have the assumption that the existence of wolf blood in the veins of the Alsatian makes the breed inherently vicious. There can be no doubt that many Australians, particularly farmers, graziers and people associated with the sheep population were convinced that such an assessment of the Alsatian was accurate.

Clearly, the basis for this was twofold. Firstly, the early British importers, by agreement with the British Kennel Club, floated the name Alsatian Wolf Dog, with its dreadful consequences for the reputation of the breed. The second factor was the dog's extremely bad publicity in Britain, due to some very poor breeding practices and irresponsible owners. Of course, as in Great Britain, this reputation was not based on entirely false premises. For instance, the late Walter Reimann, the leading Australian breed authority, felt that the reason for the ban was partly because of the ignorance and carelessness of individual owners, partly due to the opposition of the breeders of Australian Sheepdogs, and partly brought about by the importation of inferior stock, particularly in terms of character. Some early dogs were the progeny of Shepherds which, in Germany, "had been expelled from the show rings and had their breeding permits cancelled because of bad nerves and unstable temperament and hereditary faults."

LIFTING THE BAN

Eventually, reason prevailed and breed associations, such as the German Shepherd Dog Club of Victoria, led the way towards the lifting of the ban. This society also organised a great deal of fundraising, which helped to finance the campaign to bring the injustice of the ban to the attention of politicians, bureaucrats and, particularly, departmental officers. Club members argued that the import ban was based on false, illogical and emotive grounds and was totally discriminatory. The modern GSD is a domesticated dog whose natural instincts are to attach itself to its owner and family, rather than – as would a feral dog - wander off into the wilderness with the Dingoes. The original, and more recent, ancestors of the German Shepherd Dog tended the flocks and guarded them against intruders – therefore, had the GSD been a sheep-killer, it would hardly have succeeded in the tending function. As for the wolf component in the genetic make-up of the GSD, only a few crosses between wolf and Shepherd Dog are known to have existed in the history of the breed. Once this was accepted in official circles in Australia, there could be no logical reason for maintaining the ban.

By this time, the service organisations in Australia, particularly the Royal Australian Air Force, had also lobbied in the right quarters and explained how German Shepherds were protecting equipment and personnel in the Air Force. They spoke of dogs who were fully under control, very trainable, extremely intelligent and infinitely adaptable. Europe had appreciated all these qualities since the early days of the century, and it is a pity that certain parties in Australia took so long to get the message. The country missed out on the German Shepherd's police and military role over many years. Organisations, including America's Seeing Eye and the Guide Dogs for the Blind, all played their part in lobbying and helping the cause of the GSD, as well as many people in Australia's veterinary profession and universities, and success came when the ban was lifted in 1972.

The Australian experience should be a salutary warning of the dangers of using stock that is not of the highest quality, and of underestimating the enemies of the breed, particularly the media. Behaving irresponsibly with our Shepherds is merely playing into their hands. The ban was lifted, initially for twelve-month trial period, which passed without any problems, and led to its welcome end throughout the whole country.

BREED PROBLEMS AND SOLUTIONS

It must be appreciated that the state of the breed at the beginning of the 1970s was roughly equivalent to the pre-Klodo/Utz period in the rest of the world, particularly in Europe, since no blood of these two famous dogs was known to have been officially incorporated into Australian breeding. The first Australian National German Shepherd Show was held five years before the ban was lifted. Herr Hutter from Germany was engaged to judge this show, which took place at the North Sydney Oval on March 19th, 1967. The occasion was used as a concerted public relations campaign for the breed. There was a televised guard of honour, made up by lines of German Shepherd Dogs, at the City Council Town Hall and at the judges' hotel. Unprecedented radio and TV coverage was syndicated across the whole of the country and televised demonstrations of Obedience and Royal Australian Air Force dogs brought the breed's good points to the masses. For the first time, the German Shepherd was able to show its true colours on a large scale, and

Ch. Dunmonaidh Junker: Top winning GSD 'down under', a British import.

finally started to tip the scales of prejudice. It was a very astute move on the part of the GSD authorities to engage somebody of the calibre of Herr Hutter, one of the most celebrated of contemporary German judges. He went through the entry thoroughly, in a detached manner, but with a willingness to be helpful and make suggestions. At the same time, he did not conceal his opinion of the situation. The results were a shock to exhibitors and onlookers. For the first time, many learned the implications of the length and angle of bones, and their impact on movement and endurance. They were told of the importance of strength of the back, relative to the transfer of thrust. Virtually without exception, they also learned new things, such as the desirability of a dog with a full mouth, and strong, healthy dentition. Australian ringsiders, who were themselves judges, were shown most graphically that not one of their dogs was built as a trotting dog should be, with long, well-angled, dry bones and taut ligamentation. The great majority of onlookers, although aware their dogs were not up to scratch, primarily because of restrictions created by the ban, were unquestionably naive, and with all due respect, quite ignorant of the breed's real needs, and how far the Australian breed lagged behind the rest of the world, particularly Germany. Never before had they seen so many dogs penalised so heavily for weak nerves. The judge seemed to have no heart or pity. Indeed, records show that a petition to this effect, signed by a number of notable people in the breed, was circularised. Dogs with what many considered only an insignificant defect such as a missing tooth or two were penalised "severely". Many of the top winners of the period were, in retrospect, pretty to look at but not terribly well-constructed. Such dogs were dismissed out of hand, in fact, Herr Hutter put them out of the ring. The top-winning German Shepherd of the day was in fact thrown out with the first batch, and the judge kept saying that the dogs were far too fat and out of condition.

Herr Hutter stated the obvious. Only lifting the ban on imports could cure the breed's ills, and he provoked a desire to have it revoked among Australian breeders that had not previously been felt. That first National was small, compared to the subsequent competitions, and ran at a huge loss (20 per cent on turnover), but it was actually the greatest National of all, because it started the process which brought the German Shepherd in Australia towards a situation of comparability with the rest of the world.

Although onlookers had been told that, in Herr Hutter's opinion, the breed could not be upgraded to the German standard without new blood, they were advised that they could improve on what they had by carefully planned breeding and the selection and care of puppies. When we compare this first National Show in Australia with other shows judged by SV judges and judges of the equivalent outlook around the world, we see that not one single adult dog at the Show was graded 'Excellent'. The highest grade given was 'Very Good'.

A NEW DIRECTION

The German Shepherd Dog Council of Australia, affiliated to the Australian National Kennel Control (Australian Kennel Club) and also affiliated to the World Union of German Shepherd Dog Clubs (WUSV), was formed to take over the activities of the breed in Australia on a national basis. Its affiliated clubs were the ACT German Shepherd Dog Association, the German Shepherd Dog Club of Broken Hill, the Newcastle and Hunter Region German Shepherd Dog Club, the German Shepherd Dog League of New South Wales, the German Shepherd Dog Club of Northern Territory, the German Shepherd Dog Club of Queensland, the German Shepherd Dog Club of South Australia, the German Shepherd Dog Club of Tasmania, the German Shepherd Dog Club of Victoria and the German Shepherd Dog Association of Western Australia.

The current President of GSDCA is Louis Donald, who when appointed in 1976, quickly showed tremendous qualities which were necessary at this point in the development of the breed in Australia. He had ability, drive, and the absolute conviction that things had to be done and done quickly. The following is the list of schemes introduced under his Presidency. It is most impressive bearing in mind that the GSDCA consists of entirely voluntary workers with no paid officials of any kind.

1977: Breed Survey Scheme.
1979: Tattoo Scheme.
1982: Hip Dysplasia Scheme.
1983: Judges sub-committee.
1983: Obedience sub-committee.
1986: New quarterly National Review launched.
1986: Dentition Certificate.
1987: Haemophilia Certificate.
1987: Affiliation to the Australian National Kennel Control (Kennel Club).
1987: The launch of the first Main Breed Show.

THE BREED SURVEY

The establishment of the Breed Survey in Australia has resulted in the compilation of a great deal of information of help to breeders, and the following is a list of the results by sires classified into Breed Survey Class I and Class II, with the country of origin. This period covers 1977 to 1989. The table of results is very revealing, because it shows which imported dogs have had the greatest influence by virtue of their having produced animals of sufficient quality to pass the Breed Survey, either in Class I or Class II. It will be seen that most of the dogs are imports, primarily from Germany, but also from other countries including Britain. Nine Australian-bred dogs appear on the list, and this percentage is likely to increase in future years. The dogs listed as Australian-bred are, in fact, bred from imported lines, as the old Australian breeding has virtually disappeared the scene. It is noticeable that one Australian dog, Karlrach Kentucky Lad, is in the fifth position, having produced sixty-one dogs in the Breed Survey. The clear winner is Liakar Satan, a British import with 103 progeny through the Breed Survey. Of these, thirty-one dogs and twenty-eight bitches were classified as Breed Survey Class I.

GERMAN SHEPHERD DOG COUNCIL OF AUSTRALIA

ANALYSIS OF BREED SURVEYED CLASSIFIED PROGENY BY SIRE
1977 TO 1989 INCLUSIVE

SIRE	COUNTRY OF ORIGIN	CLASS I D	CLASS I B	CLASS II D	CLASS II B	TOTAL D	TOTAL B	ALL CLASSES TOTAL
Liakar Satan	Britain	31	28	15	29	46	57	103
*Condor v Arminius	Germany	15	32	10	26	25	58	83
*Ingo v Hafenlohrtal	Germany	11	28	15	28	26	56	82
*Masuta Piaute	Britain	12	19	13	19	25	38	63
*Karlrach Kentucky Lad	Australia	8	19	14	20	22	39	61
*Rintilloch Rogue	Britain	3	10	11	22	14	32	46
*Ogus de Colombo	France	6	13	12	14	18	27	45
*Phal v Aegidiendamm	Germany	10	15	6	13	16	28	44
*Alf vd Mark Brandenburg	Germany	6	10	8	18	14	28	42
*Volscain Jester	Britain	8	15	4	8	12	23	35
*Edlenblut Orkan	Australia	9	14	5	7	14	21	35
*Heiko vd Burg Hausbrunn	Germany	5	12	9	9	14	21	35
*Karlstadt Tumblin' Dice	Australia	5	11	6	12	11	23	34
Nando v Anger	Germany	9	6	4	13	13	19	32
*Cäsar v Löhnerring	Germany	7	12	4	8	11	20	31
*Bratara Sultan	Australia	7	10	3	11	10	21	31
*Pirol v Tronje	Germany	5	13	4	5	9	18	27
*Dunmonaidh Junker	Britain	6	5	3	11	9	16	25
*Nico di Val del Tiepido	Italy	4	5	8	8	12	13	25
*Voirlich Amigus	Britain	4	10	5	3	9	13	22
*Erntemond Gold Lancer	Australia	7	7	2	6	9	13	22
*Delridge Echo	Britain	5	5	7	4	12	9	21
*Barry Berlesldörfer Hang	Germany	3	3	9	6	12	9	21
*Elan del'Alta Quercia	Italy	3	8	1	8	4	16	20
*Ambala Karu	Australia	6	6	4	3	10	9	20
*Raps vd Wienerau	Germany	5	5	1	8	6	13	19
*Karlrach Satans Rites	Australia	2	2	3	11	5	13	18
*Edlenblut Fedo	Australia	5	5	4	4	9	9	18
*Wasko vd Urbecke	Germany	1	4	3	10	4	14	18
*Dirk v Clausenhang	Germany	3	1	3	9	6	10	16
*Xiwar v Oberbeckerland	Germany	0	5	1	10	1	15	16
*Rocko v Hühnegrab	Germany	2	7	3	4	5	11	16
*Hasenway Putz	Australia	4	6	3	3	7	9	16
*Vasall v Kirschental	Germany	1	6	3	4	4	10	14

	CLASS I D	CLASS I B	CLASS II D	CLASS II B	TOTAL D	TOTAL B	ALL CLASSES TOTAL
Sub-total for above 34 sires (25 imported)	218	357	206	374	424	731	1155
All other sires	314	446	281	619	595	1065	1660
TOTAL CLASSIFIED	532	803	487	993	1019	1796	2815

*Denotes Breed Surveyed

Source: Annual Breed Survey Books 1977 to 1989 inclusive.

THE FIRST MAIN BREED SHOW

Australia's first Main Breed Show was held on October 11th 1987. Many of the concepts were bold innovations: 12 Australian judges, judging 12 Classes; Open dogs and bitches gaiting off lead; pedigrees being made available to judges in Junior, Intermediate and Open Classes; bloodlines being an additional judicial consideration; Excellent Select gradings to Open exhibits who were anatomically of a predetermined high standard of breed worth, possessing the 'A' stamp for hips, Breed Survey Class I and having passed a set temperament test at the show.

Ages in the classes were attuned to European practices: 3-6 months, 6-9 months, 9-12 months, 12-18 months, 18-24 months and 24 months and over. There was the introduction of a new grading of 'Very Good Merit' to be awarded by judges in Junior and Intermediate Classes. All specialist judges were brought together at the conclusion of each Class. Special commemorative medallions were made, and outright trophies second to none. All dogs were placed and graded, sashes and trophies were awarded to the first fifteen place-getters, and a judges' seminar was instituted to discuss what lay ahead, including major faults within the Breed. An environment which brought judges, breed surveyors and breeders closer together was developed, and no inter-class or inter-sex competition permitted. 'Excellent Select' and Sieger was Edlenblut Orkan, by Edlenblut Fedo, who will be seen among the sires on the Breed Survey list. Siegerin and Excellent Select I in bitches was Landrina Majic Melody, by Karlrach Kentucky Lad, who will be seen as number five on the list of best producers in terms of Breed Survey results.

A POSITION OF STRENGTH

The Main Breed Show, Australia's equivalent of the Sieger Show, is an annual event. After the import ban was permanently lifted in 1974, Ingo v. Hafenlohrtal and Phal Aegiendamm were imported into Australia. This was indeed fortunate for Australia, though it must be understood that these dogs had bitches of much lesser quality to mate with than dogs going into the country nowadays. Most bitches had some basic problems, such as missing teeth, temperament, gun shyness and lack of firmness in the back, to name but a few. It was fortunate that the lines of Ingo and Phal combined well together, and these combinations had a fairly high success rate. Naturally, imported lines were represented by the four major bloodlines from Germany: Marko, Quanto, Canto and Mutz. As elsewhere, Canto and Quanto in particular have proved most successful, and have been now well incorporated into Australian lines.

There is absolutely no doubt that the far-sightedness, diligence, energy and vitality of Australia's German Shepherd enthusiasts have been responsible for rescuing the breed from the doom and gloom which prevailed in the period during which imports were banned. They have created one of the most advanced German Shepherd systems anywhere, and Australian control of the breed nationally through various systems, as well as the seriousness with which they view the breeding and exhibiting of German Shepherds, is something we should all admire. We can only congratulate Louis Donald and his associates on a tremendous job and we wish them well in future years.

SOUTH AFRICA

The history of the South African German Shepherd begins largely with the importation of British stock, and most were of British origin right up to the mid-seventies. However, some German animals were imported in the late fifties and early sixties, although they were little used. But the swing towards German stock began in earnest twenty years ago, and by the early eighties such stock was dominating the show scene.

THE TWO FACTIONS

The South African Kennel Club (KUSA) was at this time resisting all efforts by GSD enthusiasts to introduce such German ideas as mandatory specialist judges, outside attraction, gun-shot, etc. in the ring. This led to the formation of the German Shepherd Dog Federation of Southern Africa (Federation) in 1984. It was an organisation independent of KUSA, and registered the Shepherds of its own members, organised its own shows, and administered its own affairs. Many serious breeders and exhibitors were to join its ranks.

At this time a GSD Breed Council existed which operated in an advisory capacity, and comprised one member from each specialist club within the KUSA organisation. There was much political wrangling that resulted in five years of isolation from Germany, in particular from German judges, and a split in the breed between enthusiasts unable to decide who should be recognised as the breed's legal authority. By 1989, KUSA had granted greater autonomy to the GSD people remaining under its jurisdiction, and the gap between the two organisations narrowed. At this point, the main differences between the two groups were that, within the Federation, members controlled the breed and breed control was compulsory, whereas KUSA members were still under the control of the Federal Council of KUSA and breed control was still only voluntary.

In September of the same year, the SV in Germany realised that withholding German judges from South Africa was seriously impeding the development of the breed in that country. Under the Presidency of Herr Herman Martin, it was decided to grant the KUSA GSD Council a three-year guest membership of the World Union of German Shepherd Dog Clubs (WUSV), while the SV recognised the existing WUSV Club, the German Shepherd Dog Breeders Association (GSDBA), as the holding club of the Federation. The SV stated they would send judges to all members of the WUSV; that is to both KUSA and to the Federation. In 1990, KUSA narrowed the gap still further (on the advice of the GSD Council) by introducing certain mandatory requirements.

On information from Mike Sullivan, President of the GSD Federation of South Africa, the Federation is now the only recognised WUSV member club from South Africa. The Kennel Union (KUSA) was a guest member for three years, but full membership of WUSV by KUSA was not successful, and in the future, KUSA has no access to German SV judges. There are still negotiations afoot to bring the two sides together by giving the Federation, which now represents the majority of influential kennels and breeders, autonomy over GSDs and GSD affairs in South Africa, while at the same time seeking affiliation with KUSA. This is a landmark decision for GSDs worldwide as it means that the World Union (WUSV) actively will support specialist GSD organisations that prove their bona fides.

It is probably true to say that while KUSA has quality within its show rings, the Federation has a greater depth of quality, and though the Federation is successful with Schutzhund results, the working side of KUSA members is stronger. Most people involved at the time found the split a far from happy situation, but it was directly responsible for the change in KUSA's attitude to the German Shepherd. KUSA now accepts that the Shepherd has a different set of requirements from those of other breeds. Negotiations towards a reunification of the breed are ongoing, and may be successful in the foreseeable future. However this is achieved, the bottom line is that German Shepherd enthusiasts *must* have control of their own breed.Below is a comparative survey of the various activities of the two sides of the breed, in other words the Federation and KUSA, in South Africa. This survey covers breeding requirements, showing and breed surveys, and hip gradings.

BREEDING: Official pedigrees are issued by both organisations, to three generations in the case of KUSA and five generations with the Federation. With regard to hip grading, it should be noted that with both organisations the score *from the worst hip* is the score recognised.

SHOW GRADE: Federation: Minimum of 'Good'. KUSA: Minimum of 'Good', otherwise the animal may have been to an Assessment, or have been Breed Surveyed.

TATTOO: Federation: The animal must have been tattooed. KUSA: As of 1990, the animal must have been tattooed.

AGE RESTRICTIONS (BREEDING): Federation: Females not less than twenty months at the time of mating. Males two years at least at the time of mating. KUSA: Females, not less than 22 months at the time of whelping. Males, 18 months at least at the time of mating.

HIPS: Federation: An 'A+' and an 'AO' may be freely bred from. 'A-' is a restricted category that may currently be mated to an 'A+', Normal, or Fast Normal. (The last two are grades of the SV 'A' Stamp.) KUSA: No animal with a hip score greater than a South African Grade 2 may be bred from.

NOTE: Federation: The National Breed Committee has the power to alter the restrictions when it is deemed necessary. A Progeny Testing Scheme exists, and has power to withdraw any animal producing a high incidence of hip dysplasia from breeding.
KUSA: Up until just before publication, KUSA has controlled the frequency of the mating of bitches to one litter per year. This restriction has now been lifted.

SHOWING
FEDERATION CLASSES: 6-9 months; 9-12 months; 12-18 months; 18-24 months; Over 24 months. A gun shot test is taken by all animals from 12 months of age.
KUSA CLASSES: Minor Puppy (6-9 months); Puppy (9-12 months); Junior (12-18 months); Graduate (18-24 months); Open (24 months and over); Open Select (24 months and over with a working qualification of either BWT*, IWT**, I, II, III).
*Breed Working Trial – an easier IWT Grade I.
**International Working Trials (previously known as FCI) broadly equivalent to the Schutzhund – also known as IPO Prüfung. A gunshot test is taken from the Junior Class onwards.

HIGH AWARDS: Federation: VA Gradings are given at the annual National show only. Males must do a full test of courage. Females are expected to 'take the sleeve' of the helper, on lead if necessary. KUSA: The title of Champion is only awarded to an animal who has gained the necessary CC points under a specialist judge, *and* who also has a South African working qualification. CCs at specialist shows are only awarded to dogs or bitches who have been graded 'V' (Excellent). Therefore, the CC and RCC winners are taken from the Open and Open Select classes only.

PEDIGREES: Federation: A pedigree for each exhibit is required in the ring at the time of judging to verify the hip status. KUSA: No pedigree is allowed in the ring.

GRADING CERTIFICATES: Federation: Grading Certificates are awarded in the ring.
KUSA: Grading certificates are awarded in the ring at Specialist Shows.

CRITIQUES: Federation: Verbal critiques are given (in public).
KUSA: Verbal critiques are given at Specialist Shows (also in public).

DOUBLE HANDLING: Federation: Permitted. KUSA: Permitted at Specialist Shows only.

BREED SURVEYS: Apart from obvious things such as owners and dogs being registered with their own organisation, the following criteria must be met when presenting for a Breed Survey.

AGE: Federation: Minimum 16 months, and maximum 8 years.
KUSA: Minimum 18 months and maximum 8 years.

TATTOO: Federation: The animal must have a visible tattoo.
KUSA: The animal must have a visible tattoo.

HIPS: Federation: The animal must be in possession of a Federation-recognised pass, or an 'A' stamp. KUSA: The animal must be in possession of a South African Grade One pass or better. The 'A' stamp is recognised, as are scores from other WUSV countries, but they must fall within the accepted range.

SHOW GRADE: Federation: Minimum grading of 'Good'. KUSA: Minimum grading of 'Good'.

TEST OF COURAGE: Federation: Not required. KUSA: Required.

ENDURANCE TEST: Federation: Dogs born after 1.1.87 must have passed an endurance test before being presented for their first survey. They are presently allowed to pass this test up to six months after their survey, as it is a relatively new requirement.
KUSA: At the time of publication, this is not required. However it is possible that after 1.1.95, an animal being presented for survey will be required to have passed a 20km endurance test.

NOTE: Federation: Federation policy is that increased control of breeding in the future will not affect the minimum requirements, but will be aimed towards additional requirements for Breed Survey. KUSA: After 1.1.95, animals being presented for a Breed Survey will also require a minimum working qualification of BWT or better.

HIP GRADES: The chart below gives equivalent hip grades for the UK and South Africa's KUSA and Federation schemes. These figures are meant as a rough guide only, to aid the reader. They are in no way an official interpretation and should not be used as such. In both South African schemes, the highest scoring hip is taken as the grade awarded to the animal.

UK	KUSA	FEDERATION
0 – 6	Normal	A+
7 – 12	Grade 1	AO
13 – 25	Grade 2	A-
26 – 39	Grade 3	
40+	Grade 4	

PINK PEDIGREES: Both authorities issue the coveted Pink Pedigrees, although requirements for issue differ somewhat. Federation: Both parents are required to have passed their Breed Survey.
KUSA: The pink pedigree is issued to an animal who has:
1. A recognised and approved hip score, or grade.
2. Been Breed Surveyed.
3. Has obtained a working qualification.

GRAND VICTOR SHOWS: Prior to January 1st 1985, Grand Victor Shows were judged against

SA Ch. Rushlight Eden of Yanuka: KUSA Grand Victor 1986. British-bred top winning SA Shepherd.

A Breed, WT and Obedience Champion (KUSA) Leimon Montana IWT3 also attained breed survey Class 1 and 'V' rating under SV judges. Bred from British lines.

the Kennel Club Standard, and afterwards against the Standard of the FCI, or the World Union Standard for the German Shepherd Dog. In 1985 KUSA awarded a Floating Trophy for the Grand Victor, and it was decided that the Grand Victor Show would go to a different club or area annually. Until 1992, the Grand Victor and Grand Victrix were the Best in Show animals, and the Best Opposite Sex or the Challenge Certificate winners. Subsequently, dogs and bitches were judged separately and there was no Best of Breed as an award. Furthermore, to enter for the title of Grand Victor, a dog had to have certain minimum qualifications which were not applicable in previous years. The following is a list of Grand Victors and Victrices since 1985:-

1985
Grand Victor Ch. Quester von Haus Wipplinger SchH III
Grand Victrix Ch. Starguard Deena

Buco Van Noort: Leading KUSA sire – Winner of progeny groups Grand Victor show 1992.

Natz v. Huitze Hintdonk Sch H3, FH VA 1991: Presented a very good progeny group at the 1992 Federation National show.

1986
Grand Victor Ch. Rushlight Eden of Yanuka
Grand Victrix Correaith Jola of Halenburg
1987
Grand Victor Canto vom Schloss Weissenburg SchH III
Grand Victrix Ch. Judy von der Beilsteinmühle
1988
Grand Victor Ruthenwald Xai of Haps Hill
Grand Victrix Simnikan Xita
1989
Grand Victor Taifun v.d. Kahler Heide
Grand Victrix Cara aus dem Schwarzer Zwinger

Gayville Putz of Elsaville: This rich sable import from England was Kusa Reserve Grand Victor 1991 and top GSD 1992.

1990
Grand Victor Hausfischer Kuti
Grand Victrix Ratta v Densul of Di Casa Conti
1991
Grand Victor Ch. Irko von der Goldenen Wetterau SchH III
Grand Victrix Dio Biene of Tanah Merah (a Zimbabwean entry owned by Mrs Ilse van Erp.)
1992
Grand Victor Quai vom Spessartblick SchH III
Grand Victrix Zelka vom Murtal

KUSA TOP SHOW WINNERS
It is probably true to say that very little is known about dogs that have been bred in South Africa and exported within recent years, but there is no doubt that the standard is very high indeed. The following are some of the dogs that have figured prominently at KUSA Shows:

BUCO VAN NOORT: A consistently good producer of a very good type in both males and females and was winner of the progeny group at the Grand Victor Show of 1992. Buco is by Sieger Fanto vom Hirschel out of Ossie v. Tannenmeise, a litter sister to the great producing sire Odin v. Tannenmeise.

LEIMON MONTANA: This GSD had the distinction of being the first dog in South Africa, and possibly anywhere else, to carry the three titles of Breed, Working Trials and Obedience Champion. He also obtained the qualification of IWT III. Montana was awarded the 'V' rating six times under SV judges, the last time as a veteran, and he qualified 12 times in IWT III. He also gained a Breed Survey Class I.

In 1984 he was judged by Walter Martin of Wienerau fame, who gave this critique of Montana: "A large masculine dog, very good type and substance, firm all through, good croup, very good angulation of the forequarters and of the hindquarters, correct in the front. Very good movement."

British breeders should be proud to know that this high-achieving dog, probably unique anywhere in terms of his qualifications, was entirely bred from British lines, being by Royvon

Oro v. Batu:
Federation Sieger
1992.

Rodreigo, litter brother to Ch. Royvon's Red Rum; Rodreigo was exported to Rhodesia and became Rhodesian German Shepherd of the Year in 1979. It will be recalled that this excellent litter was sired by Ch. Delridge Erhard. The dam of Montana was Schloss Adler Omega, who was by Ch. Brinton Playboy of Hendrawen, a Premonition son, who was Rhodesian German Shepherd of the Year in 1976, 1977 and 1978. Omega's dam was a grand-daughter of Ch. Ramacon Swashbuckler, who was Supreme Champion of Crufts in 1971.

CH. RUSHLIGHT EDEN OF YANUKA: Grand Victor in 1986. He was imported from England in October 1983. He was sired by Moonwinds Fels, who was a grandson of Supreme Ch. Ramacon Swashbuckler, and a great-grandson of Derby v.d. Schinklergrenze, whose sire was Mutz a. d. Kückstrasse. The dam of Moonwinds Fels was a very fine imported Champion, Banja vom Hil-ka-forst by Reza v. d. Wienerau, a combination of Quanto/Canto breeding. Ch. Rushlight Eden's dam had Ch. Druidswood Consort as double grandparents, one through the Ch. Shedocast Condor.

'Asa', as he was known in South Africa, was not used a great deal, mainly because of prejudice against English breeding, but from his few studs he produced an excellent type. Two of his sons, Ch. Majuta Ajax and Ch. Majuta Bomber of Aerojohn, gained between them 30 Best of Breeds, 27 CCs and 17 RCCs. Ajax was Top GSD Veteran of 1992 and Reserve Veteran of the Year (all breeds). All the progeny of Asa which were campaigned gained V grades and today's sixth-generation stock are gaining top awards at specialist shows.

Roy had the privilege of judging Asa at the Diamond Jubilee Show in Cape Town in 1984, and gave him the CC and Best of Breed. On the same weekend, Asa attended four shows and won Challenge Certificates at every one, under four different judges.

QUAI VOM SPESSARTBLICK: This is a son of Exl von Batu, who became a British Champion. He is a son of double Sieger Uran vom Wildsteiger Land. The dam of Quai is Jessy vom Spessartblick, a Canto v. d. Wienerau grand-daughter through the 1978 Sieger Canto von Arminius.

GAYVILLE PUTZ OF ELSAVILLE: Another British-bred dog that has done well in South Africa. He was Top GSD in 1992 and reserve to the Grand Victor at the KUSA Show of 1991. He is a very rich sable, very masculine, with excellent forequarter and hind angulation, and with extremely good proportions. Putz is by Rebroc Davos, a grandson of 1983 Sieger Dingo vom Haus Gero, out of Ch. Gayville Dixie winner of four CCs and six Reserve CCs, Best of Breed at Crufts in 1988, and a daughter of the imported Meik von der Talquelle, who also gained his English title.

HASSO VOM GLOCKENER MOOR: Considered to have been one of the best producers in recent years.

IRKO V. D. GOLDENEN WETTERAU: Grand Victor in 1991. Son of the Federation Dog Fimo aus der Eremitenklause, Irko is a strong and substantial male, with a good head and expression, a firm back, slightly steep croup, good forehand and very good hindquarter angulation, a very good mover (critique from UK judge, Malcolm Griffiths). Irko is by Fimo aus der Eremitenklause, a son of Queno von Arminius, litter brother to Quando von Arminius, whose dam is a daughter of Erk vom Holtkamper See.

IBAR VAN NOORT: Considered to be a good dog; he has not been in South Africa very long but is also considered to have produced some good youngsters, particularly females. He is by double Sieger Uran vom Wildsteiger Land out of Illa vom Haus Pari, a daughter of Sieger Dingo vom Haus Gero.

FEDERATION SIEGERS AND SIEGERINS
We have already stated that the quality of the dogs on the KUSA side is very good. We should add that the quality on the Federation side is perhaps in greater depth. The following is a list of Federation Siegers and Siegerins from 1990 when VA grading began.

SIEGER
1990: Klaus v. Vaalhoek
1991: Natz v. Haus Hintdonk
1992: Oro v. Batu

SIEGERIN
1990: Claire v. d. Burg Reichenstein
1991: Connie v. Neuen Berg
1992:Connie v. Neuen Berg

1992 FEDERATION NATIONAL SIEGER SHOW
The following is a list of VA males and females, from the Federation National Sieger Show of 1992.

MALES
VA1: Oro v. Batu. SchH2; Breed Survey, Class 1; Hip grading, Normal; Sire, Mark vom Haus Beck; Dam, Fina vom Turntal
VA2: Kveno Obmostni. SchH3; Hips, Fast Normal; Breed Survey, Class 1; date of birth, 31.1.88; Sire, Sieger Eiko vom Kirschental; Dam, Jalta von der Kahler Heide.
VA3: Joker vom Steckenborn. Hips, Fast Normal; date of birth, 19.7.89; No further details available. He is understood to have been returned to Germany and obtained his SchH2.
VA4: Chicko von Grehenheim. SchH1; Hips, A+; Breed Survey, Class 1; date of birth, 16.3.89; Sire, Double Sieger Uran vom Wildsteiger Land; Dam, Cocki v. d. Kahler Heide.

VA5: Amany von Dulcamara. SchH3; Hips, Normal; Breed Survey, Class 1; date of birth, 25.6.88; by Natz von Huize Hintdonk (son of Uran vom Wildsteiger Land) out of Nonja vom Uferbaum.

FEMALES

VA1 and Siegerin: Connie von Neuen Berg. Hips, Ao; Breed Survey, Class 1; date of birth, 9.6.88; Sire, Fanto vom Südblick; Dam, Anusch von der Beilsteinmühle (a daughter of Tell vom Grossen Sand).

VA2: Yalta von der Holzheimer Linde. Hips, Normal; Breed Survey, Class 1; date of birth,6.10.90; Sire, Quero vom Wiesenborn (a son of Fando vom Südblick); Dam, Alfi von der Dörnchenburg.

VA3: Lea vom Flutgraben. SchH1; Hips, Normal; Breed Survey, Class 1; date of birth, 16.3.89; Sire, Harko von der Wilhelmswarte (a grandson of Double Sieger Uran vom Wildsteiger Land); Dam, Salke von der Kahler Heide, a granddaughter of Uran through Sieger Eiko vom Kirschental.

VA4: Zelli von der Holzheimer Linde. IPO1; Hips, Normal; Breed Survey, Class 1; date of birth, 30.9.90; Sire, Cimbo von der Burg Reichenstein (a son of Double Sieger Quando von Arminius); Dam, Kira von der Holzheimer Linde (a granddaughter of Double Sieger Uran vom Wildsteiger Land).

VA5: Kennelm Britt. Hips, Ao; Breed Survey, Class 1; date of birth, 7.ll.89; Sire, Ruthenwald Xai; Dam, Spice of Simnikan.

VA6: Eja di Casa Conti. Hips, A+; date of birth, 10.8.90; Sire, Natz von Huize Hintdonk; Dam, Kira von der Kahler Heide.

VA7: Bo von der Herderskring. VH1; Hips, Normal; date of birth, 11.7.86; Sire, Double Sieger Quando von Arminius; Dam, Quidi von der Herderskring (a daughter of VA Onex von Batu).

VA8: Zina von der Kahler Heide. SchH1; date of birth, 12.12.87. No further details on this bitch.

VA9: Herra vom Kiefern-Eck. SchH1; Hips, A+; Breed Survey, Class 1; date of birth, 25.1.89; Sire, Klaus von Vaalhoek (a grandson of Irk von der Wienerau through Cäsar vom Haus Schmittmann); Dam, Anja vom Kiefern-Eck.

VA10: Jiva vom Kiefern-Eck. Hips, A+; Breed Survey, Class 1; date of birth, 21.5.89; Sire, Klaus von Vaalhoek,; Dam, Iris von der Heimat (a great-great-grand-daughter of Quanto von der Wienerau).

INFLUENTIAL FEDERATION DOGS

AMSEL VON DER KAHLER HEIDE SchH1: Arrived in South Africa in 1987 in whelp to Uran, and produced the Q litter, Grehenheim, Quera and Quina. Quera was the Federation's Vice Siegerin in 1990 and at the 1991 Show her litter sister Quina was Vice Siegerin.

NATZ VON HUIZE HINTDONK: Presented a superb progeny group at the 1992 National Show, and at eight years of age, looked a real showman. (Sire, Double Sieger Uran vom Wildsteiger Land out of Heike v. Tannenmeise).

FIMO A. D. EREMITENKLAUSE SchH3: This dog went V12 at the Sieger Show before being imported into South Africa. He had been awarded 55 'V' gradings in Germany. Although now in Norway, his influence remains through his many 'V' rated progeny in South Africa. At the Federation 1992 National Show, Fimo was still able to present a progeny group despite being absent for nearly three years. It is interesting to note that the KUSA 1991 Grand Victor Irko v. d. Goldenen Wetterau is a Fimo son. Fimo is by Queno von Arminius, a brother to Quando, out of Racki von der Kahler Heide.

VICKY VOM HAUS GERO: The Federation's first Siegerin. Sire, Double Sieger Uran; Dam,

Lucki vom Haus Gero, a daughter of Sieger Axel v. d. Hainsterbach.

GUNDO VON DER TEUFELSKANZEL SchH3: A very fine male who is considered to have had an enormous influence on the breed in South Africa. This is seen through his grandchildren and great-great-grandchildren who are achieving high awards today.

CÄSAR V. HAUS SCHMITTMANN SchH1: Considered to have had a major influence on the breed in South Africa and is found in many pedigrees today, mainly through his son Klaus v. Vaalhoek, who became the Federation Sieger of 1990. Also a daughter, in-bred father to daughter to him, Gina v. Grehenheim, who was an excellent brood producing eight 'V' sons and seven 'V' daughters in five litters. Sadly, Cäsar died prematurely at just seven years of age.

QUERO V. BATU SchH3: He won very well in Junior Classes in Germany. When he came to South Africa, he started his career with KUSA but later transferred to the Federation. He is considered to have been a very good producer of females and some good males. Quero is by Canto vom Bilderstöckchen, a grandson of Canto through Sieger Canto von Arminius, out of Diana von Batu, a great-grand-daughter of Bernd vom Lierberg through Boss vom Amalienhof.

ZILLY VON DER TEUFELSKANZEL SchH1: Considered to have been an excellent producer, particularly to Cäsar vom Haus Schmittmann. She was particularly prepotent for good type, conformation and temperament. She is by the Canto grandson Heiko vom Loherstein, whose dam Brixi vom Loher-stein was sired by VA Kai vom Silberbrand (Marko vom Cellerland). The dam of Zilly is Laika di Val Sole, a daughter of Quanto von der Wienerau.

QUANTO V. ARMINIUS: Imported in 1979. He won the progeny group under Dr Ernst Beck in 1982, but his show and stud career was cut short by a tick bite, which caused a bad infection and left the dog lame. He is still found in the pedigrees of today's dogs. Quanto is by Herzog von Adeloga, a son of the 1973 Sieger Dick von Adeloga, out of Gitte v. Gründel, a grand-daughter of Mutz von der Pelztierfarm through Jonny von der Rheinhalle.

QUERO V. KOPENKAMP: Born on 13.2.70, he had a very good career in the ring and was often up against Quero v. Batu. He produced good males and females but critics consider that the progeny showed a little length in the body, and perhaps a little over-angulation in the hindquarters.

WORKING QUALIFICATIONS
We end this look at the South African scene by referring to the working qualifications which can be obtained in that country. The Working Trials system is similar to that in Britain. So far as the Federation is concerned, the schedule of the Schutzhund Prüfung is worked in exactly the same way as it is in Germany and all other countries including Great Britain, who use the Schutzhund programme. However, KUSA has a slightly different system for working their dogs in this discipline, which was known as FCI. It was introduced to South Africa in 1983/84 by Johan Gallant, a Belgian, whose breed was Giant Schnauzers. The FCI designation was later changed to IWT, and although IWT rules are virtually identical to those of Schutzhund, it is not exactly the same. The controlling body for IWT in Europe is the FCI, and on that continent it is called IPO.

The first FCI in Cape Town was held on June 3rd 1984. Except for Mr Gallant's home province of Natal, FCI seemed to get off to a fairly slow start. Training classes, competitors and judges were very dependent on Working Trials, and FCI I, II and III were the qualifications awarded. In 1989 the rules were amended and the name changed to International Working Trials. In 1991 the rules were amended again, this time to bring the system into line with FCI rules currently in operation in Europe. IWT administration, which previously was under the control of Obedience and Working Trials, was separated. The introduction of a compulsory working qualification for KUSA GSD Breed Champions and the Open Select Class helped to increase the importance of IWT in South Africa. The minimum recognised working qualification for a German Shepherd is the Breed Working Trial (BWT), which is held only by specialist clubs. A breed judge is in attendance to check that the dog is a worthy breed specimen, and an IWT judge oversees the working side. It is believed to be slightly below the standard of IWT Grade I.

In the qualifications required for GSDs under the new system, Obedience and Working Trials are not recognised, with the exception of PD. As for KUSA's attitude to IWT, there was some early opposition. It was feared that unsuitable dogs and handlers would be trained and the public could use IWT as a way to get their dogs attack-trained. This debate resulted in IWT administrators taking some very responsible decisions. In 1989, they started to formalise a programme to train qualified helpers or assistants.

It was made quite clear that training methods were to be based on the prey instinct of the dog. In training, the arm-pad is given as a reward to the dog, taking the focus off the man. After a session, the helper makes friends with the dog. In this method of training, minimal aggression is directed towards the person. This scheme came into force in 1990, and a helper has to pass a written and practical exam in order to become qualified. A club cannot hold a training session without a qualified helper in attendance and only qualified helpers can officiate at a Trial. Each qualified helper is licensed by KUSA, and they have a personal record card which includes their photograph. Every appointment at a Trial, completed to the satisfaction of the officiating judge, is recorded on the card. In order to keep the licence valid, helpers must have a minimum of one entry a year on their record card. It is now up to both clubs and the qualified helpers to act in a responsible manner and there has been no opposition to this scheme since it was introduced. The IWT helpers, a number of whom are ex-PD 'assailants' anyway, do all the PD work. It is also compulsory for a PD assailant in a trial to be qualified and the IWT qualification is accepted.

Chapter Six

GENERAL OWNERSHIP AND MAINTENANCE

Before buying a puppy, a German Shepherd Dog or any other breed, certain considerations must be taken into account. Firstly, remember that you are acquiring this dog for life, possibly as long as fifteen or sixteen years. You are purchasing a living being, which is going to be completely dependent on you for its food, housing, exercise, training and affection. You must ask yourself: "Can I give sufficient attention and time as a daily commitment, and not just now and then?" If the answer is "yes", take it one stage further and weigh up the responsibilities of dog ownership.

A PUPPY'S NEEDS

Are you in a financial position to be able to keep your dog? Yearly inoculations, food, vetinarary bills and boarding kennels (if you decide to go abroad for your holiday) must all be taken into consideration. If you plan to keep your puppy outside, there is the cost of a kennel and fencing for the run, plus general maintenance. These are just a few items to consider, and there will probably be quite a few more expenses which will crop up as time goes by. If you are buying a puppy, you, or somebody else, must be constantly there for the first few months of its life. More behavioural problems are caused by puppies being left on their own for long periods with no companionship, than by almost anything else. Puppies, like children, get bored and will then get into mischief and start to chew, usually your new shoes or settee, or they will bark and howl causing neighbours to complain. Your puppy needs your companionship, and, in this way, it will bond to you and make future training that much easier.

A puppy needs regular feeding and, as soon as it has been fed, it must be given the opportunity to go outside and relieve itself. If you only have time to give the puppy its food and then dash back to work, you will never have a house-trained puppy. Eight-week-old puppies do not need much exercise, but they do need play-time, which usually consists of half an hour's hectic running around, chewing, playing with toys, digging up the garden, or whatever. Fatigue overtakes them and they will then flop down in a deep sleep, and will not want to be disturbed for some considerable time. Decide where you want the puppy to sleep and put it there. The puppy will soon recognise its own place and will always go there when it needs a rest. The period between two months and six months is a crucial time of learning for your puppy, and the more you can teach him during this period, the better-trained your puppy will be in adult life. We will be dealing with puppy training in a later chapter, but from what has been written so far, you can see how important it is for somebody to be with your puppy, from the moment it first arrives in your home.

LIVING QUARTERS

Before you buy your puppy, you must decide whether it will be living in the house with you, whether it will sleep outside at night and come in during the day, or whether it will live entirely outside. Whichever option you choose, suitable accommodation must be prepared before the puppy's arrival.

OUTSIDE KENNEL: The kennel should be located as near to the house as possible, preferably backing on to the prevailing wind and, in the Northern Hemisphere, preferably facing south. Of course, the reverse applies in the Southern Hemisphere with regard to the sun, but still make sure the kennel backs on to the wind. The ideal is a kennel built of brick and breeze-blocks, with cavity walls and a double roof, to insulate against both excessive heat and cold. For the cavity walls use brick on the outside, and breeze-blocks inside. This will cut down costs considerably, and don't forget a damp course both in the walls and under the floor. This will ensure a dry kennel. A concrete floor is best, but ensure that there is sufficient fall towards the door, making hosing-down easy.

If the dog is going to spend long periods shut in the kennel, a window is necessary. Make the door high enough for you to walk in without bending over, and check that it fits well enough to avoid draughts. A German Shepherd can put up with extreme cold, but not draughts and damp, and if you don't eliminate them you will soon pay the price in vet's bills. A metal door is an advantage, and saves a lot of chewed doors and door frames. For the same reason, we are against wooden kennels, although there are quite a few good makes on the market. If you decide on a wooden kennel, take the precaution of lining it with sheet metal, which is not too expensive and very easy to install. It will save an awful lot of expense at a later stage. Remember, a wooden kennel must be creosoted every year to keep it rainproof and rotproof. If you take these precautions, your wooden kennel will last you for many years.

Use unbreakable perspex for the window in your brick kennel, and construct it so that it can open outwards. To stop the dog jumping out, make an inside frame of welded mesh. Remember, at first your puppy will be too small to jump out of windows, but you are making your kennel for the future, and you will find that, by six to eight months of age, the pup will have grown into quite a hefty animal, well able to get out of a window. If you are buying a wooden kennel, it will already have a window, probably perspex, and either welded mesh or bars on the inside. The type of kennel we have described is ideal in a temperate climate such as the UK. In tropical or very hot countries, modifications are necessary. Site your kennel in a shady area, out of the sun if possible. Double walls and roof are still desirable, but make certain there is plenty of ventilation to give maximum airflow. Contact your local builder about building materials, to ensure that your kennel remains as cool as possible. Likewise, if you live in a country with extremes of temperature – hot days and cold nights for instance – adaptations must be made accordingly. Advice from your local kennel owners and builders is the best bet.

CONVERTING A GARDEN SHED: It is sometimes possible to convert a garden shed into a kennel, but be certain that it is draught and damp-proof, and that there is no possibility of the puppy chewing its way out unless you are lucky enough to have a puppy that doesn't chew! Also, make sure the floor is concrete (with damp course) or wooden, as lying on an earth floor could be fatal to your young puppy.

MODULAR UNITS: Another type of kennel is the modular unit, which consists of concrete slabs in standard heights and depths, according to what you require. You can either have just one kennel, or a block which can be extended at a later stage. Modular units require a concrete base. The advantage of this type of kennel is that, because it comes in prefabricated slabs, it is both easy and quick to assemble and, if at any time you decide to move, it is possible to dismantle it and take it with you. You can get advice from your local supplier on cost and delivery.

KENNEL RUN: The run will, of course, be the same for either brick or wooden kennels. The surface can either be left as grass, gravel, concrete, or paving stones. We favour concrete, for the following reasons. Grass quickly turns to mud in the winter and dogs love digging holes, so after a relatively short length of time your lovely grass run looks more like a ploughed field! Gravel is OK for the older dog, but puppies are inclined to eat pebbles, which can cause very serious problems, leading to possible surgery. Gravel can quickly get weedy, and there is a problem with cleaning. So concrete or paving stones are preferable. Again, make certain that you have sufficient slope for easy cleaning with a hose. The area should be surrounded by a chain-link or welded mesh fence, of 1.5 metres minimum height. An entrance at one end, consisting of a gate which will open either way, will complete your run. Welded-mesh, although more expensive than chain-link, can be bought in panels which include a gate. It is well worth the extra expense, as welded-mesh is far more durable than chain-link and will last indefinitely.

BED BOARD: It is a good idea to make a bed board to go inside the kennel. It is easy to make, and can be regularly scrubbed. A rug or the fleecy, synthetic bedding will make a comfortable, warm bed for winter, and in summer it can be left bare. Shavings make a very good bed, and will keep your puppy dry and smelling sweet, but they can cause problems blowing all over the place, and they can also be a nuisance to dispose of. We burn them, but this can be a bit impractical in a built-up area. One of the large plastic beds, obtainable from trade stands at most dog shows and also pet shops, lined with a rug or synthetic bedding, can make very cosy sleeping quarters and is easy to keep clean.

INSIDE ACCOMMODATION
Until such time as your puppy is house-trained, keep it somewhere that can be easily cleaned. Carpets, especially fitted carpets, are fatal. Once a puppy has wet on a carpet, it will continue to go back to the same spot, despite careful cleansing with disinfectant. This makes house-training a much harder task than normal. A good idea is to make a crate measuring 40 cm wide x 80 cm long x 50 cm high. For the frame, use wood 2.5 cm x 2.5 cm, and attach 2.5 cm x 2.5 cm lightweight welded mesh. Add a door opening at one end, and you have your crate.

It is easy and inexpensive to make, and will be a great help to you until your puppy is house-trained and has also learned to behave himself. Crates can be bought – probably from your local pet shop – and are reasonably priced, but it is obviously cheaper to make your own. Put plenty of newspaper inside, and at one end place some bedding. The fleecy, synthetic type is ideal as moisture will soak through, and so the puppy will stay dry even if it soils the bed. House-training is dealt with in a later chapter.

PUPPIES AND CHILDREN
Puppies make excellent companions for children but, and this is most important, the child or children must be taught to respect the puppy. Do not let children go on playing until the animal is absolutely exhausted. Over-tired puppies can get irritable and sometimes snappy, and it is then that accidents can happen. The puppy will be blamed for something that is not its fault. Remember, your children will need training in animal care and understanding in the same way that the puppy must be taught to respect your children. Teach children and adults alike not to disturb the puppy once it has gone to its bed – this must be a haven where the puppy can remain undisturbed for as long as it likes. A puppy can be left safely in its crate during the night and rest periods; it cannot come to any harm, nor can it damage your property. Give your puppy a toy to play with, and it will remain happy for quite some time, but no young dog should be left for long periods. Your puppy needs companionship and affection, so before you purchase, make certain that you and your family can give it just that.

Children and German Shepherds will get on well together, as long as they both learn to respect each other.

EXERCISE

To start with, your puppy will not need much exercise. Play training, followed by a romp around the garden for 10-15 minutes, two or three times a day, will be sufficient. But as your puppy gets older it will need more. As soon as the pup has completed its course of inoculation, it will also need socialisation, which means getting it used to travelling in your car, experiencing traffic, other dogs and the hubbub of life in general. All this takes time, but to establish a happy relationship between you and your dog, it must be done. One evening a week should be spent at a puppy kindergarten – if you can find one – or at a dog-training club. Some clubs will not let you start training your puppy until it is six months of age, but will let you take it along, provided you persuade it to sit quietly as a spectator, with the aim of getting used to seeing other dogs and people. It's much better than nothing, but a puppy kindergarten is the real answer. To progress with your training needs daily practice. Two or three sessions a day is best, and this all takes time.

As your puppy gets older, it will need more exercise and, as an adult, it will need at least one good walk a day. We are not suggesting that it needs ten miles-plus every day, but three to four miles is a minimum to keep a dog fit and healthy. If you intend to work in Trials, Schutzhund or Breed, you will need to do those ten miles – but not if you are keeping your German Shepherd as a companion/pet. When buying a Shepherd, you must realise that they are highly intelligent animals, they have been bred to work, and, like other dogs in the same category, they need mental stimulation to keep them out of mischief. Like children, a bored dog will find something to do – usually something you do not approve of – alternatively the dog could become bad-tempered and irritable, and then trouble will start.

Taking on a puppy is a responsibility which cannot be taken lightly. If you feel that you can

Exercising your German Shepherds is one of the great pleasures of owning a dog.

comply with the needs of a German Shepherd – and enjoy doing it – go ahead and purchase your puppy. You will find that you have a wonderful companion/guard, who would willingly give its life for you. It will keep you and your family fit, and give you all a lot of pleasure for many years to come. However, if you feel dubious about some of the points we have made, forget about buying a dog. Remember, puppies grow up, they do not remain the cute bundle of fluff which you brought home at eight weeks old. If you do not have the time or the inclination to give the much-needed affection, care and training, you will find that your cute little puppy will grow into a delinquent, who is destructive. You will be unable to control the animal, and yet another dog, through no fault of its own, will find its way to a rescue centre. Most of the time, the owners are to blame for the misdemeanours of their pets, not the dogs, so don't let yourself join the ever-increasing band of bad dog owners.

NUTRITION
Broadly speaking, there are three basic methods of feeding, which are as follows:- complete diets, canned meat plus biscuit meal, and a flesh diet, consisting of fish, red meat, chicken etc.

COMPLETE DIETS
There are many of these, some of which are 'expanded' and others flaked. New brands are constantly coming on to the market, and prices vary considerably. Study the formula, which should be printed on every bag, and see what it contains. Some brands use soya bean meal as their chief source of protein, which we have found can lead to overheating and skin complaints. Look at the fat content, and also make certain that the food contains all the vitamins, trace elements and calcium necessary for your Shepherd's well-being. The 'expanded' feeds are usually in pellet form, and go through a special process which makes them very easy to digest. The flaked varieties

of complete diets usually contain a fair amount of flaked maize, some of which will be undigested and seen in the dogs motions. These feeds must be soaked,whereas the pellet forms can be fed dry or slightly dampened. One of the big advantages of any complete feed is that it caters for dogs of all ages and ways of life, whether family pets, working dogs or whatever. The feeds consist of a careful blend of protein, fat, carbohydrates, and vitamins, made up into a balanced formula. If you follow the feeding instructions given on the bag, you know you are providing a correctly-balanced diet. Another advantage is that they are very easy to prepare, they are always fresh, and you do not have any problems of disposal, as you do with canned meat.

CANNED MEAT

There are many different varieties of canned meat, some of very high quality, and others not so high. Dogs seem to love it, but some brands are definitely the cause of stomach upsets, which makes us wonder what actually goes into them. Most brands suggest a suitable mixer meal to go with the tinned meat, and it is best to follow their suggestions. Again, the formula of both the contents of the tins and mixer meal can be studied, and you can make certain that you are feeding all the necessary ingredients to keep your dog fit and healthy.

FLESH DIET

A flesh diet usually consists of red meat such as beef, raw tripe (the cow's stomach), sheep paunches or stomach (which must be cooked because of the danger of tapeworm), and minced chicken or fish. As the dog is a carnivorous animal, its digestive system is best suited to a flesh diet. However, these days both the availability and storage of any form of meat is difficult. If tripe is used, it must be 'green', which means that it has not been processed for human consumption and still contains a considerable amount of partially digested grass. The dogs certainly love it and do very well on it, but the big snag is that in hot weather or climates, it very quickly becomes fly-blown and rotten, so refrigeration is an absolute must. This applies equally to all forms of flesh. If you are using a flesh diet, feed it raw, if possible, but if you must cook it, add the gravy in which it was cooked, as this contains many vitamins and trace elements which would otherwise be lost. These days, most pet shops sell frozen raw minced tripe and chicken in small quantities, which makes the storage problem much easier. All you have to do is take out the quantity you require, let it defrost and then feed, thus making certain the meat is always fresh. A good-quality biscuit meal must be given with the meat, and, for young, growing dogs, a vitamin supplement and bonemeal must always be added. This is most important if you want a well-boned, healthy dog.

Fish is also good for your dog and perfectly safe to feed raw but, if cooked, all the bones must be removed, as they can easily become stuck in the throat and cause a lot of trouble. Raw herrings are an excellent source of fat, most dogs love them and find them very nourishing. If you feed minced chicken, check that it does not come from caponized stock, or else fertility problems for both dog at stud or brood bitch might ensue. A raw flesh diet is possibly the most natural form of food, and it is practical if you only have one or two dogs. But if you travel around with your dogs, or own several, defrosting and storage can become quite a problem. For this reason we have settled for a complete feed diet, so that we know exactly what we are feeding, and that it is always fresh.

Milk is an unnatural diet for a dog once it has been weaned, but the odd drink of milk now and again will not come amiss, and your GSD will love it. Dogs also enjoy eggs. Though we have never used them on a regular basis, we have found scrambled eggs very useful as a meal for an animal which has been ill. Cooked fish and chicken also make an excellent convalescent diet, provided that all bones have been removed before feeding. We are often asked about bones. Yes, we do feed them and a good marrowbone will do wonders in keeping your dog's teeth clean, as well as keeping it happy for an indefinite length of time. But, a word of warning. Always feed bones raw and avoid smaller ones which can splinter easily. Never allow your dog to eat rabbit or chicken bones, raw or cooked. These bones splinter very easily, and one lodged in the throat or stomach could be fatal.

SUMMARY OF FEEDING

Some people give their dogs a vegetarian diet, and some manufacturers cater for this in their range of complete diets. We have never used one, and therefore cannot comment on the results. However, with so many different foods available, we cannot really see the point in feeding a vegetarian diet to an animal that is after all carnivorous. Over the years, we have tried a variety of different diets with varying results, but have eventually settled for a certain brand of complete diet which, although not cheap, we have found very successful with our dogs and therefore see no reason to change. If you have several dogs, cost must be taken into account. The makers of the more expensive complete foods claim that, because of the process involved, your dog will need less to keep it in tip-top condition. In our experience, this is not necessarily the case. But we have found that with the cheaper flaked foods, an awful lot passes through the dogs undigested and is therefore wasted.

To sum up, availability and storage is the problem with raw meat. With canned meat, especially if you have several dogs, there is the difficulty of getting rid of the empty cans. So what is the answer? Our advice is to continue to feed your puppy on the food prescribed by the breeder. Later, if you have, or have had, other dogs and your method of feeding them has been successful, then by all means change to the diet you have faith in when your puppy has settled in. Do not chop and change from one food to another. Bearing in mind both cost and availability, decide on which food you intend to use and stick to it.

Chapter Seven

CHOOSING A PUPPY

Once you have decided that you have suitable premises, finance, time and energy, the next step is to find that elusive puppy which is ideal for you. This can prove a daunting task and, alas, far too many people see Alsatian puppies advertised for sale in their local paper, and off they go. The prospective buyer has no idea what he/she is looking for, not having seen a GSD litter before, so they do not know what well-reared puppies should look like. They are unaware of what questions to ask about such things as temperament, hip dysplasia, and bloodlines. Such a buyer has nothing to go on except the sweet little puppy which comes trotting up to say hello, and the very good sales talk delivered by the breeder, convincing them that this is the litter of the century, and that there is nothing like it anywhere else in the country. And so a price is agreed, and the buyer goes off with the puppy. No diet sheet, registration card, inoculation certificate, tattoo card, pedigree or insurance is given, and therefore the buyer has no idea whether this puppy is even a pure-bred GSD. Without such documentation, the so-called GSD puppy may well turn out eventually to display the characteristics of another breed, and then it will be too late to do anything about it. But let us hasten to add that a prospective buyer might just as easily be lucky and find the ideal puppy. Unfortunately, this would be the exception rather than the rule. Reputable breeders do not have to advertise in their local papers. In fact, most never have to advertise, and usually have a waiting list of prospective buyers.

FINDING A BREEDER
So, how do you go about finding these elusive breeders who never advertise? Actually, this is not strictly true. The leading Breed Clubs of every country publish handbooks, and in these, among other interesting articles, you will find all the leading kennels advertising their stock, including stud dogs, prospective litters, and any young stock they might have available at the time of going to press. These advertisments will usually include wins in Breed, Working Trials, Obedience and so on, as well as details of hip scores. This will give you some idea of the type of Shepherd each kennel is producing. The ideal kennels are those breeding for both correct type and working ability.

To obtain a handbook, get in touch with your country's Kennel Club and ask for the address of the premier national GSD Breed Club. If there is more than one club they will send you particulars of all of them. You will probably find you have a Club nearby, which you could visit on training night. Most of the dogs taking part in the class will be locally-bred. If you like what you see, or if there is one particular GSD that you really fall for, find out more about its pedigree, then contact its breeder and, if possible, pay a visit. In the meantime, go to your local library and see what literature they have on the German Shepherd. There have been many good books written on the subject, and you will find the extra research is worthwhile.

Having read all the recommended books, you may find yourself muddled by all this information and feeling that, if you follow all the advice you have read, you will never succeed in buying a puppy. So let us try and sort out some of the knowledge you will acquire from these books. First of all, carefully read through the Breed Standard, which is the blueprint of what your puppy should look like when adult and fully mature. There will probably be a lot of discussion about various bloodlines, which can be very confusing for a first-time Shepherd owner, so forget about them for the time being. As you become more interested in the breed, you will get to know some of the most influential bloodlines and those names, which were at first just a jumble of words, will gradually slot into place. When you visit a kennel, the owners will probably show you pedigrees, and explain the relative merits of the various dogs and bitches in them. You will find that many of the same names crop up, especially in the fourth and fifth generations.

The Shepherd, as is obvious from its name, is a German breed. To achieve the very high quality in both construction and working ability, the Germans have bred back on to what can be described as pillars of the breed, in other words, dogs and bitches which are not only very good examples of the breed themselves, but which produce equally good specimens which will safeguard the future. Every few years, a new Shepherd will appear and become yet another pillar and so continue the progress of the breed. You will find that it in turn carries the bloodlines of many of the great dogs of the past.

Germany is the motherland of the breed, and we consider it true to say that every Shepherd in the world has German ancestry. Over the years, certain countries have developed the breed along different lines, even to the extent of altering the Standard to suit their own purposes. In the UK, enthusiasts are divided, with one side favouring the old-fashioned Alsatian, and the other adhering to the German conception of the breed. Most countries throughout the world are now members of the WUSV, and abide by its rules, which are compulsory in Germany through the SV (German Breed Club), but are not binding in this country. However, more and more British breeders are X-raying, tattooing and Breed Surveying their stock, which has resulted in a vast improvement in both type and temperament.

WHAT TO AVOID
There are certain things which should be avoided when choosing your puppy:

DO NOT buy from a kennel, or anywhere else, which fails to X-ray their Shepherds for Hip Dysplasia. The GSD is one of the breeds affected by this condition although the situation has greatly improved, thanks to continuous breeding of animals with low hip scores. It is now rare to hear of six-month-old puppies being put down because of bad hips. Countries have different systems of hip grading. The UK's method of scoring involves each hip being scored individually, to make up a total of 106. The higher the score, the worse the hips. In Germany there is a system of three grades of A stamp: 'normal' (the best), 'near normal', and 'still acceptable'. No Shepherd can be bred from unless it possesses one of these grades. The USA has yet another method. Dogs are X-rayed at two years of age, not at twelve months as is the case in the UK and Germany. If they meet a certain standard, they receive an OFA certificate and number. Most other countries favour either the UK or the German system.

DO NOT buy from unregistered stock. Although the puppies will be cheaper, there is no guarantee that they are pure-bred Shepherds. Somewhere along the line there could easily be some other breed, and these characteristics might surface as your puppy matures, so that the adult dog might not really look like a Shepherd.

DO NOT buy unless you are offered a six-week insurance policy to cover all risks, included in the purchase price. Even with the best-reared puppies things can go wrong, but, if you have an insurance policy, both your veterinary bills and the purchase price will be reimbursed, if you should be so unlucky as to lose your puppy. This is small consolation, but at least you will not be out of pocket. Insuring puppies is not common practice in the USA.

DO NOT buy a puppy unless it has been tattooed with an identification number. Many a lost or stolen puppy has been safely returned to its owners because of its tattoo number.

DO NOT buy from any breeder who is not prepared to show you the puppies' mother. You can't always see the father because most breeders use somebody else's stud dog, so if you want to see the sire, you will have to contact his owner and visit separately.

YOUR REQUIREMENTS

You have contacted your local Breed Club, and have received a list of breeders in your area and also some further away. You have obtained a handbook, studied the adverts, and perhaps seen the photo of a Shepherd that seems to be just what you are looking for. Before contacting the breeder, decide exactly what you want your dog for. Do you want to start showing in Breed, or perhaps you want a Shepherd to work in Working Trials, Schutzhund or Obedience? Maybe you want a Shepherd as a family pet, companion and guard dog. Whatever you decide, let the breeder know.

SHOW STOCK

No honest breeder, if you say you are interested in showing your dog, will knowingly sell you a puppy with a serious show fault. That puppy carries the breeder's prefix, which means that every time you take it into a show ring it will act as an advert for the breeder, good or bad, according to where it is placed. The show fault might be one of construction – lacking hind angulation, faulty croup or whatever – which would be penalised in the Breed ring, but would in no way affect its ability to work, or to make an excellent family pet.

WORKING DOG OR PET

If you want a Shepherd to work, the honest breeder will point out the puppy who is full of go, interested in everything, and who will fetch and carry the toys you throw. In order to achieve success in whichever form of work you intend to do, you must have a pup which wants to work and to please you. Without that basic desire, you will have a hard task ahead. The puppy who just wants to be with you, and enjoys being cuddled, will make an ideal companion and family pet. You will be able to teach it the basic obedience required for a pet, and this type of pup is unlikely to make as much mischief as its more energetic and inquisitive littermate.

TEMPERAMENT

There are some character/temperament tests for puppies, which can be done at seven weeks of age, individually, in a strange place, by an independent tester. These consist of six or eight different tests, and each puppy is marked on its reactions. According to breeders who have used them, the results indicate what types of homes will best suit each puppy, which can then be placed accordingly. We feel that these tests will probably tell you the character/temperament of each puppy at that moment, but we wonder whether they are a reliable guide to the future? After all, so much can happen to the puppy in its new home to alter future behaviour patterns. We are a bit dubious about the merits of such tests, but if they are properly executed, they might possibly constitute some sort of guide. They can do no harm, and if breeders have faith in them, fair enough.

MALE OR FEMALE?

Your next consideration is which sex to choose. With bitches there is the difficulty of seasons, but this can be avoided by having the bitch spayed. Bitches are smaller and lighter than dogs, and so are possibly easier to train. If you are hoping to breed, then you will obviously choose a bitch. As guards, dogs are probably preferable. Their size and strength act as a good deterrent. Dogs have the unfortunate habit of cocking their legs on lamp-posts, trees and gates, but this can be controlled by training. Another unfortunate habit is making a beeline for a bitch in season, anywhere in the vicinity, despite your best efforts to stop them. Dogs eat more, and take up more space than bitches. Having said all this, we feel that a good Shepherd is a good Shepherd, regardless of gender. It really is up to you.

COLOUR
Colour sometimes plays a very important part in the choice of a puppy. The colours recognised by the Standard are: black-and-gold, golden sable, grey sable, bi-colours, all-blacks, and black-and-fawn. Those which are not recognised are: whites, blues, browns, and brindles. The serious breeder will breed for correct colour, and you will find that the litters you see will not contain any of the unrecognised colours. We have never bred a white, but have had the occasional blue, which, if the litter is of reasonable size, is put down at birth. There are breeders in this country breeding whites. In fact, there is a Breed Club especially for whites, and the puppies fetch a lot of money. If you decide to buy a white, whether dog or bitch, you would be inadvisable to breed from it, as you would be perpetuating a serious fault. There is nothing to stop you showing one of the unrecognised colours, but no responsible judge would give the animal a second look, however good your Shepherd might be in construction. However, there is nothing to stop your dog competing in Working Trials, Agility, or Obedience, where colour plays no part.

COAT
One last consideration is type of coat. Basically, there are two types. The correct coat has a woolly undercoat with a harsh weather-resistant top coat. The alternative is the long coat, which is most attractive, and preferred by many people. There are certain disadvantages to long coats. Often, the outer coat is soft and not really weatherproof. They also take far more grooming, especially in bad weather when mud sticks to the featherings and becomes a problem to brush out. As with an incorrect colour, you would not get very far in the show ring with a long-coated GSD, but you see many working successfully. They constitute a fault in the breed, but they do crop up from time to time with all breeders, despite efforts not to breed them. It is easy to tell, at four to five weeks of age, which puppies will have long coats.

CONTACTING BREEDERS
You have decided on which colour, sex and type of coat you prefer, and you have a list of breeders who you think are producing what you require. The next step is to contact them, and find out whether they have any puppies available now, or in the near future. Tell the breeder what you are looking for and, if you can, make an appointment to go and visit their kennels. When you arrive, most breeders will be only too pleased to show you the mother, or prospective mother, of a litter, as well as any other relations they happen to have. Now you can check their temperaments. All the Shepherds shown to you by a breeder should come up to you happily wagging their tails. If any show excessive signs of nervousness or aggression, go elsewhere. The last thing you want is to buy a puppy from kennels whose inmates have questionable temperaments. You can be sure of one thing. If the adults show temperament faults, so will the puppies – although it might not be apparent when they are babies.

  If the temperaments seem OK, and the breeding stock have good hips, take a quick look round to see whether the kennels are clean, and that the dogs are in good condition and regularly groomed.

In a well-run kennel there should be no smell. If there is, go elsewhere. Dirty kennels and premises breed disease, and you never know what puppies reared there might be carrying. A litter of puppies should be clean, bright-eyed and lively. Most breeders probably will not let you pick a puppy up for fear of disease, but they will be happy for you to look. If you like the litter, and you have discussed the pedigree with the breeder, find out how many are booked and what choice you would have. Remember, just because you have the final choice of puppy as all the others are booked, it does not mean that particular puppy will be the worst. In a well-reared, even litter there will be no bad puppies, and the one you fancy might just be the one that nobody else wants. If the puppies look thin and small, with little spindly legs, or if they are scratching and you see loose motions in the run, think again. But, for the breeders' sake, do not go from from one kennel to another on the same day. Disease can very easily be passed from one place to another, especially when the puppies are about eight weeks of age. At that stage they are ready to go to their new homes, and have lost practically all the immunity received from their dams.

After visiting several kennels, you will have decided where to go for your puppy. You must then find out when the breeder will be having another litter. If what you have seen at your chosen kennel is just what you want, and if they have no puppies at that moment, be prepared to wait, rather than go to somewhere less good. You have ascertained that the breeder of your choice only breeds from X-rayed stock with low hip scores, has all the puppies tattooed and registered, and is willing to help you choose the puppy that suits your needs. Find out when their next bitch is due to whelp, and telephone a few days after the birth. You have already selected the colour and sex you want, so the breeder will let you know what they have in the litter. You can then pay the required deposit, which will guarantee you a puppy. As far as choice is concerned, we operate on a first-come, first-served basis, so that whoever pays the first deposit gets the first choice of puppy.

IMPORTANT CHECKS
TEETH: When the time comes to choose your puppy, do not forget to check its mouth for a correct bite. Even at an early age, your puppy should have what is known as a scissor bite, which means that the top jaw should protrude slightly over the bottom jaw. If there is a slight gap, this will probably correct itself when the adult teeth come through, as the bottom jaw continues growing for longer than the top jaw. If there is too big a gap, or if the bottom jaw is in front of the top – uncommon in Shepherds – think again. Faulty dentition, if serious, can cause a lot of problems in adult life. Canine teeth can grow into the roof of the mouth, in some cases making the GSD unable to eat or pick things up, and thus totally unsuitable for working. Alas, at this age, it is impossible to know whether the puppies will have full dentition. You can only be certain when they are six months of age and finished teething.
TESTICLES: If you have decided on a dog, check that both testicles have descended into the scrotum which should have happened by eight weeks. It is possible for testicles to descend at a later age, and, if your puppy is not entire at eight weeks, he will not necessarily stay that way. However, if you intend to show your puppy, do not take the chance, as most judges consider non-entirety a serious show fault.

Such problems sound alarming to the first-time Shepherd buyer, who must be wondering whether he or she will ever find the ideal specimen. Your safeguard is to go to a reputable breeder, who is breeding from stock with good hips, sound temperament, correct dentition, and so on. Remember, any good breeder will have a prefix carried by all stock they breed, and that is their trademark for top quality puppies. A few bad Shepherds carrying a breeder's prefix very quickly results in a bad name which will adversely affect future sales. Of course, every breeder, has from time to time, produced the faults mentioned, and if they maintain otherwise, you should beware.

But you are much more likely to get a well-reared puppy, free from faults, from a well-known breeder, than by following up an advertisement in the local press. The latter is probably much cheaper, and you might be lucky, but we feel that it is not worth the risk involved. If something does go wrong with your puppy, reputable breeders will do their best for you, even replacing the puppy, whereas the majority of the local advertisement breeders will just shrug their shoulders and put it down to bad luck. You will then be left holding the proverbial baby.

HOME BREEDING

When you are choosing a puppy from a home-bred litter, obviously many of the same guidelines apply as when you are buying, and, if you follow the advice in our chapter on rearing, your litter will be strong, healthy, bright-eyed, energetic and clean. You have decided what futures you envisage for your puppies, and which sex, coat and colour you intend to keep. We spend a lot of time with the puppies, right from birth, so that we can assess their characters, temperament and body construction. We are looking for a dual-purpose Shepherd, who can both work and do well in the show ring. We are not worried about colour, as we believe in the saying "A good dog cannot be a bad colour". But we do want a correct coat, so any long coats in the litter are immediately put to one side and not considered for us to keep.

TEMPERAMENT

From about five weeks of age, you will begin to see differences in movement and temperament within the litter. The puppy who, when you call, clears off in the opposite direction, will probably be very independent and quite difficult to train, whereas the one that stays at your side, and follows you around waiting for a cuddle, will make an excellent pet. So what are we looking for?

For working, we want a pup which is lively, interested in different objects, but not too independent, and one that will go out and inspect different toys thrown to it, and even pick one up and bring it back to you. We want a puppy who will take hold of a rag or old glove and have a tug-of-war, proudly trotting around with the prize when you let go. As we believe in play-training with toys, it is a great advantage to have a puppy which, from a very early age, wants to play with you and other objects. You will notice that your litter will contain a mixture of those who want to play, those who play in a half-hearted sort of way but soon give up, and those who are just not interested. Choose the one that wants to play if you are looking for a working dog, but make sure it is also constructionally the best, if you are going for the dual-purpose Shepherd.

CONSTRUCTION

It is a much harder task to pick an eight-week puppy which, when fully mature, is going to turn into a near-perfect example of the Standard. So, what do we look for? We spend a lot of time watching the pups moving around. Study their toplines. Do they keep their height at the withers, or, when they move, are their bottoms higher than their withers? Are their croups reasonably long, or do they appear rather square with a high tail set? Above all, when they are moving, are they striding out well in front, at the same time getting their hind legs well underneath their bodies and thrusting with them. If they take short, little strides with both front and back legs, they are probably lacking in angles of shoulder and hindquarters. We are looking for a puppy which has a good length of stride, keeps a straight topline, gently sloping from withers to tail, without any lumps or hollows. There might be those who think it is impossible to find a puppy like this. But we can assure you that if, when you mated your bitch, you took construction and movement into consideration, and if parents and grandparents were also good specimens of the breed, you will find a puppy in your litter with the attributes we have described. We have bred eight British

Champions, all of which were picked as eight-week-old puppies, so it is possible to find a good breed specimen at that age. We firmly believe that if your eight-week puppy is a miniature of what it should look like when adult, it will make the grade sooner or later. It might go through stages of looking awful – puppies between eight and sixteen weeks often do – but it will return to its original promise. A good-moving puppy will be constructionally correct. As breed specimens, forget about short-stepping puppies with incorrect back lines.

We also want good sexual characteristics, and you should be easily able to tell the difference between a dog and bitch by looking at their heads. Look for a fairly broad head, with a good stop (the bit between the eyes). The length of muzzle should be roughly the same as the distance from the eyes to the top of the head. Puppies with narrow heads and long muzzles, whether dogs or bitches, will not finish up with good heads.

EARS
Correct ear carriage is another thing that you cannot really be certain of until the puppy is six months old and finished teething. But even at eight weeks, we like to see the ears beginning to lift. Beware of large ears which hang down from the base, and make the puppy look more like a Labrador Retriever than a German Shepherd. Ears like these can sometimes take a long time to go up, if ever, without help. Weak ears which flap about in the breeze when the Shepherd is moving are a problem in the breed, and rumour has it that breeders in some countries are routinely taping the ears of the whole litter at an early age, to improve ear carriage.

Even at an early age puppies should show good sex characteristics – there is no problem telling which is the dog and which is the bitch in these slightly older.Dunmoinadh puppies.

A nine-week-old puppy illustrating excellent bone, lovely straight forelegs and very good ear carriage.

FROM PUPPY TO ADULT
A promising puppy (left) showing correct topline, croup, hind and fore angulation.

Shootersway Tiberius as a mature adult, fulfilling all his early promise. D.G. Banyard.

If you want to tape an ear, take a polystyrene cup, cut it in half, and then shape it to the size of the inside of the ear which you intend to help. Stick it in with a rubber-solution glue, and leave for about three weeks, by which time it will probably have fallen out anyway. This will work, except for really soft ears, but do not do it unless it is essential, and always give the ears a good chance of coming up naturally. It would be advisable to seek expert advice the first time you tape an ear, as much damage can occur if you do it badly. If you are unlucky enough to have bred a Shepherd with bad ear carriage, do not breed from it, as the chances are that it will reproduce the same fault in the offspring. If you decide to mate the dam again, make certain that you choose a stud dog with very good ear carriage, who is also known to produce good ear carriage.

One word of warning, if you see, or have, a litter of puppies which have all their ears up at about six weeks of age, take care. We have always found there is something wrong if this is the case. Either they are about to fall ill, or they are sickly, badly-reared puppies, which lack bone and stamina. We do not know whether other breeders have had the same experience, but litters we have seen, or the odd puppy of ours, whose ears have suddenly gone up at that age, have always had something the matter with them. It might simply be that the litter needs worming, but it could be something more serious. Do not confuse this with ears which are beginning to lift or are perhaps half up. We are talking about ears which are erect, like those of an adult Shepherd.

SUMMARY

Make good temperament your first consideration. Without this, however good your puppy is in other respects, you will have a problem in later life whichever field you decide to go in for. Your next two considerations should be to choose from a well-reared litter, and to ensure the puppy is bred from stock with low hip scores. Make these your three basic requirements, then look for the other faults and virtues we have discussed.

Chapter Eight

ELEMENTARY TRAINING AND SOCIALISATION

Most people would define training as: "Making the dog do what I want he to." Our definition is: "Making the dog *want* to do what I want him to". Adding this word makes a world of difference. The concept of motivating the dog must always be foremost in your mind, especially in elementary training from eight weeks of age. So, how do we achieve he? First of all, let us look at things from the puppy's point of view. He has been taken away from his mother and siblings by strange people, subjected to a car journey and thrust into a completely strange environment with none of the sights, or smells, that he has been accustomed to from birth. He is on his own in a strange new world. A puppy lives by his instincts, which are eating, sleeping, warmth and a will to survive. And, most important of all, reacting to a pack leader which, from now on, must be you. You are the means by which he can fulfil all his instincts, so make certain that you do your best to meet the puppy's needs.

IN-BUILT DRIVES
A German Shepherd puppy has three natural drives, namely prey, defence and social. The social drive is easy to describe. It means being friendly with man and other animals. The prey drive is the desire to chase after whatever is moving. Humans cultivate this drive when encouraging a puppy to play and chase toys. We must be careful, however, not to let the prey drive get out of hand, thus encouraging the young dog to chase other things. Never let your puppy chase anything except his toys. The defence drive is usually not too obvious in a very young puppy, but it needs controlling. This drive is usually the cause of biting in an adult dog, and must be carefully monitored. Although we want the adult dog to protect us when necessary, we do not want the defence drive to get out of control. Excessive mouthing of your hand or clothes can often lead to a pronounced defence drive in the adult dog, so stop it in your young puppy by transferring to the prey drive. More about this later. These drives are natural instincts in your Shepherd, and can be channelled to your advantage in both elementary and advanced training work.

Always remember that during the first few weeks with you, the puppy has an awful lot to learn and find out. Before coming to you, he had no idea that there was another world outside the one in which he was born. His pack leader was, first of all his mother, then, after he had been weaned, the breeder. Now, your puppy must find a new pack leader – you. He has to get used to new surroundings, a new bed, new feeding arrangements and a multitude of other things. Above all, your puppy must learn the difference between right and wrong, a situation he has not previously encountered, other than the occasional ticking-off from his mother.

TEMPERAMENT
Most puppies of good temperament will adapt to new surroundings very quickly, but occasionally you will get the odd one who, in spite of having a good temperament, will take his time and look around as if sizing things up or inspecting. These are usually the more thoughtful ones, and the

trait will be a characteristic of his behaviour throughout his life. Such puppies are usually very independent, and require very careful training. This is not the sort who demands a lot of fuss – and this sometimes upsets the new owner – but the puppy will come up to you for attention in his own time. Once a bond has been formed with the new owner, this type become very loyal, make excellent workers, and will not forsake you for anybody else. But you must make certain that you are the pack leader right from the word go.

At the other extreme are the very friendly puppies who come into your home as if they had never been elsewhere. Their attitude is "fools rush in where angels fear to tread", and they will go up to everybody, be into everything, and will enjoy as much attention and fuss as you are prepared to give. This sort also make excellent workers, but will probably not learn as quickly as their more serious-minded littermates. Because they are interested in everybody and everything, they lack concentration, which makes training hard work, but once you have focused their attention on you, such a puppy will become a keen and willing worker. Then, of course, you have a wealth of different characters in between – a mixture of both types. We hope, however, that after reading this book, you will not have picked a nervous dog!

BRINGING THE PUPPY HOME
Before collecting your pup, you will have decided whether he will be kept in the house or live outside, and made suitable arrangements.

SLEEPING QUARTERS
If the puppy is to sleep outside, make certain that the place is really warm, especially if the weather is frosty, when it would be advisable to have some form of heating in the kennel. Remember, your puppy has had brothers and sisters to snuggle up against. These have all disappeared, and a puppy on his own can get very cold, not only in cold climates. Some breeders recommend giving the puppy a hot-water bottle (covered) to create the illusion of another puppy, but we are not sure that this is successful. By the end of the night, the bottle gets very cold and uncomfortable, defeating the object of the exercise.

EQUIPMENT
You will need feeding and water-bowls, both preferably made of stainless-steel and not plastic. Puppies love chewing plastic, and swallowing pieces could cause serious trouble. A wire brush, a fairly broad-toothed comb for grooming, and the all-important collar and lead are all you will need in the way of equipment at this stage. We start off with either a leather or nylon collar, and a good-quality bridle leather lead, about 152cm long by 1.5 or 2cm thick, with a trigger-clip for attaching to the collar. The lead will not be cheap, but will last you a lifetime. Some trainers recommend a check-chain, but we do not advise you to use one on a small puppy. A check-chain can be a very helpful training aid, but only on older dogs, and in the hands of an expert. If you speak to your vet, you will find that he has probably treated dogs with quite severe neck injuries, due to the misuse of a check-chain. Do not forget that your name, address and telephone number must be attached to the collar. This is now law in the UK, and you can be fined if your dog is picked up without this form of identification.

A variety of different leads are now on sale, and the ones to avoid are the chain and nylon leads. If your dog pulls, both sorts can cut your hands badly. Rope leads are better but, again, we find them rather slippery and so advise you to stick to leather, expensive though it may be. Another useful addition is a Flexi-lead, which will extend and retract at will. They come in three different lengths, and the one we favour is 370cm. This gives your puppy a good deal of freedom, and yet is still safe if the dog is not reliable on the recall. We suggest that your puppy is kept on either a

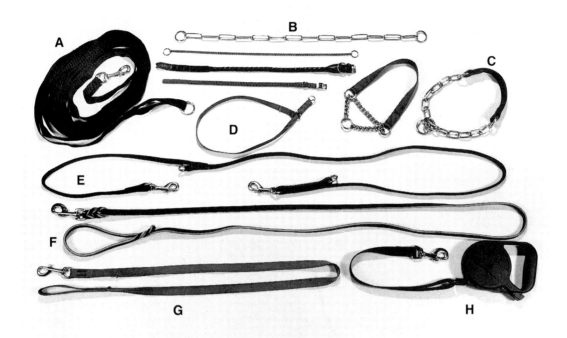

TRAINING EQUIPMENT

A. A 5-metre line, useful for early training.
B. A long-linked check chain for more advanced training, a fine check-chain, a leather collar, a nylon collar.
C. Half-nylon, half-chain collar – ideal for early training.
D. A 'pulling' collar used for showing.
E. A training leather lead. Note the various rings which allow you to lengthen and shorten the lead.
F .A 2-metre leather lead for early training.
G. A nylon lead.
H. A flexi-lead, invaluable for using before your puppy is reliable on the 'Come' command.

Flexi-lead or a long line, until you are a 100 per cent certain that he will come back to you when called – in all circumstances and despite any distractions.

NAMING
Another thing to consider is what you are going to call your puppy. He will have a registered name, but this might not be suitable as a pet name. You should choose a name of only one or two syllables. Sometimes an abbreviation of his registered name is suitable, and can easily be used in conjunction with a command when training.

HOUSE-TRAINING

Your new puppy is home, you have decided on a name, his bed is all ready, you have food and water-bowls, and a collar and lead. You will know from his diet sheet at what times he is used to being fed, and you will have a supply of the food on which he has been reared, either from the breeder or another source. Your first task, if your puppy is to live in the house, will be house-training. Puppies want to relieve themselves at certain times, always when they wake up and after they have been fed, so make a point of taking your puppy out at these times, and staying with him until he has performed. Then give lots of praise and a game before you take him back inside again. The praise and the game are both very important – the praise because he has performed, and the game so that the puppy does not expect to go straight back into the house as soon as he has relieved himself. If you persist with this routine, your puppy will soon learn that to relieve himself quickly will result in a game, and therefore pleasure.

However, as an eight-week-old puppy will probably not be able to last throughout the night, you must take the precaution of putting some newspaper down by the door. As mentioned in a previous chapter, watch out for carpeted floors! But, please, do not resort to 'rubbing the puppy's nose in it', which is sometimes recommended as a method of house-training. If you try this practice, and the puppy comes up to you with his head down and tail between his legs, you might be tempted to argue that he knows he has done wrong and is therefore learning. But, on the contrary, the puppy has no clue what he has done wrong as the accident probably happened several hours previously, and his attitude towards you suggests only that he is frightened about what might happen. We feel nose-rubbing is a disgusting method of house-training which will get you nowhere. It will succeed only in making your puppy apprehensive of you, which is the last thing you want. Shepherd puppies learn to be clean very quickly, and if you make a routine of taking your puppy out every time he wakes up, after meals, and after play-time, you will have a house-trained puppy in a matter of a week or two.

TEACHING A PUPPY TO SIT

An eight-week-old puppy will need feeding four times a day, so if you make him sit for every meal, he will soon learn the meaning of "Sit". To teach the command, hold the food bowl high above your puppy's head, and one of two things will probably happen. He will either sit down immediately, or jump up. If he sits at once, give the command "Sit", and put the food down straight away, praising the puppy as you do so. If he jumps up, ignore the fact and do not say anything. He will soon tire of that, and try sitting instead. As before, put the food down, and praise. If your puppy backs away, stand him quite close to a wall so that he backs into it, which will probably make him sit at once. The first few times you will have to be patient, but your puppy will soon realise that no sit means no food. This is the whole basis of using titbits or toys in our training methods, to achieve our aim of making the dog want to do what you want him to do. He wants his food, so he learns to sit, and he will be fed.

It is useful to have a pocket of titbits always handy for training purposes. A new puppy will follow you around, so, when you see your pup coming after you, turn round quickly, give the command "Come", then give him a titbit and plenty of praise. If you have done your 'sit for food' exercise, you will find that your puppy will come straight to you and sit in between your legs, especially if you hold your titbit at about knee-level. Do not give him a command to sit, and if he does not sit, do not worry. This exercise is the start of the Recall, and you do not want to confuse the puppy by adding another command such as "Sit". But from our experience, you will soon find that he will automatically sit. The pup's thought process is: "If I sit in front of my pack leader I will get food, so that is what I will do."

Another way of introducing the "Come" command again features food. Get somebody to hold your puppy, show him the bowl of food, and then back away for about ten metres. As you give the command "Come," tell your helper to let go of the puppy, and he will come bounding towards you, probably jumping up. Wait until your puppy sits in front of you, then give him food and praise. Assuming you have already bought a collar, it is now time to put it on so that your puppy gets thoroughly used to it before you start lead training. We always take the collar off at night, but leave it on during the day.

TOYS AND PLAY

Provide the puppy with some toys, such as an old leather glove, a sock knotted in the middle, a piece of plastic hosepipe, a squeaky toy, or a piece of wood. You will notice we have not included a ball. Balls, especially small ones, can be rather dangerous, as they occasionally get stuck in the throat, and could suffocate a pup. In our opinion, it is better to be safe than sorry. At a later stage, a football can be introduced. Dogs love to chase them, and running after a football can be a very useful form of exercise.

Get down on the floor and have a good rough-and-tumble with your puppy, but also have two or three toys handy. After a few minutes, get the puppy's attention on one of the toys, then throw it about two feet away from you and encourage your puppy to go and fetch. If the pup fails to bring the toy back, because you are close to him, you can very easily take the object away from the puppy. Put the toy away, say nothing, and walk away from the puppy, which will soon realise that if he does not bring the toy back, it means the end of the game and no reward. If, on the other hand, he does bring the toy back, give a titbit, lots of praise and throw another toy.

Do not do this more than three times in any one session, or throw the toy more than about two feet away from you, and do not give any command. This way, if your puppy does not bring the toy back, he will not be disobeying a command, which is most important at this stage. If, however, the puppy shows no interest in the toys, try getting him to chase after a knotted sock by pulling it along the ground and encouraging the puppy to grab hold of it. Let him tug on the sock, praising him for doing so, and then let the puppy have it. There are some puppies which are not keen on playing with toys, and it can take quite some time before you succeed with them, but be patient. You will win in the end, and if you can get your puppy really toy-conscious, it will make a big difference to your future training.

SOCIALISATION

From the moment you first get your puppy, continue his socialisation. Socialisation and training must go hand in hand. If you have bought your puppy from a breeder who believes in socialising puppies, he will probably be used to washing-machines, hoovers and other household fitments. Encourage your pup to come up and sniff such machines by giving a titbit when he gets close. If the puppy backs away do not praise him, otherwise he will get the idea that he gets praise for backing off. Out in the garden, your puppy can get used to a different set of strange objects, such as gardening tools. One word of warning though, never let your puppy get too close to a mowing machine or a rotary cutter. If you have an inquisitive animal, it is all too easy for a paw to be cut off or a nose damaged.

GROOMING

Grooming is another aspect of socialisation, so right from the start, get your puppy used to being groomed. Start with just a brush, stroking down each flank, and making sure that the puppy stands still. Then praise, give a titbit and have a game. Gradually increase the brush strokes until the puppy will stand still, letting you brush him all over, including the tail and inside of legs. Grooming also includes an inspection of ears, mouth and the picking up of feet. Make these examinations a daily routine, to get the puppy thoroughly used to being handled. This ensures that the animal will allow a vet to examine ears or mouth without any fuss.

CAR TRAINING

Until inoculations are complete, you cannot take the puppy out on the streets, but you can get him used to the car. The first time you put your puppy into the car, let him eat one of his meals there. He will then associate the car with something pleasant, and will soon be eager to get into it. After a few days. take your puppy for a short drive – not more than about 200 yards (100m) – and then feed him, still in the car. Gradually increase the length of the drive, until you are able to take your puppy shopping or into town, thus getting him used to other cars around yours. Take the precaution of putting paper down in the car, in case your puppy is sick, although we have found that car training as we have described, will help prevent car sickness. There are, unfortunately, some dogs which will be sick whatever you do, and we have found that only age and maturity will correct this unpleasant behaviour.

Never leave your puppy for any length of time in a car in full sunlight. Even in temperate climates, the inside will soon become like an oven and you will return to a dead puppy. It is possible to buy dog cages to fit into the back of any make of car. This will allow you to leave the tail-gate open, assuming you have an estate car, and some form of cover on the top of the car will keep your puppy reasonably cool.

LEAVING THE PUPPY

Another thing to aim for is getting your puppy used to being shut in a room on his own. Do not try to rush this by leaving him for too long at a time. The best way to tackle this, is to put the pup into a room with a toy to play with, so that he associates being on his own with something pleasant. After a few minutes go in, praise him, give him a titbit, then let him out and have a good game. If he starts to cry, do not go into the room, but wait until he is quiet, even if only for a few seconds, before going in and praising him. If you go in while the puppy is still crying, you will be rewarding him for doing so, creating a problem for yourself.

CHEWING

Chewing furniture is a bad habit, so keep a watchful eye on your puppy and as soon as he tries to chew your valuable Chippendale chair (or even your old sofa), say "No" very firmly, and give a toy to distract his attention. Prevention is better than cure when it comes to chewing, so take the precaution of removing anything which you think he might fancy, such as shoes, tea-towels or such like. Put yourself into your puppy's position for a moment. He has toys on the floor which you not only allow, but encourage him to play with. Imagine his confusion when you are praising him for playing with toys one moment,and the next you are chastising him for doing what seems to be exactly the same thing! Unfortunately, puppies are not able to tell the difference between your brand new shoes and an old slipper, if both are on the floor. One of the advantages of having a new puppy is that he makes you much tidier!

LEAD TRAINING

When the puppy is thoroughly used to his collar, attach the leather lead – no chain leads – to the clip on the collar and just let him drag it around for a few minutes. Be careful that it does not catch on furniture if inside, or a tree or bush outside. Whatever you do, at this stage you must prevent a sudden jerk which can happen if the lead snags on something. When the puppy appears to ignore the lead, take hold of it but do not put any pressure on, just follow the puppy around. In the meantime, begin to practise without the lead, the start of Heelwork, by holding a titbit in your left hand and encouraging your puppy to walk at your left side, his front legs roughly level with yours. Let him walk like this for just a few paces, then give him a titbit, lots of praise and have a game. After a few minutes, repeat the exercise. You will find that in a very short time, the puppy will be doing excellent Heelwork and watching your every hand movement. Do not do this exercise more than two or three times in a training session, and, to start with, be content with just a few paces which can gradually be extended. Give the puppy the titbit while he is on the move, because you are praising him for doing so.

With this exercise, it is sometimes a good idea to use a favourite toy instead of a titbit, so that when your puppy has walked for a few paces you can throw the toy and let him chase after it. What if the puppy jumps up and tries to grab the titbit or toy from your hand? Say "No" very firmly, put the toy/titbit away, and stand still. When your puppy has calmed down, try again. Even if he can only manage two or three steps, give praise, but make certain that you do not reward him for jumping up. A young puppy will very quickly learn that he only gets the titbit when he has all four feet on the ground.

REVIEW
By now your puppy should be sitting well for his meal, probably without needing a command. As soon as you go in with his food-bowl, he comes and sits in front of you. Now, try showing him a titbit, and saying "Sit". If he sits at an angle to you, straighten yourself to him, so that he is sitting straight in between your legs, looking up at you. Wait a few seconds, give a titbit, praise and then play a game. Repeat two or three times. The puppy will soon realise that sitting straight in front of you is a pleasurable experience. You are sowing the seeds of a puppy which will always come when called, and sit straight in front of you.

By now, we hope you have grasped our method of training by encouraging the puppy to want to do what we want him to do. We are using a process of positive reinforcement, by giving titbits and toys as rewards for the puppy doing what we ask him to do. There is no pressure or punishment involved at any time, and the puppy is doing what he is asked to do, because he wants his titbit or a game with his toy.

PROBLEMS
What if the puppy will not do these exercises? This is a question we are often asked, and it can sometimes be a hard one to answer. If you have followed the pattern of training we suggest, why has a problem arisen at all? Let us suggest some questions you can ask yourself. Have you tried to progress too fast, starting some new exercise before the puppy has really learnt the meaning of the one you are at present teaching? Have you inadvertently praised your puppy for doing the wrong thing? Has he at any time been frightened or hurt while doing an exercise? Have you given any commands which your puppy has not obeyed? And probably most important of all, have you developed sufficient motivation in the puppy to make him want to please you?

MOTIVATION
What is motivation and how do we achieve it? The dictionary definition is: "to stimulate interest of or in." This is exactly what we are trying to do by using toys and titbits. But some puppies are much harder to motivate than others, and we know from experience that it can take a lot of time and hard work on your part to achieve it. However, every puppy can be motivated by something, and it is up to you to find out what turns him on. Try all sorts of different toys, and find out which your puppy likes best. Do not leave a lot of toys lying around, otherwise you might find that, because he can play with toys when and if he wants, your puppy will not be interested in playing with you. Always remember, the toy is yours and your puppy is allowed to play with it only at

your discretion. If you take this attitude, the puppy will appreciate the toy and the game far more, which is the first step towards motivation.

A big mistake made by trainers – not always beginner trainers – is to progress too fast with the various exercises. Puppies learn quickly, but each exercise must be mastered thoroughly. A puppy must become "fixed" on one skill before proceeding to another, otherwise you will end up with a very muddled animal who is not sure of anything. If, when training, you accidentally tread on your puppy's toes, or in any way frighten or hurt him while doing an exercise, you will have taken a backward step which could take some time to rectify. Whichever problems you have, there is only one satisfactory solution, and that is to go back to the beginning and start all over again. By doing this, you will soon see where you went wrong, and be able to correct your previous mistakes.

PROGRESS
Now is the time to recap and see what progress we have made. Your puppy will sit in front of you, come when called, do a few paces of elementary Heelwork, and is quite happy wearing a collar with lead attached. He loves playing with, and bringing back, his different toys, and you have identified the favourite toy, so that you can keep it as a training aid. You have also been socialising your puppy; he is happy in the car, will stay in a room on his own for a short time, and is getting used to all sorts of different sounds both inside and outside the house. If not already house-trained, he is well on the way to being so. How long does this take, days, weeks or even months? This very much depends on the temperament and character of the puppy, and your own patience and perseverance. As a rough guide, and if you have trained regularly two or three times a day, your puppy should have achieved what is outlined above in about three to four weeks.

TRAINING CLUBS
The next stage is to get the puppy accustomed to walking without pulling on a lead, so that when he has completed his inoculations, you can take him for a walk down the road to improve his socialisation with regard to traffic, meeting strange people, dogs, and noise. Now is the time to look around and see if you can find a club which runs a puppy kindergarten. This is a class run for inoculated puppies, up to the age of six months. The training should be based on the methods we have been using, but the big advantage of going to a class is that your puppy will mix with other puppies, see different people and be subjected to lots of different distractions. You will soon see how much your puppy has learned, and how well motivated he is. You could be in for quite a shock when you find that your pup, which is perfectly-behaved at home, seems to have forgotten all he has ever been taught. Do not despair. With perseverance, you will soon see he is behaving properly.

MORE LEAD TRAINING
You will often find that when you first take hold of the lead and the puppy feels the sudden restriction, he will start jumping about like a bucking bronco. Do not try and pull him towards you, just follow him around for a few minutes, keeping the lead quite slack. When he has calmed down, encourage him to come towards you using a titbit or his toy. Give lots of praise when he has come, then unclip the lead and have a game. After a few minutes, repeat the exercise once or twice more. When the puppy is happy doing this, try your Heelwork, still using titbits or a toy, and encouraging the puppy to look up at you, as he does off lead, but be careful to keep the lead slack. Once he is heeling successfully, if only for a few paces, try putting in a "Sit" command. Hopefully, if you have been continuing with your "sit for food," your puppy will know what the command means and will sit. If not, a little gentle pressure on his croup will help him to get the idea. Immediately he is sitting down, reward with lots of praise and a game. Repeat two or three times.

ATTENTION

When practising Heelwork, do not always include a "Sit," and sometimes, when using a toy and while on the move, throw it a few paces in front of you, and let your puppy chase after it. Hold the lead in your left hand, have the toy in your right hand, and swing your arm as you walk. The dog's attention should be rivetted on the toy, waiting for you to throw it. This is the way to get good Heelwork, with the puppy's attention always on you. Remember, as soon as you have lost his attention, throw the toy or give a titbit, and end your session. Heelwork is rather boring at the best of times, so do not overdo it.

THE DOWN

Keep the puppy sitting at your side, with the lead in your left hand. Have a titbit in your right hand, let the puppy sniff it, and, on the command "Down," move your right hand down to the ground letting the puppy follow it. When he is lying down, let him have the food and praise. Sometimes, you might find that a little gentle pressure on his withers with your left hand will help him go down. When praising, make certain your puppy stays down, even if only for a few seconds. We use a release command such as "OK" before ending the exercise, and letting the dog get up. It is very useful in the Stay exercises to have some sort of release command, to stop the tendency of your puppy to jump up as soon as you get back to him. He will then realise that he must stay in the Down position, until you give your release command. Once he has learnt to go down at your side, without pressure on the withers, you can start teaching a Down-Stay.

STAYS

Give the command "Stay", put your left foot on the lead as close as possible to the collar, and stand up straight. Once the puppy is settled, repeat the command "Stay" and, with your left foot still on the lead, take one step to the right. Wait for a few seconds, bring your right foot back to your left and praise the puppy, who will still be in the Down position. Give the release command and have a game, before repeating the exercise again. When your puppy is steady in the Down position, slowly move your left foot to join your right. You are now standing a pace away from your puppy. Return to him, and, as before, praise him in the Down position, not letting him get up until you give your release command. Then give lots of praise, a titbit, and have a game.

Gradually, as your puppy becomes steady in this exercise, move further away and increase the length of time you leave him. You can also walk round him, and when you are certain he is quite steady, drop the lead. But a word of warning. Progress slowly, making certain that your puppy is absolutely steady in the Stay, before increasing both the distance and the length of time you leave him. Once your puppy gets the idea that he can break his Stay, it can be very hard to achieve a reliable Stay again. You will have to go back to the beginning, and start all over again. The Stay exercise is a very important one, for both competition animals and for pets, so take our advice and make haste slowly.

You can teach the Sit-Stay at the same time as the Down-Stay. Sit your dog, hold the lead in your left hand, straight above the puppy's head. Give the command "Stay," and, as in the Down-Stay, move your right foot a pace away, keeping your left foot stationary. When the puppy is steady, give a further command of "Stay," and move your left foot to join your right. After a few seconds, return to him, as with the Down-Stay, use your release command, then give a titbit and lots of praise. Continue instructions as those for the Down-Stay.

THE RECALL

We can now commence a slightly more formal type of Recall. Your puppy is coming when called, either to a titbit or his food, and should know what the command "Come" means. Get the puppy

ELEMENTARY TRAINING
DEMONSTRATED BY ANN MUNKS
AND SHOOTERSWAY INDI, AGED FOUR MONTHS.

Teaching the Down.
Notice the titbit in Ann's hand.

Teaching the Sit, using food.

The Recall.

Sit-Stays: The puppy is still on the lead. Notice Indi's attention on her handler.

sitting at your side as in the Sit-Stay exercise, holding the lead in your left hand. Give a firm command of "Sit," and stand right in front of him. Stay there for a few seconds, give a titbit, and move back to his side. Release the pup and have a good game. Repeat two or three times. Whatever you do, do not give the command "Stay." "Stay" is *only* used when you leave a puppy, and then return to him. The completion of this exercise is calling the puppy to you. He can very easily become muddled if, on the one hand, you are praising him for remaining stationary, and the next moment praising him for coming to you, so do take care not to use the "Stay" command when doing a Recall. Another important point is never to do a Recall exercise after you have done a Stay. If you think about it, you can see why. One moment you are making the puppy stay stationary and chastising him if he does not, and then you are calling him from the same position, and getting annoyed if he does not obey you. So, always do a different exercise between a Stay and a Recall to avoid confusion in the puppy's mind.

When the puppy is steady sitting in front of you, give a further command of "Sit", and step back to the end of the lead. Wait for a few seconds, return to your puppy's side and then the usual praise, titbit and game. You can now try this variation. Again give the command "Sit", then stand in front of your puppy and give a titbit. Give the command "Come", simultaneously running backwards for a few paces and then halting. Keep your lead short, underneath the pup's nose, and held in your left hand. This way you will be able to guide him into sitting straight in front of you. Have a titbit ready, held in your right hand slightly above the level of your puppy's nose, so that he is looking up at you. As soon as he has sat, give him the titbit, go back to his side, give praise and a game. Alternate these two exercises, so that he is never quite certain which one you are going to do, and always finish your Recall session by making your puppy sit while you back off to the end of the lead without calling him. This will prevent anticipation on the part of the puppy which, if allowed to happen, can be very difficult to correct.

Once you have perfected these two exercises you can then try, using the same commands and titbits, going to the end of the lead, dropping it, and stepping back a further two or three paces. Wait for a few seconds, call your puppy, give a titbit when he is sitting straight in front of you, and return to his side. Give lots of praise and have a game, before repeating the exercise. If at any stage of the Recall exercise, your puppy gets up and follows you, it means that you have progressed too quickly and left your puppy before he was really steady in the Sit. Your answer is to go back to square one, and start again, this time making certain you do not progress too fast.

GAMES

When discussing early training, we have constantly mentioned "having a good game." By this, we mean playing with a toy, letting the puppy tug on a piece of rope or old sock, throwing a squeaky toy, and as many different objects as you can think of. Do not ever chase after a puppy who is carrying something. If he will not bring the toy back to you, just turn your back on him and walk away. Chasing after a puppy makes him think that this is the right thing to do, and all part of the game, but you will be making a rod for your own back if you let this happen even once. But if you have been doing what we suggested earlier, your puppy should be coming back happily to you.

You can now try, with your puppy on the lead, throwing out his favourite toy, and giving the command "Fetch it". Then encourage your puppy back to you, so that he is sitting straight in front of you still holding the toy. If he spits the toy out gently put it back into his mouth with the command "Hold", wait a few seconds, give the command "Give", and take the toy. Then give a titbit, but no verbal praise. Praise the puppy while he is actually holding the toy, not when he gives it back, otherwise you will be praising him for doing the wrong thing, which is the last thing we want. Your puppy must learn that he only gets praise for holding the article, and not letting it go. On no account either praise your puppy or give a titbit if he spits the article out. Your puppy will soon get the idea that he only gets a titbit if he holds the toy until you issue the command "Give".

This is the introduction to the Retrieve, which can cause a lot of problems. If you teach the command "Hold" on the puppy's favourite toy, you should have little or no problem in getting him to hold a dumbbell. Include some hard articles, such as a piece of broomstick, or even a six inch nail, among your puppy's toys. But, above all, get your puppy really crazy on toys and articles, as this will be invaluable in more advanced training. Your puppy is now approaching six months of age, and you will be taking him out for walks in the country. Take his favourite toy with you, and throw it into some long grass, encouraging your puppy to find it. Puppies usually love doing this, and it is a valuable introduction to both searching and tracking, if you intend to train for Working Trials. (More about these exercises in Chapter 12.)

MEETING STRANGERS
Of course, while training your puppy, you must not forget his socialisation. Get him used to the postman, milkman, dustman and any other person who is a regular visitor to your house. Give the person concerned a titbit, encourage the puppy to go up to him/her, and the pup will immediately receive a titbit. It will soon click in the puppy's mind that these people are friends, and nice to know. Likewise with children. Shepherds, if not brought up with children, often have a fear of them. To avoid this happening, take your puppy to the nearest school when the children are leaving, and just let him sit quietly, some way away, watching the children go by. If you have friends with children, introduce your puppy to them in the same way as you did with the postman. Start this as soon as the puppy has finished his inoculations, and is reasonably happy on the lead.

DEALING WITH PROBLEMS
We have mentioned methods of getting your puppy used to being left alone, and also how to stop him chewing furniture, and so on. But there are other problems which we must consider and correct, such as a puppy who jumps up on you or your friends, steals food, or rushes through a door in front of you. Chasing cats can sometimes be a problem too.

How are we to deal with these problems? Firstly, it is important to remember that your puppy does not realise he is doing wrong. The problems we have mentioned might be annoying to you, but are all perfectly natural reactions to circumstances which he will encounter in everyday life. He is not doing any of these things to upset you, but, until you have taught him not to do them, he does not know that he is doing wrong.

An excellent aid to correcting the above faults are the Mikki dog training discs designed by one of the founder members of the APBC (Association of Pet Behaviour Counsellors.) If you cannnot buy the discs, a fairly heavy check-chain will work quite well.

JUMPING UP
Get a friend who knows your puppy well to come in, and let the dog go and greet the person. As soon as the puppy jumps up, throw the check-chain on the floor behind him and give the command "No". As soon as the puppy has all four feet on the ground, praise him and let your friend stroke him too. He will soon realise that a fuss will be made of him only when he has all four feet on the ground. Other methods can be tried if this does not work. As the puppy jumps up, bring your knee up smartly into his chest, and again when all four feet are on the ground, praise as usual. A third method which sometimes works is to catch hold of his front paws as he jumps up, squeeze until he cries, then let him get down and praise as usual. Persevere with throwing the discs or check-chains, as this is by far the best method of dealing with this particular problem and causes no pain to your puppy. The element of surprise is the important factor.
STEALING FOOD

This can be dealt with in a similar manner. Of course, by far the best thing is to keep all food, both yours and the puppy's, well out of the way. As we have said before, prevention is better than cure. But stealing might not be confined only to food, so let us see what we can do about it. Put the food, or whatever, in a place where the puppy can easily see it. Keep a little way away, and, when your puppy jumps up, throw the discs/check-chain on to the floor behind him, giving the command "Leave". When the puppy has obeyed, give praise and have a game with his favourite toy.

RUSHING AHEAD

The habit of rushing through a door in front of you is an annoying one, which needs to be corrected right from the word go. As the puppy rushes towards the door, throw the discs/check-chain in front of him. Make the puppy sit, then go through the door, and call your pup after you. He will quickly get the idea that you always go through doors first and he follows. Another successful method is, as soon as you open the door and the puppy tries to rush through, you shut the door on his nose. As before make him sit, and when you have gone through first, let him follow. Then give the usual titbit and have a game.

MOUTHING

Young puppies will often take hold of your hand or fingers, which can be quite painful. If you watch puppies in the nest, you will notice they spend a lot of time mouthing each other, not to hurt but just as a game. This is what your puppy is doing to you, merely treating you as one of his littermates. To stop this, give a firm command of "No", take your hand away, and distract your puppy with his toy. In this case, we advise against giving a titbit, because the puppy might think he is being praised for biting you and not for letting go! When he grabs your trouser legs or laces, act in the same manner. Mouthing could turn into a serious problem as the puppy gets older, so make a point of stopping it right from the start. This is the defence drive beginning to become apparent, and by distracting his attention on to a toy, we are diverting one instinct (defense) towards another (prey).

CHASING CATS

Chasing cats, or anything else for that matter, is a basic behavioural pattern (prey drive) of any dog, but it must be stopped at all costs, before it becomes a dangerous one which could cause an accident. Have your puppy on a long line or Flexi-lead. As soon as he starts to run, throw the discs/check-chain behind him and give the command "Come". When he has returned, reward him with the usual praise, titbit, and have a game. If your puppy does not respond to the discs, wait till he has got to the end of the line, stand still and you will find that, at the speed he is going, he will stop very suddenly. Call him back to you and praise him.

If you are using a nylon line, wear gloves. A sudden check, or even the line running through your hands, can be very painful and give you a nasty burn. But always try to distract your puppy's attention by producing his toy, before he has actually started to run. Another thing you can do is to put him in the Down-Stay until whatever he wants to chase has disappeared. Joggers and cyclists can often cause a problem. When your puppy's Heelwork is reasonably good, take him out somewhere where you are likely to meet both. As soon as he shows any interest in either, simultaneously give the command "Leave" and drop the discs/check-chain behind him. Get him thoroughly used to joggers and cyclists, so that he can walk past both without taking any notice of them at all.

These problems are not going to be cured in a single lesson, and so you must have patience and persevere. You will win in the end, but sometimes it can take quite a long time. When using the discs or a check-chain, the element of surprise is of great importance, so make sure you give no command until you have actually thrown them. And, of course, as soon as your puppy has reacted favourably, be lavish with your praise. Always ensure that you do not praise until he has responded.

GUNFIRE

Further socialisation involves exposing them to loud bangs and other such noises. A cap-pistol can be very useful in this respect. To start with, get a friend to fire it quite far away from your puppy, who is on the lead, and see what the reaction is. If your puppy does not take any notice, gradually move closer until the person with the pistol is only a few yards away. If, on the other hand, the puppy does show signs of fear, move the gun further away and do not let the gun be brought closer, until he has got used to the sound. A lot of people make the mistake of trying to comfort the puppy by making a fuss of him, but all you are doing is praising him for backing away. So, stand quite still and let him find his own level. As soon as you have finished with the gun, have a game, throwing your puppy's favourite toy and making much of him.

To help the puppy get used to the gun, if you live in the country, find out where your local farmers have put some crow-scarers and take your puppy for a walk nearby. If you have a clay-pigeon shoot in your area, take him near that too, but remember, not too close to begin with, and only for a short time. If your puppy is nervous of a gun, take care to progress very slowly. Two or three shots once a week is quite sufficient. Try letting your puppy play with his favourite toy while the gun is being fired, so that he is concentrating on something he enjoys. It is sometimes said that a gun-shy dog can never be cured. We have proved this wrong, but it does take a lot of time and patience to overcome.

Another useful introduction to noise is hitting a saucepan with a wooden spoon. Do it softly at first, watching the puppy's reaction the whole time, and if he shows no fear, progress in the same way as the gun test. Similarly, throwing coke or beer cans around can also be beneficial. But do not overdo any of these suggestions, otherwise you could do more harm than good and give your puppy a real complex about noise. Puppies of sound temperament will soon get used to unusual noises, and within a very short time will completely ignore them. If there is a good puppy kindergarten in your area, your dog will encounter different kinds of temperament tests, including noise, which will be most beneficial to his socialisation. At our puppy kindergarten, we also include putting them on a table for examination of ears, teeth and feet, as well as letting them all loose, under supervision, in a large pen so that they can get used to different puppies and breeds.

If you have followed our training programme, you should now have a puppy who walks to heel on a loose lead, does a Sit and Down-Stay, an elementary Recall and retrieves his toy. At the moment, all on the lead. Let us just deal with some problems which you may have encountered.

PROBLEMS ENCOUNTERED IN HEELWORK

Pulling on the lead is one of these, and we get an awful lot of dog owners who come to us with this problem. There are two things to try for this fault. Every time your puppy starts to go forward, give him the command "Heel", pull him back to the Sit position at your side, praise him and give him the usual titbit. In a relatively short time, your puppy will realise that little or no progress will be made as long as he pulls on the lead.

Another way is to let your pup go out to the full length of the lead, say nothing and give no command, but you do a smart about-turn when he gets to the end, thus jerking him. When he gets back, you give praise. If the puppy goes off to the right, you turn left, and similarly when he goes left, you turn smartly right. In both these cases, give praise and a titbit when he gets back to you, but continue walking the whole time. Your puppy will soon realise that it is much nicer staying with you than rushing out to the end of his lead. Sometimes, you might find the reverse happens, and the puppy lags behind, even to the extent of sticking all four feet into the ground and not moving at all. Try to encourage him with titbits and toys, but if he still refuses to move, pull him forward until he is with you, and then praise. No puppy likes being dragged, and before long you will find that he will be walking at your side.

Crabbing, which means the puppy constantly crossing in front of you, can sometimes cause problems. The reason for this is that you are probably holding the toy or titbit in your right hand, and your puppy is coming across you to try and get hold of one or other of them. Shorten your lead, holding it in your left hand so that the puppy cannnot come across you. Keep your toys and titbits in your left pocket, so that he has no incentive to look to your right hand. A puppy who has his attention on you, as those that crab usually do, will soon be doing very good Heelwork. Much better to have this fault than a puppy who pulls or lags.

CROOKED SITS

Sooner or later we all encounter crooked sits, and here are some ways of correcting this. Right from the beginning, you have been teaching your puppy to sit in front of you for his food, so he quite naturally thinks that when you say "Sit," this is what you mean. He must now understand that when walking at your side, the command "Sit" means he should stay at your side, and not turn at right angles to you. So, when giving he the command "Sit," have your left hand ready to push his bottom down straight. At the same time, practice your Heelwork in a tight left-handed circle, which will automatically help your puppy to sit straight. Offer no praise, titbit or game when he sits crooked, only give praise for sitting correctly. Try walking very close to a wall, so that the puppy is forced to sit straight or hit his bottom against the wall. Crooked sits can be quite difficult to correct so, except when first getting him to sit at your side, do not let it happen in the first place. Do not praise your dog, or give a titbit or a toy when he sits crooked, only praise for sitting straight.

BREAKING STAYS

If your puppy has started to break his Stays, as mentioned earlier in this chapter, there is only one thing you can do, and that is to start all over again, with your puppy staying, both in the Sit and the Down, at your side.

Until your puppy is 100 per cent certain about coming when called, keep him on a long-line or a Flexi-lead. This way, you have complete control, and your puppy never gets the idea that he can get away from you. Obviously, this does not apply in his own garden but whatever you do, do not chase after him. He will take this to be a huge game and great fun, and you wiil end up only making matters worse. The puppy cannnot come to any harm in your garden, so if you think he is not going to come when you call him, do not give a command, just walk away from him and go back into the house. (More about Recall in Chapter 10.)

Throughout all your training, remember that you are the pack leader, and whether in formal training or just in everyday life, see that you only give one command which, if your puppy does not obey instantly, should be followed by compulsion. Constant nagging at your puppy will achieve nothing – you are only teaching him to disobey you.

We have gone into considerable detail about training in this chapter, and if you have followed the lessons carefully, you should now have a reasonably well-trained puppy who knows all the basics and is ready to progress to more advanced work. These basics, if well-executed, will give you a well-behaved puppy which can take his place in society, and not disgrace you in any situation. These days, it is imperative that none of our dogs disgrace us in public through lack of

The 'A' Frame: Most puppies love running up and down this, and we allow this if a puppy is happy to do so. Make sure the pup does not try and jump off the side or from the top.

training. Whether you want your puppy solely as a pet/guard, or you intend to enter into the competition world, it is essential these days to have a well-trained dog.

Chapter Nine

CHOOSING A DISCIPLINE AND EQUIPMENT

At this stage in your training, you will probably have to decide in which discipline you intend to concentrate. Let us hasten to add that it is perfectly possible to work in more than one discipline at the same time, and it is not unusual to find people doing so. In the UK, most of the dogs working in Schutzhund III have also worked successfully in Working Trials TD or PD stakes, or have done both in the past. Likewise, quite a few of our top Obedience dogs also have Working Trials qualifications. As far as Schutzhund is concerned, the UK abides by the Tests and Rules as required by the SV (Germany). The British Kennel Club are vehemently against any form of Schutzhund, and at the time of this book going to press, anybody connected with the sport could be severely penalised. The extraordinary thing is that although the Kennel Club is totally against the Protection phase in the sport of Schutzhund, it is quite happy to support Working Trials PD, which also has Protection work. In fact, the Kennel Club runs a yearly Trial for the best TD and PD dog of the year! In countries where Schutzhund is practised, the Tests will be as we describe.

EQUIPMENT
Whatever discipline you decide to go in for, you must consider the equipment you will need.

WORKING TRIALS
You should already have acquired a good-quality lead and check-chain or collar, as well as a square-ended dumbbell either made of wood or plastic. If you have managed to find a good club which specialises in Working Trials, you will have had the use of their jumps – Clear Jump, Long Jump and Scale. As you progress, you will need to acquire some of your own. If you are a good carpenter you could probably make some, but if not, your Working Trials Club could recommend somebody who will make you a set at a reasonable price. Make certain that the Clear Jump has at least two bars with the lowest bar about 25cm from the ground and slots 8cm apart for increasing the height.

SCALE
The Scale should consist of twelve boards,15cm in width and 91.5cm wide, which slide into two upright posts, one at either end. These can be made of wood or metal, whichever you prefer. The posts must be supported by a diagonal bar on either side, fitted to a base-bar which needs to be pegged into the ground to stop the Scale tipping over when at maximum height. It is a good idea to have another board 8cm wide to make the increase in height as gradual as possible. To us, 15cm does not look much, but in the eyes of your Shepherd, as the Scale gets higher, it can seem enormous.

LONG JUMP
This consists of five slats ranging from 92cm in width for the first and lowest one to 112cm for the

last and highest slat. Each slat is 15cm wide, with the first slat at an angle of 10cm lowest edge to 16cm for the highest edge. The angle of the last board is 20cm for the lowest edge slanting to 26cm for the highest edge. The three slats in between are of relative height, angle and length to give your Shepherd the impression that it is one long jump.

THE 'A' FRAME

The 'A' frame is a piece of equipment required for Schutzhund but not Working Trials. It is useful to have as an introduction to the Scale, and also as a means of getting your dog fit. If you have found somebody to make your Scale, they will also be able to make an 'A' frame. You will find measurements and a diagram in the WUSV Evaluation Regulations, a manual which gives particulars of all Schutzhund tests, and also a diagram of the one-metre Clear Jump. It is obtainable from your national SV or Schutzhund Club.

TRACKING LINE AND HARNESS

As you progress with Nosework, you will require a tracking harness and a ten-metre long line. The tracking harness can be made from either webbing or leather. The line should be strong, not too fine and can be either nylon, webbing or leather. Leather lines are expensive and need care and attention otherwise they get hard and brittle, so we favour a nylon line which dries quickly and stays very supple. But whatever material you decide upon, make sure it is not too fine. A fine line can burn your hands badly if it runs through them quickly.

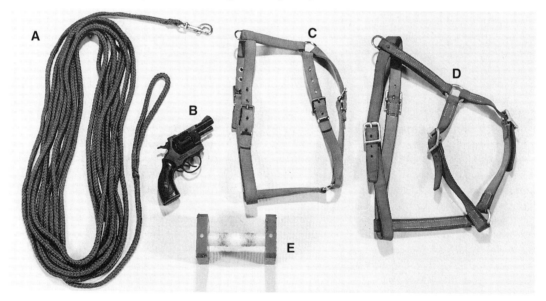

WORKING TRIALS EQUIPMENT
A. 10-METRE TRACKING LINE.
B. GUN.
C. WEBBING TRACKING HARNESS.
D. LEATHER TRACKING HARNESS.
E. PLASTIC DUMBBELL.

POSTS

You need four or five posts for your Search square (one spare for the beginning of your track) which you can easily make. Take a one-metre length of broomstick, drill a hole in one end and insert a 15cm nail. Cut off the end of the nail and you have a post. Paint it white for easy visibility.

GUN

To make certain your Shepherd is not gun-shy, introduce this at an early age. Far away to start with and, when you are sure your dog is not afraid, gradually move closer. What you need is a starting pistol, although at first a toy cap pistol is perfectly adequate.

SEARCH ARTICLES

Start collecting these as soon as you have decided which discipline you are working for. Clothes pegs, corks, plastic and metal teaspoons and sparking plugs all come in handy.

SCHUTZHUND

As in all disciplines, a check-chain/collar is required, but for Schutzhund a broad strong leather collar is also needed for protection work. The tracking harness and line are the same as those required for Working Trials, although in Schutzhund it is not necessary to work your dog with a tracking harness. The gun is the same.

DUMBBELLS

Four wooden dumbbells are required of regulation size and weight (approx. 350g, 650g, one kilo, and two kilos). As you progress beyond Schutzhund I, heavier dumbbells are required both for negotiating the Clear Jump and the Scale. It is a good idea to acquire a set so that your Shepherd can get used to retrieving heavier dumbbells.

BITE-BARS

This is a piece of coarse sacking, tightly rolled up and glued together, about 22cm long and 13cm in diameter, although they can vary in both length and diameter. A bite-bar is easy to make and a very useful piece of equipment which can be used as an introduction to the Retrieve, as well as for protection training. In protection training, when your Shepherd is confident in both holding and retrieving a bite-bar, you move on to what can only be described as a 'sausage' – a longer and thicker version of the bite-bar, but with a tape attached to one end to form a handle. It is made from strong, coarse hessian, filled with any substance to make it firm for the dog to take hold of. It is sewn at both ends and down one side in a pronounced ridge, and is approximately 60cm long and 22cm in diameter. The ridge down the side is a first introduction to the large bite-bar which runs along the full length of the inside of a sleeve. The webbing handle makes it easy to swing the sausage around, encouraging and training your Shepherd to jump for it. The official name for what we have described as a 'sausage' is a bite-roll.

SLEEVES

These are made in a variety of different types, depending on the stage of training your Shepherd has reached. The first version of a sleeve can be made yourself and consists of sacking, well-padded with several layers of felt, to fit over your arm and hand. You must use sufficient felt to protect yourself because a dog, even early in its training, can take a hard hold of the sleeve. This is, after all, what we want. For more advanced protection work, a much harder, stronger sleeve with a bite-bar down one side of it is required. These are made either for the right or left arm, according to how you want to work. More about this in the chapter on Protection training.

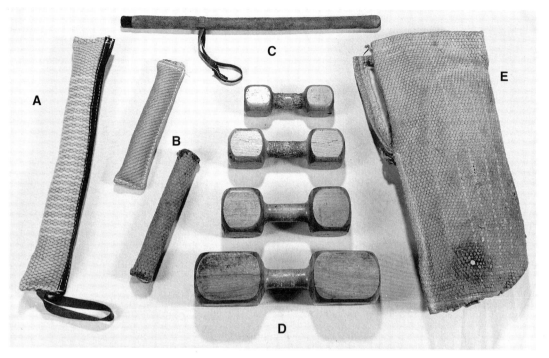

SCHUTZHUND EQUIPMENT

A. BITE-ROLL.
B. TWO TYPES OF BITE-BARS.
C. WHIP.
D. WOODEN DUMBBELLS OF VARIOUS WEIGHTS.
E. PROTECTIVE SLEEVE.

PROTECTIVE SUITING
This is padded, and made to cover your legs and the whole of your body except your arms. It is not so much to protect you from being bitten, although obviously this can happen, but unless you are suitably protected, a dog jumping for the arm can give you some nasty scratches with its front claws. You, as the Trainer, will not require protective suiting, but your all-important Helper does.

WHIPS
In Protection work when the dog is on the sleeve, it is struck on its flanks and shoulders with a whip. This sounds cruel, and perhaps some people reading this book will be horrified. But it is not nearly as bad as it sounds. To start with, all the Helper does is to wave the whip on both sides of the dog and then, as the dog gets used to it, the Helper will stroke him with the whip. The whip is 63cm long, 10cm in diameter, and made of flexible material covered with either suede or leather. It is a good idea to get your Shepherd used to having the whip waved around when he has learnt to take a hard hold of the 'sausage', and not let go.

HIDES
In Schutzhund III, the Shepherd is required to inspect six hides, three on one side and three on the

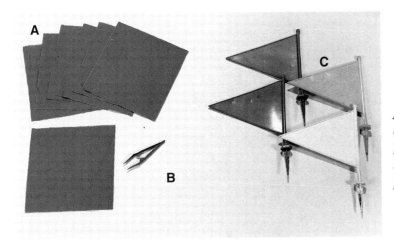

*OBEDIENCE
EQUIPMENT
A. WEIGHTED SCENT
CLOTHS.
B. TONGS.
C. SENDAWAY BOX
MARKER.*

other side of the training area, with the aim of finding the hidden criminal, who will be in the end hide. Hides come in a variety of different shapes and sizes, and are made from many different materials. All have two things in common, they are high enough to hide a man standing upright and they incorporate two sides of a right angle, so the Helper can be hidden until the dog comes round to the front. Portable hides can be made of canvas over a light metal frame, or two doors can be hinged together to form a right angle.

The equipment we have described for Schutzhund is what is required, but it is not necessary for you to purchase it all. At a certain stage in your Protection training, you will need the advice and help of an experienced Helper, for it is the Helper who trains your dog and not you. Our advice to you is to join your local Schutzhund branch – most countries have one – where you will find they have hides, protective suits, sleeves and, most important of all, experienced helpers. Any Schutzhund Club will also have the regulation 'A' frame and solid Clear Jump, but for practice at home, it is a good idea to have at least the latter.

OBEDIENCE

Very little equipment is needed. You have your collar/check-chain, lead and dumbbell, which is all you require until Test A. For Test A and above, you need weighted scent cloths, tongs and Sendaway box markers.

The scent cloth is preferably made out of cotton, for easy washing. It is approximately 15cm by 15cm, not more than 25cm square and has a weight sewn into a corner, to stop it blowing away in an outside ring. Sometimes pegs are used for this, or even stones. You will need a pair of tongs or gloves so that the cloths remain completely sterile when put down in the ring. Each cloth used by a dog, or any mouthed during competition, must be washed before being used again. When clean, store all scent cloths in an airtight box or plastic bag so they remain sterile.

Sendaway markers are used to mark the square that a dog is sent to when doing this exercise. A variety of different items are used, including small plastic flags, plastic mugs, small traffic cones, and wooden posts. It is a good idea to get (or make yourself) some of these items, so as to accustom your Shepherd to going into a square marked out by unusual articles. These are the only things you will require for Obedience.

Much of the equipment required for the three disciplines can be supplied by your local Working Trials, Obedience or Schutzhund branches, so there is no need for you to go to terrific expense, certainly not in the early stages of your training.

Chapter Ten

INTERMEDIATE TRAINING

If you have followed the training in the last chapter, your puppy, at the age of around eight months, will be reasonably proficient in Heelwork, elementary recalls, retrieves and stays – all on the lead. It is usually at this stage that we are asked: "Why go on to more complicated exercises, when all we want is a well-behaved pet? Our answer to this is quite simple. First of all, unless your dog is 100 per cent perfect in the above exercises *off* the lead, you cannot say that he is a well-behaved dog! From three to nine months of age, your Shepherd has done most things just because he wants to please you, and not only because you say so. But at this age he is starting to think for himself, and realises that when he is off the lead, he does not have to come back to you until he wants to. He can get up and run away from you in a Stay, and so on. The transition from working on the lead to off must be careful, and no mistakes must be made.

GENERAL PRINCIPLES
Another most important point is that your puppy is far less likely to get into trouble if you are giving him something to think about. Many owners think that taking their Shepherd out for an hour's walk once a day is sufficient, but they completely forget about providing any exercise for his mind. Never forget that the German Shepherd is bred as a working dog, and therefore needs the stimulus of work to keep him fit, healthy and happy.

In the last chapter, we stressed the importance of the owner being the pack leader. Doing more advanced exercises, as well as the ones you have already learnt with precision, will really stamp you as pack leader and make your puppy realise that he cannot just do what he likes. You, as the owner, will get immense satisfaction out of possessing a well-behaved dog which will do anything you want him to, as well as gaining respect from your dog. During this stage, continue socialisation, taking your puppy with you whenever possible, and subjecting him to as many unusual situations as possible. Do not only work your Shepherd at home, or at the dog training class you attend, but practise in a variety of different places such as parks and picnic areas. You can even practise some exercises, such as Heelwork and Stays, in the street.

By now, your Shepherd should be behaving himself in the house, not minding being left on his own, not stealing, chewing or jumping up on you or your visitors. The puppy will also let you go through the door first, without trying to push past you. Incidentally, it has been said to us that if your Shepherd is being sent in to search a building for a criminal or any other intruder, you do not want him to wait for you to go in first! But how many of us are ever in a position to be asked to search a building with our dog? If you are a police, army or air force dog handler, your dog will be expected to search buildings, but the dog will be given the command to do so. In his home environment, he will still let you go through a door first like any well-mannered Shepherd should. Nothing is more annoying than when taking a tray of drinks into your guests, your dog charges through in front of you, causing you to drop the lot! But what happens if somebody breaks into your house? Obviously, you want the dog to go down first to investigate. When teaching your dog

Socialisation is a vital part of early training – this six-month-old puppy is unperturbed by the presence of the deer.

to let you go through the door first, you have given him a command to come through after you. Now all you have to do is to open the door – which you would have to do in any case – stand aside, and tell the dog to go through.

Another statement we hear from people interested in showing the dog in breed as well as working is: "I do not want to teach my dog to sit at my side, otherwise every time I stop in the ring, my dog will sit." A very simple answer to this one – teach your dog to stand as he will have to learn for a judge's inspection, and then give the command every time you come to a halt in the Breed ring.

One misconception we encounter is what we call rag-work. This consists of the dog tugging at a rag, an old sock, sack, or anything made of material. Many people seem to think that if a Shepherd tugs at a rag or whatever, you are teaching him to become aggressive. Give your puppies a piece of material or a rubber tug, and what happens? Two or three take hold of it and try to get sole possession. The puppy who wins trots off with the article, either to chew it, or start the whole game again with another of its littermates. And what is so wrong about that? When you are playing "tug" with your puppy, all you are doing is taking the place of one of his littermates. Playing with rags or toys, and letting your Shepherd tug at them, is a wonderful way of improving motivation as well as the prey drive, which is so essential in a good protection dog. It will certainly not make your dog aggressive or vicious. On the contrary, it will develop his attitude towards an object rather than a person, which is what is needed for Schutzhund protection work.

Now you and your dog have got beyond the puppy stage, you will probably come across certain problems. In a book of this size we cannot possibly tell you all the answers, and so it is up to you to solve them for yourself. To us, this is part of the fascination of dog training. Every dog is different in character and temperament, and cannot be treated in the same way. For example, let us take two dogs, both of good character and temperament. One will respond favourably to firm handling in a particular exercise but, if you do the same to the other, he will dig his toes into the ground, go sulky, and fail to respond at all, and you will find that you have taken a backward step which could take quite some time to rectify. So study your Shepherd, find out what turns him on, and train him accordingly. The key to most of your problems is still the magic word motivation. Get your Shepherd crazy about toys of all descriptions, and spend a lot of time playing with them.

Some dogs are far harder to motivate than others, but all can be with patience and time. A well-motivated dog is a joy to train, so persevere. When doing more advanced work, a Shepherd who is toy crazy will make things much easier for you.

HEELWORK
Having got to the stage of starting Heelwork off the lead, footwork plays an important part in success. Up till now, all you have been doing is starting your Heelwork by moving off with your left foot. If, throughout your early work, you have always done this you will find that your Shepherd will automatically move forward with your left leg. With Stays and Recalls you leave, moving off on your right leg, and your dog will stay still. In other words, your Shepherd is working to your left leg. So now, when executing right, left and about-turns, you must always lead off with your left leg. Follow the diagram carefully, and practise it away from your Shepherd until it becomes a habit. You can perfect footwork when doing odd jobs, which entail walking, in the house and garden.

   Start lead-free work, as you did when you first started training your puppy, in a confined space, such as the house, back-yard or garden. Do not let your Shepherd wander away, and if he does, catch hold of his collar using your left hand, and give a smart jerk which will soon bring him back into line, and then, of course, give the usual praise and fuss. When you have perfected this, take your Shepherd to the park or field, and, with the lead still attached to your Shepherd, put the lead into your pocket or throw it over your shoulder. Then commence your Heelwork, using voice commands only, and not touching your Shepherd unless really necessary. At this stage just keep to a straight line, plus about-turns, making sure that your footwork is correct, and when coming to a halt, bringing your left foot up to your right. Make sure that you have your Shepherd's attention the whole time and, as described in the previous chapter, reward with toys or titbits and a game. Now, as you are walking along with your Shepherd's attention on you, unclip the lead without the dog realising and continue with your Heelwork. If your Shepherd tries to run away, put him immediately back on the lead and return to the previous exercise. He is not yet ready to work off lead. Whatever you do, do not let the dog run off as, once he realises that he can get away from you, you will have created a real problem for yourself.

   As you progress, cut down on titbits; sometimes use a toy instead, and sometimes just give verbal praise. This will keep your Shepherd guessing, and increase his attention on you. But as soon as his attention wanes, immediately show him his toy, or throw it, stop the exercise and have a game. With the repetition of Heelwork with Sits, your Shepherd will probably soon start sitting without a command when you come to a halt. Cut out some of your verbal commands, but continue to use them when you start, and when approaching a corner or an about-turn. And, of course, when the exercise has been executed correctly, give verbal praise. You are now aiming for Heelwork both on and off the lead, without any extra commands other than at the start of the exercise. With the exception of the three elementary classes in Obedience, all Heelwork in Advanced Obedience, Working Trials, and Schutzhund has to be executed without any extra commands.Do not do too much Heelwork during any one training session, as it is an exercise which can very easily become boring to your Shepherd. A bored Shepherd will start to lag or work wide, both of which are faults which are difficult to correct, so do not let them occur in the first place. Keep your Shepherd's attention on you with the aid of a toy or titbit. Up and down, with a couple of about-turns, is all you need in any one session. Make certain your footwork for the about-turns is correct, otherwise you will only confuse your dog. Plenty of praise, and also titbits or toys, can help to bring your Shepherd round close to your side. Double about-turns (doing a full circle and ending up facing the same way) can be very helpful in improving these. But you must practise your left and right turns separately.

All three dogs are doing good Heelwork with their attention on their handlers.

TURNS

With the lead in your left hand, tell your Shepherd to "Sit." Take two paces forward and turn to the left. Give the command "Heel" and, at the same time, take one step back with your left foot, keeping the right foot stationary, and guide your Shepherd, with an anti-clockwise motion of the lead, round to your side. On completion of the turn, bring your left foot back to your right, and command your Shepherd to "Sit", making certain that he finishes sitting straight at your side. When this stage has been learnt, repeat the above instructions, but only take one step forward before turning to the left. In the final stage, you stand facing to the left immediately in front of your dog, and repeat the above.

Your dog has been heeling and sitting fast, so it is now time to try standing in front of him, facing to the left and not moving your left leg when you heel your Shepherd. You will find that he will swivel round on his front legs and sit next to you. Now try, as you give the command "Heel", to take two paces forward. For these two final stages, you might find that you can help your Shepherd by pushing his bottom round with your left hand. The important thing in this exercise is to make certain that your Shepherd is moving quickly and sitting straight at your side at every stage. Do not try and progress too fast, but make certain both you and your dog are proficient in every stage before progressing to the next. This is an exercise that can become very boring, so perform it no more than two or three times in any one session, and make certain to give plenty of praise and have a good game between each turn.

The left about-turn is just one stage on from the left turn. You are standing straight in front of your Shepherd, facing to the left. As you give the command "Heel", place your left foot at right angles to your right and as your dog swivels round, before he has a chance to sit, take a step forward with your right foot, bringing your left foot forward to join him and telling your dog to "Sit". The right turn can be practised in exactly the same way but, instead of turning to the left, you turn right and you take a step forward with your left foot instead of one back. The progression is the same.

Do not incorporate either turn into your Heelwork pattern, until both left and right turns are perfected. If at any stage your Shepherd starts to lag or become disinterested, you will know that either you have been doing too much, or else your dog needs more motivation. In this case, stop all Heelwork practise for the time being, and concentrate on motivation. When you feel that your dog is full of bounce and happy again, start off with short distances, showing your Shepherd the toy and throwing it, and then letting him run out for it while you are both still on the move. If he jumps up do not take any notice – we want keenness, not precision.

SPEED

Our next phase in Heelwork is working at the three different paces – normal, fast and slow. You must take care to move at the right pace to suit your Shepherd. For normal pace, stride well out so that he is gaiting at your side, not too slow or fast, but comfortable for both you and your dog. For the slow pace, take long strides and see that your Shepherd is walking. If you go too slow, he will constantly try to sit, and if too fast, he will break into an amble. The fast pace means you running and your dog trotting in an extended gait, at your side. Study the pace at which your dog is most comfortable at all three speeds, and match your pace to his. A video is very useful in ascertaining the right pace.

In most of the early classes in Obedience and Working Trials, you will halt in between each different speed, but in all Schutzhund classes you go from one speed to another without a halt, so practise both ways.

COMPETITION HEELWORK

Whichever form of competition you intend to go in for, good Heelwork is important. There are slight differences between Obedience, Working Trials, and Schutzhund but, if your groundwork has been thorough and your Shepherd is well-motivated, you will have no difficulty in going from one to another.

In Obedience, Heelwork must be very precise, with your dog staying in exactly the same position in relation to your body at whatever speed, and when executing turns of all sorts. In the Advanced Classes, no extra commands are allowed, whether verbal or in the form of hand or body signals, all of which are very heavily penalised. Likewise in Working Trials and Schutzhund, no extra commands or body signals are allowed, but neither require quite the same precision as Obedience.

After CD, there is no Heel On Lead, and the steward will usually take both your lead and collar/check-chain at the start of the Control Section. The judges like to see a dog working happily, and most will forgive the odd crooked sit or wide about-turn. It is wise to train your dog to work without a collar or check-chain before entering Trials.

For Schutzhund Heelwork, the basic difference is the about-turns. The dog does a right about-turn as in Obedience or Working Trials, but the handler does a left about-turn. This requires slight alteration in your footwork, or else your Shepherd might think you are about to turn left. A dog that does a good about-turn will have no difficulty in managing this. After all, it is the handler who is turning in a different direction and not the dog. The German about-turn is not allowed in Obedience or Working Trials, but you must do the German about-turn when competing in Schutzhund. For Schutzhund, the lead must be held in the left hand at all times.

In all Classes of Obedience and Working Trials, a steward will be calling out commands for halts, about-turns, and so on. In Schutzhund, you have no steward but you have a set pattern which is the same for all classes and never changes, whether you are competing in Schutzhund I, II or III.

STAYS

When your Shepherd is reliable in both Sit and Down-Stays with the lead on the ground, you can gradually increase the length of time and distances you leave him. Unclip the lead, but leave it on the ground two or three times before you take it away with you. If your dog shows any sign of unrest, go back to him immediately and try again. Whatever you do, do not let him get up. If he does, you have left him too far and for too long, so go back to both shorter distances and times. Breaking Stays can create real problems, and the only solution is to go right back to square one and start again.

Assuming your Shepherd is steady when left for a reasonable length of time and distance off the lead, it is now time for you to go out of sight. As you disappear, give a firm command of "Stay", keep out of sight for about two seconds, and then go straight back to your dog's side. Do not let him jump up as soon as you return – another bad habit – but before praising him, count to ten and then praise him in the Down position. Give your release command before letting him get up. Your dog will soon realise that you are coming back, so now you can start staying away for longer periods. Sometimes, on returning, give another command of "Stay" and leave him again. If you do this, you will make him realise that returning does not mean that the exercise is finished. On completion, do not forget your release command of "OK" or whatever you decide to use, so the dog knows when the exercise is over.

When you are quite certain your Shepherd knows the meaning of the word "Stay", try a Stand-Stay. Have the dog sitting at your side, hold the lead in your right hand, give a long-drawn-out command of "Sta-a-and" and, with your left hand under his belly, gently lift him into the Stand position. Make certain that the front legs remain stationary, with the hindlegs taking a step backward into the Stand position. Praise and have a game, and then try again. It is important that the front legs remain still, so, if necessary, restrain your Shepherd from moving forward with the

Sit-stays well executed.

use of the lead. After a few days, you will find that you will only have to apply a small amount of pressure for your dog to stand. Ultimately, the movement of your left hand, plus the command, will make him stand. To complete the Stand-Stay, continue as you did with the Sit and Down-Stays. Another way of making your dog stand is to loop a lead, held in the left hand, under his belly, and then proceed as above using your lead instead of your hand to bring him into the Stand position.

   Practise the following exercise to consolidate your Stays. When sitting your dog during Heelwork, tell him to "Stay" and circle round him before continuing. You can make a bigger circle as he gets steadier. This exercise can also be practised with your dog in the other two positions. Make certain that your Shepherd goes Down, Sits and Stands quickly and without any hesitation. This leads on to more advanced exercises which are dealt with later. So it is worth your while to make certain they are done correctly. All three disciplines require Stays, but all are different.

OBEDIENCE STAYS: With the exception of the Test C Stand, which is incorporated with the Heelwork, each class will do their Stays as a group. In the three earlier classes, handlers are in sight, but from Test A onwards they are out of sight, with the exception of the Sit-Stay in Test A and the Stand-Stay in Test B. The length of time increases as you get to the higher classes.

WORKING TRIALS: In Working Trials, as in Obedience, each class do their Stays in a group. All are out of sight, and CD is the only class to require a Sit-Stay. The other classes are all the same – a ten-minute Down-Stay out of sight. There is no Stand-Stay in Working Trials.

SCHUTZHUND: The big difference between Schutzhund and the other two disciplines is that the Stays are performed individually, and not as a group. Your Shepherd is required to do a Down-Stay while the next competitor is working the Control Section. The Instant Sit is incorporated in the Heelwork for Schutzhund I and II, with the handler giving the dog a command of "Sit" while moving. The handler continues walking for a further thirty paces, about-turns and halts, returning to the dog on the judge's command. The dog must sit instantly without the handler interrupting his/her pace. Schutzhund III requires the above, plus the same exercise performed in a Stand-Stay while doing normal Heelwork. A similar exercise is required in Test C Obedience and is described as Advanced Stand, Sit and Down.

RECALL
If your Shepherd is steady on his Recall and will wait for your command before coming, you can now try taking the lead off. Only short distances to start with, and have a titbit ready for him to come to. If you think he is coming in crooked, take a step or two backward so that you can bring him in straight. Do not always call him, keep him guessing, and sometimes just walk back to his side, without calling him. For every time that you call your Shepherd, make a point of returning to him without calling him three or four times. This way you will stop anticipation, which is a very common fault and can be quite hard to correct.

   To improve the Present (sitting straight in front of you), practise the following exercise. Tell your Shepherd to sit, stand right in front of him and give him a titbit, then take two steps back and one to the right. Put your left foot forward, keeping your right stationary, call your dog and have a titbit ready to give him when he sits straight in front of you. Your leg is there to stop him sitting crooked. Repeat two or three times, and then have a game with his toy. The same can be done with you moving to the left. When your Shepherd is coming in straight, you will find you do not need to put a foot forward.

   Once he gets really proficient, you can try taking two paces forward and then turning to the right

KEMJON ARKO – 'ZAK' CDEX, UDEX, WDEX, TD (EX) AND HANDLER CHRIS GREGORY DEMONSTRATING THE FINISH.

The left-hand Finish.

The right-hand Finish.

or left. This is much harder for your dog, and should not be tried too soon. Try this as a variation to the above exercise. Stand straight in front of your dog, tell him to come, and as you move backwards, weave to the right and left before coming to a halt. Use a titbit if required. When doing a Recall always stand with your feet slightly apart. This exercise is rather boring for your Shepherd, so make certain you have plenty of fun and games in between each attempt, and do not practise it too often. Three or four times a week is quite sufficient. A good Present is important and is used in other exercises as well as the Recall. A bad Present could lose you quite a few marks in competition, so it is worthwhile making certain you have a good one.

THE FINISH
In conjunction with the Recall, another exercise your Shepherd has to learn is the Finish. The dog, having sat in front of you, must then go round on the command of "Heel", and sit straight at your left side. He can either go round to the right or to the left.

LEFT FINISH: With your dog sitting straight in front of you, hold your lead in your left hand. Give the command "Heel", step back with your left foot and with an anti-clockwise motion of your left hand, bring the dog round to your side moving your left foot back to your right foot, at the same time transferring your lead back to your right hand and giving the command "Sit". The dog will learn to swivel round on his front feet to sit at your side. A titbit can be used to bring him round if desired. The movement of the left foot back is to give the dog a bit of impetus but, once he has learnt the exercise, this can be left out. If you find that your Shepherd is sitting crooked, use your left hand to straighten him before he sits down. The practise for this is very similar to the work you do on left turns, and you will find that the dog will quickly learn this Finish having previously performed the other.

RIGHT FINISH: In the right-hand Finish, the dog must still finish sitting at your left side. With your Shepherd sitting in front of you, hold the lead in your right hand. Give the command "Heel", step back with your right foot and, as the dog goes behind you, transfer your lead to your left hand and bring your right foot back to your left. As he comes round to your left side, transfer the lead back to your right hand at the same time as giving the command "Sit". Your left hand can be used to help the dog sit straight. Once your Shepherd really knows what a Finish means, and comes round and sits quickly at your side, you can then try off the lead and also with you standing still. If at any time your dog either sits or comes round slowly, put him back on the lead and give him plenty of encouragement. As with the Present, this is a boring exercise, so do not practise it too often and, as before, have a good game in between each attempt.

SCHUTZHUND RECALL
The Recall to front is used in the three first classes of Obedience and in CD Working Trials. Extra commands are allowed in Obedience, but not in Working Trials or Schutzhund. The Schutzhund Recall is slightly different. The chief difference between Schutzhund and the other two disciplines is that in all Schutzhund classes, the Recall is incorporated with Heelwork. In the BH, Schutzhund I and II, the Recall is the same. The BH Test has no Tracking or Protection, and is only concerned with Control and the Shepherd's attitude to traffic and crowds. All Shepherds have to pass this before they can work in Schutzhund I. Its object is to assess temperament, character and whether the dog is suitable to start Protection work.

The Schutzhund Recall is as follows. Start with your dog sitting at your side off lead. At normal pace, proceed with your Shepherd for a minimum of ten paces, then drop him in the Down position, continue walking a further thirty paces, then about-turn and halt. On the judge's command, call your dog. The Present and Finish are the same as for Working Trials and Obedience.

The exercise you have practised to consolidate your Stay is the same as for this, so your Shepherd should have no difficulty achieving this Recall. When you have got him going down instantly on command, instead of circling him, walk straight on for a few paces, then about-turn and return to the dog. If your Shepherd gets up at any time, go back to circling him, as you have obviously progressed too quickly. The important part is to get a quick Down, so try this. With your Shepherd only a few paces away, give the "Down" command. If he does not drop immediately, approach him and apply pressure until he goes down. At the beginning, this is best tried in a confined space, such as a room in your house or a back-yard.

If your Shepherd goes down instantly, go up to him, praise him, and give a titbit while the dog is still in the Down position. Give your release command and have a good game. Repeat three or four times. When your Shepherd Downs instantly a few paces away from you, gradually increase your distance. Then try outside in your garden, and finally when you are taking him out for a walk. The Instant Down is a most important exercise, which all dogs should learn – it can avoid many an accident. For instance, if your dog sees a cat or another dog and is about to chase it, if you can put him in the Down instantly, you might possibly have saved a fight or a dead cat.

In Schutzhund III there are two Recalls. The first is as for Schutzhund I and II, but for the second one your Shepherd is in the Stand position instead of the Down, and instead of heeling at normal pace, you heel at fast pace. Command your dog to "Stand" and, without stopping, continue at fast pace for a further thirty or more paces, then about-turn and halt. The rest is the same as before. Teach this exercise as you did the Sit and the Down, but make certain your Shepherd is really reliable in his Stand-Stay before you start walking or running away from him.

TEST A RECALL

The Recall required in Test A Obedience is another you will have to master, if you intend to enter Competitive Obedience. Actually, we think this is a much better Recall for pet owners than the Recall to front, as it consists of calling the dog to heel while continuing walking. If you think about it, it is far easier to call your Shepherd to heel having finished his daily walk or during his exercise, than having him sit.

What does a Test A Recall consist of? Your Shepherd is put in the Sit or Down position – your choice – while you proceed forward without your dog. You could be asked to turn to the right or left, or both, before being told to call your dog ,who should come smartly to heel and stay there until you are told by the steward or judge to halt. Do not try this exercise until you are certain your Shepherd is 100 per cent reliable on his Sit and Down-Stay. If he is not, you will be doomed to failure, not only in this test, but you will be ruining your Stays as well.

With the lead on, put your Shepherd in the Sit or Down – *do not* tell him to stay – and with your right foot, step forward. When you have come to the end of the lead give him the command "Heel", simultaneously giving a quick jerk to the lead, and continue walking until the dog has joined you. After a further two or three paces, you can give the command "Sit". By careful use of the lead, you can make certain that your Shepherd comes fast and close to you, as well as sitting straight at your side when you stop. Then have the usual game, and try again. When the dog is coming in fast without you jerking the lead, try this. As he reaches you, turn smartly to the right and, after two paces, halt. You can do the same turning left, but be careful that your Shepherd tucks his bottom well into your side on the turn. The correct use of the lead can make all the difference to a good or bad Test A Recall, so think carefully and know exactly what you are going to do before attempting it.

When you are certain that your Shepherd knows exactly what you want and is coming in fast, you can try taking the lead off. Follow the same routine as before, but do not always halt soon after the dog has reached you, rather continue with your Heelwork, including more turns in both directions, as well as about-turns. The usual problem with this Recall is the dog anticipating your command. As you did with your Recall to front, do not always call him, but, having done a turn or two, go back to him. If the dog is never quite certain when or if you are going to call him, he is far less likely to anticipate. But progress slowly, making certain that you have consolidated each section before going on to the next. This way, you should have no problem with a Test A Recall. As with all Test A work, you are allowed no extra command. The only command you can give is "Heel" when calling your dog.

THE RETRIEVE

This exercise seems to cause many problems for the Shepherd, some of which can be quite hard to correct. Running out and not picking up the dumbbell; refusing to go out at all; bringing it back but dropping it in front of you; picking it up and then running off with it – these are just some of the problems we encounter. We feel the secret of success with this exercise is the early fun training with a variety of different toys. If, by the time you come to a formal retrieve, your Shepherd is happy chasing toys and bringing them back to you – and this is the important point – without

Zak performing a Retrieve with a 2-kilo dumbbell.

dropping them, it is not difficult to substitute a dumbbell for a toy.

For a reliable retrieve, you must teach the hold. It is not necessary to start with a dumbbell. Use something hard like a bit of broomstick or a bite-bar. Get your Shepherd sitting at your left hand-side and, holding the article in your right hand, press it against the dog's front teeth, at the same time give the command "Hold". If your dog shows resistance, gently prise the mouth open with your left hand and slip the article in. Give plenty of praise while the dog is holding the article and then, after a few seconds, tell him to "Give" and take the object out of the dog's mouth. Remember, you are praising your Shepherd for holding the article, *not* for giving it up. Practise the hold three or four times, and then have a game.

If you find it difficult to get your Shepherd to hold when sitting at your side, try this. With both you and your Shepherd facing the same direction, sit the dog in between your legs and proceed as before. If your dog tries to back away, stand against a wall. By holding his head up and tickling his chest, you will make him less likely to spit the article out. If he resists holding anything hard, try winding an old sock or glove round the article or the shaft of the dumbbell. This will make it easier for him to hold. If you are throwing toys, do not give any command, and then if the dog does not bring them back, he is not disobeying you. Whatever you do, if your Shepherd brings the toy back but drops it at your feet, do not pick it up and throw it again. Put it in your pocket and say nothing. But if your Shepherd brings it back without dropping it, lavish much praise, take the article and throw it again. From now on, only throw an article if the dog has held it until you have told him to "Give".

If you practise the Hold every day, you will find that within a few days your Shepherd will be reaching out to take the article as you give the command. This is the first step to success. Now is the time to replace your article with a dumbbell. When the dog is reaching out happily for the dumbbell, start moving it closer to the ground until ultimately it is on the floor and your Shepherd is picking it up confidently from there. If your Shepherd stands during this stage, let him. It is far easier for him to pick up the dumbbell from a stand position than from a sit. The important point is picking up and holding the dumbbell. Now you can go on to the next stage.

With your dog walking, not heeling, at your side, and while still on the move, present it with the dumbbell and tell him to hold. Continue for a few more paces, making certain that the dumbbell is not dropped, and then give the command "Sit". Stand in front of the dog, wait for a few seconds and then give the command "Give", and take the dumbbell. Now, as with the previous exercise, you can gradually move the dumbbell closer to the ground until your Shepherd is picking it up from there, without any hesitation and while still on the move. This is usually the hardest part to achieve, but will come with patience and perseverance.

You can also practise a Recall to front with the dog holding the dumbbell but, whatever happens, do not let him drop it. When these exercises are being executed keenly, with the dog showing no tendency to drop the dumbbell, put him on a long line, tell him to sit, walk out a few paces, place the dumbbell on the ground and continue walking for a further half-dozen paces, then about-turn and halt. Call your dog, and immediately give the command "Hold". If you have done your homework properly, he will pick the dumbbell up on his way to you and present it in the usual manner. Alternate this exercise with the following:

With the dog still on a long line, tell him to "Sit", walk out about four metres, place the dumbbell on the ground, go back to your dog, give the the command "Hold", and you will find that he will run out, pick up the dumbbell and come back to you. Praise your Shepherd, but if there is any hesitation about coming back, tell him to "Come" as for a Recall, continuing the praise the whole time. The long line is important because, if your Shepherd decides to run off, you still have control. If, at any time, he drops the dumbbell, you will know you have progressed too quickly, so go back a step or two.

When you are confident your Shepherd is picking up the dumbbell and coming back to you fast, the time has come to dispense with the long line. At first, try your dog in the house – a fairly long hall is ideal – or in any other confined space you have available. Once you are certain you have a reliable retrieve in a confined space, you can try outside. Only throw the dumbbell a short distance to start with. A reliable Retrieve is imperative for whichever discipline you intend to work for, so it is worthwhile spending time to achieve this. The Retrieve is the basis of a successful search in Working Trials, and scent in Obedience. It may take weeks or even months before you achieve success, but it is worthwhile persevering because you need a reliable Retrieve for competition for all disciplines.

PROBLEMS WITH THE RETRIEVE

SLOWNESS: If your Shepherd is sluggish about going out to pick up the dumbbell, try attaching a line to the dumbbell and pull it along the ground for your dog to follow. Most dogs will respond to this as you are using the 'prey drive', an instinct possessed by all dogs, to achieve success. Pick up the dumbbell, and encourage the dog to come to you by applying pressure on the line.

KEEPING HOLD: Sometimes you will find that you have a Shepherd who, having brought the dumbbell back to you, will not let you take it. To correct this, have a titbit ready so that on the command "Give" you can replace the dumbbell with the titbit. Twisting the dumbbell in the dog's mouth will sometimes work, but be careful that, as you take it, the dog does not jump up to grab it again. You can also try blowing, or even pinching his nose, to make him release the dumbbell.

ANTICIPATION: In the Competition Retrieve, the dog must sit at your side until you are given the command, either by the judge or a steward, to send him. Anticipation is a common fault. When teaching the Retrieve, this does not matter. In fact, if your Shepherd is not too keen to go after his dumbbell, we suggest you throw your dumbbell and send your dog simultaneously. But to correct anticipation put your fingers through his collar/check-chain to stop him moving, and then do an about-turn on the spot before sending him. Another way is to tell your dog to sit, throw the dumbbell, then go out to pick it up yourself. If you have serious problems, try this, getting a friend to help you. Sit the dog at your side, but do not give any commands, just throw the dumbbell from one to another. Your Shepherd will probably get up and try to catch it. Do not chastise him, but sit him again and repeat. You will find that your dog will soon get bored when he finds he cannot get hold of the dumbbell and will remain sitting. Give lots of praise, and repeat the whole process, ending up with the usual game when success has been achieved. Anticipation is annoying, but at least it tells you that your Shepherd is keen to retrieve, so do not be too hard in your correction. A dog like this is much better than one that will not go out. With the exception of the higher classes of all disciplines, you will not lose many marks for anticipation. By the time you have reached those heights, you will, hopefully, have corrected the fault.

MOUTHING: This is another common fault. To correct this, try the following. With your Shepherd sitting in front of you and you holding the dumbbell, press a finger in between the jaw bones giving a firm command of "No" as soon as he starts mouthing. As soon as he stops mouthing, release the pressure and then praise. Alternatively, use one of the heavy German dumbbells for the retrieve, but watch your toes in case the dog drops it during the Present. There are a variety of different dumbbells for you to choose from, ranging from wood to plastic. We favour wooden ones, but, if your Shepherd tends to chew, try a plastic dumbbell instead. Square-ended ones are best, but whichever one you choose, make certain there is sufficient clearance from the shaft to the ground for easy picking up.

THE COMPETITION RETRIEVE

This consists of the dog sitting at your side, and on the steward's command you throw your dumbbell. The steward will give you another command, you will tell your dog "Hold", and he will go out, pick up the dumbbell, bring it back, sitting in front of you as for a Recall. You will be told when to take the dumbbell, and again, on the steward's command, you will send the dog to heel. This is the Retrieve required in Obedience and Working Trials. In Working Trials and from Test A onwards in Obedience, no extra commands are allowed. The Schutzhund Retrieve is done with dumbbells of different weights over the Clear Jump, and in Schutzhund II and III, over the 'A' frame, as well as from the ground. No extra commands are allowed.

SEARCH

When exercising your Shepherd, you have been throwing articles into long grass for him to find. Once you have a reliable Retrieve, encourage your dog to bring the articles back without dropping them. Then try throwing two in at the same time and, when the dog brings out one, send him back to find the other. Do be careful not to overdo this, or to use very small articles. Above all, make it easy and pleasurable for your dog, and stop while he is still eager to go out and find them. You will never get anywhere if you allow your dog to become bored. We will be studying the Search in greater detail in the chapter on Nosework, but the above is an excellent way of encouraging a dog to search, as long as you make certain that he brings the articles back to you without dropping them. Once your Shepherd has learnt the command "Hold", whatever he goes out to find or fetch must be brought back to hand. There is no need for a formal Present as long as he waits, holding the article, until you tell him to "Give".

AGILITY CLEAR JUMP

Your Shepherd is now eleven or twelve months old, and his bone structure is well on the way to becoming fully calcified (hard), so it is safe to start jumping him. Before this age, it will have done no harm for the dog to jump small heights of not more than half a metre. In fact, as you have found out by now, young Shepherds jump about and over things at a very early age without coming to any harm. However, as an exercise, it is best left until this age. Before progressing to higher Clear Jumps, the Long Jump, or the Scale, make certain that your Shepherd is really fit and never jump him on hard surfaces. Untold damage can be done to shoulders and elbows in this way.

Start with the Clear Jump at about half a metre. Sit the dog in front of the jump, one metre away, and give him the command "Over" ("Up", "Jump", etc.), and walk over the obstacle with your Shepherd at your side. Give much praise and have the usual game. If your Shepherd shows reluctance to jump, throw his favourite toy over in front of him. This usually succeeds, as well as making the dog jump over straight. If, on the other hand, your dog gets panicky, as some do, lay the bar on the ground and walk over it several times. Then put the bar at about a quarter of a metre or lower, and encourage him to go over that. You will find that most Shepherds love jumping once they realise what they have got to do.

Right from when you first start jumping your Shepherd, see that he is in complete control. By this, we mean sitting or standing the dog in front of the jump and not letting him move until you give the command you have chosen to mean 'jump'. The big mistake many beginners make in Agility is to think that the dog needs a long run at the obstacle. Far from it! The chances are that, given a long run at the jump, he will take off miles too soon, then flatten out, thus knocking the jump for six! Your Shepherd must learn to arch his back and tuck his hind legs well under for good clearance. As you heighten the jump, you will learn, by careful observation, the correct distance to enable your Shepherd to clear a one-metre high jump. Some need two strides, others only one before take-off. But progress slowly, taking care not to heighten the jump before your Shepherd is jumping happily and with complete confidence at the lower height.

When this is accomplished with the dog still on the lead or long line, try sending him over with you staying on the take-off side. Nip round smartly as soon as the dog has landed and be lavish with your praise. In competitive Working Trials your Shepherd, having negotiated the jump must, on your command, stay in the Stand, Sit or Down position (your choice), until you are told to rejoin him. If your control is good, which it should be by now, this should not cause any problems. Once the dog is jumping happily, and you have decided which position he finds most natural to wait in, give him the relevant command as soon as the jump has been accomplished. There are two exercises involved in agility, the jump and then the stay, so remember to praise as soon as the dog has landed and again when he has remained in the position of your choice. When you are confident that your Shepherd understands, and is successfully carrying out what is required, you can try him off lead. Once you have complete control at a low height, you can start increasing the height but only by about 7cm at a time, until your dog is easily clearing the full metre, which is what is required in both Schutzhund and Working Trials. In Schutzhund, the dumbbell is thrown over a solid fence with your Shepherd jumping both ways to retrieve it. Do not try this until you are 100 per cent certain that your Shepherd is reliable in both his retrieve and jumping off lead. In Working Trials the one-metre clear jump is never solid, but consists of one, or sometimes two, bars between two upright posts.

LONG JUMP

This is only found in Working Trials. It consists of five slats, increasing in height from front to back, and set at such an angle that, from the dog's viewpoint, it looks like one continuous expanse of obstacle. In competition, your Shepherd is expected to clear a jump three metres long and, as with the Clear Jump, remain in the position of your choice on the other side until you are told to rejoin him.

ZAK DEMONSTRATES THE JUMPS REQUIRED IN WORKING TRIALS

ABOVE: *The 3ft Clear Jump.*

BELOW: *The 9ft Long Jump.*

RIGHT: *The 6ft Scale.*

TEACHING GRETEL TO SCALE WITH THE USE OF THE 'A' FRAME.

TOP LEFT: The 'A' Frame is vertical up against the scale and is now standing at 2.5m.

ABOVE: On the summit.

LEFT: Sliding the front feet down the ramp. A ramp is used to avoid jarring the forequarters when coming off a height of 2.5m.

Start with just three slats fairly close together. With your dog on the lead, tell him to sit about 1 5 metres away from the jump, give him your chosen command, and run with him towards the slats, encouraging him to clear them while you run along the right hand-side. When your dog lands, give lots of praise, have a game, and repeat the exercise. Some trainers use different commands for each jump, but we use the same, including that for the scale and 'A' frame, and we find it makes no difference. As your Shepherd gains confidence, increase the length by adding another slat until you are using all five. Then increase the distance between them until the dog is jumping the full three metres. When he is jumping three metres happily and without hesitation, still on a lead or long line, the time has come to try off lead. For the first few attempts, shorten the distance again until you know you have full control, and also that your Shepherd is clearing it easily and jumping straight every time. Control on landing is required as with the Clear Jump. So far, you have been running at your dog's side, but now start gradually letting him forge ahead of you until you are remaining stationary. If you place your Shepherd's favourite toy on the other side, this will give him the incentive as well as keeping him straight. Some dogs tend to jump out to the side instead of going straight, so, if this happens, put your dog back on the lead and start again. You have increased the length too quickly. Another common fault is paddling through instead of jumping. To correct this, put one of the slats on top of another to increase the height.

As you increase the length, carefully study the distance your Shepherd needs to start at in order to clear the jump. Some need a far longer run than others. If you are too far away, your dog will have to take a short stride before take-off, which could make him hit the end slat and if too close, he will take off too far away and the result will be the same – hitting the end slat. Once you know the correct distance your dog needs before take-off, make certain you always set your dog up in the right place. This is most important.

SCALE

Once your Shepherd is clearing the one-metre Clear Jump, you can start him on the Scale. Start the height at one metre, and encourage him to jump over and back again. It does not matter, at this stage, if he is not scaling, for, as you add more boards, you will find the dog will automatically start to scale when he gets to a certain height. If he becomes hesitant about scaling, get a friend to hold him on one side while you go to the other side and call him over. Whatever you do, do not let your Shepherd slip backwards. Make certain that whoever is helping you is ready to give your dog a push on the backside if he appears to be struggling. Slipping backwards off the scale will put a dog off quicker than anything else.

Increase the height gradually by about 15cm or less at a time, but make certain your Shepherd is scaling keenly and with ease before doing so. As with the other jumps, throwing a favourite toy over will encourage him to scale. Progress slowly, and make certain your Shepherd is scaling confidently at every height. For competition, your Shepherd must scale both ways, waiting on the far side in the position of your choice until told to return by the judge. So it is advisable to get him scaling from either side from the start, but as soon as he is doing so confidently both ways, you can begin getting control on one side. Whichever position you choose, stick to it. Sometimes, instead of calling your dog back over the scale, go round, praise him and have a game. Doing this helps to eliminate anticipation, which could lose you valuable marks in competition. The use of the toy on the landing side will help to keep your dog straight, thus giving him more chance of successfully coming back over the scale. As he comes back over, take a few steps back so that he can finish with a Present, as learnt in the Recall, and then go to heel. A Present and a Finish are not essential, and you will not lose marks for not doing them, but it does look smart and creates a very good impression.

As with the other jumps, you must calculate the distance from the scale your dog is best suited to, for both the take-off and the return. The dog, having negotiated the scale, will probably take a few steps forward before halting in the position of your choice. Run round the scale so that you can make him stop in the correct place for the return. Placing the toy in that place will help.

THE 'A' FRAME

This consists of a couple of solid boards, usually with slats on them, about one metre wide, shaped, as the name implies, like an 'A' with the peak being two metres high. The angle should be movable so that to start with, you can lay the boards practically flat and the dog can get used to walking on an unusual surface before increasing the height.

Most dogs love climbing an 'A' frame, and it makes an excellent prelude to the Scale, as well as getting the dog fit. Some dogs will panic when first faced with an unusual surface so, once again, get the help of a friend. Put two leads on the dog, giving one to your helper and keeping the other yourself. With one of you on either side of the 'A' frame, which is almost flat on the ground, walk your Shepherd over and back again. Give much praise and the usual game. Repeat once or twice, and then leave until the next day. Do not increase the height until your dog is going both ways without the use of a helper. When your Shepherd is going over and coming back with the 'A' frame at a reasonable height, try off lead, and then (as with the Scale) introduce the control and gradually increase the height.

If your Shepherd is unhappy scaling but enjoys going over the 'A' frame, try putting the 'A' frame over the Scale. Start with it low so that your Shepherd can easily run up and down it, and, as before, gradually increase the height. When the Scale is two metres high, your 'A' frame will be practically vertical. If you can get it vertical, all the better. When your dog is confidently negotiating the 'A' frame at more than two metres, take it away and your Shepherd should go over the Scale without any difficulty. This is an excellent way of training your dog to run up and down the Scale, without jumping off the top. The 'A' frame is not an exercise required in Working Trials, but it is required in Schutzhund. Here the Shepherd is required to retrieve a dumbbell over the 'A' frame. As with the Clear Jump, do not try and put the two together until your Shepherd is reliable at both going over the 'A' frame, and retrieving a dumbbell.

GENERAL POINTS ON JUMPING

When tackling any sort of jumping there are some things to remember:

1. Always use a dead check-chain or collar and be careful never to let the lead or long line get caught around the jump. Even when on a dead check-chain, a sudden jerk on your Shepherd's neck will make him think he has done something wrong. It could put the dog off or make him very hesitant of trying again.
2. Ensure that your dog is really fit before doing too much jumping.
3. Do not work all obstacles every day. Do one obstacle a day, moving to another until your Shepherd is familiar with all the apparatus.
4. Make certain your Shepherd enjoys his jumping, and is eager to try again after one attempt. As soon as he shows the slightest sign of boredom or becomes anxious, stop.
5. Take your time, and do not increase the height or length of your obstacles too soon.
6. You cannot enter Working Trials until your Shepherd is 18 months old, so you have plenty of time to work up to the required heights and length of the jumps.

Having read this chapter and carefully followed the methods we suggest, your Shepherd should be working well off the lead, coming when called, doing Stays out of sight and, above all, retrieving a dumbbell and whatever other articles you throw for him. Our next chapter consists of the more advanced exercises required in all three disciplines.

Chapter Eleven

ADVANCED TRAINING

Continue with the approach suggested in the Chapter 9 for Heelwork, Recalls, Stays and Retrieves, but work for more precision. If your Shepherd is watching you the whole time, precision is not difficult to achieve but, if not, you must go back to more fun training with toys and titbits. Remember, in all exercises, short sessions of concentrated work, ensuring the correctness of whatever your dog does, are much better than the endless nagging that some handlers resort to. Nagging will merely make the dog more and more bored. Vary the speed in Heelwork, which always keeps a dog on his toes, and then give plenty of praise and a game.

Lengthen the time and distance you are out of sight in the Stays and, on returning, make certain your Shepherd does not jump up to greet you. Every so often, do your Stays – Stand, Sit and Down – within sight so to help build up your dog's confidence. With all types of Recalls, as with Heelwork, work towards cutting out all commands. Be careful, however, to watch body commands, such as turning your head, waving an arm, and so on. If your Shepherd really needs a command, vocally or by use of your hand, give it. This is much better than letting him make a mistake or get confused.

Your dog should now be happy retrieving most articles, including a dumbbell, so introduce more metal objects such as a 15cm nail, a sparking plug, or whatever else you can find that will not hurt the dog's mouth when it is picked up. Start getting your Shepherd used to retrieving a dumbbell over an obstacle. Begin with whatever jump you like, Clear Jump or A frame at a low height, and wait until your dog is both jumping over, and bringing the dumbbell back enthusiastically, before you increase the height. If you have worked at the two separate parts, jumping and retrieving, until you are certain that your Shepherd understands what to do, and is also executing both exercises with enthusiasm, you should have no problem in putting the two together. Likewise, with the Clear Jump, Long Jump and Scale, do not increase the height or length of any of them until your Shepherd is jumping with confidence, and you have perfect control on the landing side. Of course, always remember the fun and games in between each exercise.

The important thing about training is for you to work out a plan. Do not do every exercise every day. Decide what you are going to do on any one particular day, and then do the rest the following day. Work on your finishes, left, right and about-turns on one day and, on the next concentrate on Heelwork in a straight line with about-turns, varying the speed, and making certain you have your Shepherd's full attention.

THE SENDAWAY

All three disciplines require this exercise. For Obedience it is usually a short one, depending on the size of the rings. The target is usually to a square, roughly lm x lm, marked at each corner with small plastic flags, traffic cones, stakes or similar objects. In Working Trials, the distance can be anything up to and beyond 200m, possibly marked by a fencing post, a tree or even a different-coloured patch on the ground. In the early stakes, the distance is much shorter and there is usually

Rope-tugs suitable for all stages of training.

a clear marker such as a traffic cone, white post or a plastic bag in a hedge. The Schutzhund Sendaway is much shorter and, whereas in the other two disciplines the dog is sent from a stationary position, in Schutzhund both you and your Shepherd are moving. As soon as you give the command, you remain stationary and your dog continues in a straight line until commanded to go down. The judge then tells the handler to rejoin the dog. The length is increased for each stake.

Unless it is very carefully taught, the Sendaway can cause some confusion in the dog's mind. Up till now, except for the Retrieve and Search/Scent in which the Shepherd is going out to fetch something, we have spent our time persuading our dogs to keep as close as possible to us. Now, quite the reverse is the case. We are making our dogs go away from us, ultimately to nothing. Therefore, we must make it very clear to our Shepherds exactly what we mean when teaching this exercise. There are several ways of teaching a Sendaway, most of which stress the importance of an Instant Down at a distance. Methods vary considerably, and in a book of this size, we do not have the space to consider every one in detail. What follows is a brief description of various methods, and a detailed look at the one we find most successful.

One method is to take your dog out on his walk then, when he is a distance away from you, command him to Down. Go up to the dog, praise him, put him on a lead, and move about 1.5m away from where he has gone down. Point your dog towards the spot, using your hands as blinkers on either side of his eyes, and give your chosen command – "Get off," "Away", "Go", "Voraus" (German), or "Out" – and let him go. If the dog is puzzled, take him out on the lead. If he goes away happily, increase the distance by moving further back and repeat two or three times. Choose a different place every day.

Another method is to put a post firmly into the ground, put your Shepherd down by the post, then attach him to a long line which runs round the post. With your dog still on the long line, go two or three metres away from the post and send him back, giving a smart jerk on the line to encourage the dog to move. Then Down him at the post. When your Shepherd understands what is required, try off-lead and gradually increase the distance. Yet another method is to put something of yours, like a coat, in front of some sort of a barrier (a hedge, wall, or fence) and send your dog to it, making certain your Shepherd goes down as soon as he gets to your marker. Food or a toy can be put on the marker to encourage the dog to go. When the dog understands what you want, increase the distance you are away and then gradually cut down the size of the marker. A variation of this is to put your marker in the middle of a field and send your dog back to it, going round the

Your Shepherd must get used to retrieving different articles including metal objects.

clock and increasing the distance on every Sendaway. All these methods entail putting the dog down in a certain place before starting, and then sending the dog back to that place. Then go up to the dog and praise him, but never call him back. With all these methods, a very reliable Instant Down is essential.

For success with the Sendaway, we like to give the puppy the idea of going away from us at an early age and, we try to make certain the puppy wants to leave, thus avoiding a stressful situation. What better than to persuade him with food? Sometimes, when making the puppy sit and come for his meals, we do it the other way round. Put the bowl of food down about three or four metres away from the puppy, sit him straight facing the food, then give your chosen command and let him go. Give much praise when he gets there, and while he is eating the food. You are teaching your puppy a command which, if you practise this exercise regularly, he will soon learn and associate with leaving you.

Another good idea, especially for owners who want to specialise in Obedience is to send your puppy to his bed, assuming that he lives indoors. Put a titbit in the middle of his blanket, and send the puppy to that, as described above. You will soon be able to dispense with the titbit, and send him straight to his blanket. When your puppy is going to his bed without any hesitation, put a marker at each corner to simulate an Obedience Sendaway box. As yet, we have not used this method, but it seems a very good idea and one well worth trying.

Having practised one of the above methods, you now have a Shepherd who is quite happy to leave you on command, and go to a suitably-marked spot with an Instant Down when the dog gets to whatever marker you are using. We split this exercise into two sections, firstly leaving you, and then going down when he gets to a particular marker or place. We want the Shepherd to go out keenly and with pleasure, so until he is doing this over quite a considerable distance, we run out after him and then give much praise and have a game when we get there. The Instant Down should

Polly retrieving a 2-kilo dumbbell over an A frame.

be practised separately. Only when your Shepherd is dropping instantly when quite some way away, do you put the two together. Please note, you should not call your dog back from the Sendaway marker, as this will only lead to anticipation. When competing in both Working Trials and Obedience, the dog must be called back, but, if you have practised your Recalls to front and to heel, this will cause you no problems.

OBEDIENCE SENDAWAY

Using your markers, make a box about one metre square and in the middle place a piece of carpet, on which you have put your Shepherd's favourite titbit. If your Shepherd's Stays are reliable, leave him in a Down-Stay and let him see you putting down the carpet, plus titbit. If not, get somebody to hold the dog. Whatever you do, do not let your dog break his Stay and run after you. When you have put your marker down, return to your dog. Either a Sit or Stand is the best position from which to send your Shepherd, but whichever you choose, make certain that his body is in a straight line with the direction in which you want him to go. This is most important because, if your dog is either standing or sitting crooked, he will probably run to the marker in an arc instead of going straight, and we do not want this to happen!

To start with, a distance of two metres is enough but, as your Shepherd gets the idea, move further back from the box, until you are about ten metres away and your dog is going out fast and straight. Please note – you move back, the box always remains in the same position. Follow your dog out, then give much praise and have a game when he gets there. Now put the titbit under the carpet and repeat. If there is any hesitation, go back to a shorter distance. Next, take the titbit away, but give your Shepherd one when he gets there. When your dog is doing 10m with no titbit under the carpet, you can start cutting down the size of the carpet until there is nothing left. Then remove the markers. When you do this, you might find that on the first few attempts it is advisable

Zak being set up for an Obedience Sendaway. Notice the position of the handler's hands; she is making sure that Zak is looking straight at the box, which in this Sendaway, is being marked by four plastic flags.

to put a small piece of carpet down again. Once your Shepherd has really got the idea, move your square to a different place and repeat the above. You will find that, as you progress, you will be able to dispense with the early part of the exercise and send the dog a reasonable distance to a small square of carpet with no titbit every time you move to a new location. Any sign of hesitation or lack of speed means you have been progressing too fast, so go back to the beginning. In this exercise, both speed and accuracy are essential to get good marks in competition.

In the meantime, you have been practising your Instant Down. When you are quite certain that both the Down and your Sendaway are perfect, you can start putting the two together. Not every time, as anticipation of the command "Down" can sometimes make for a slow Sendaway.

In Obedience, your Sendaway is usually fairly short and nearly always to a box. The box can be marked by all sorts of different things, so get your Shepherd used to peculiar objects marking the box. Sometimes, there will not be a box to go to, hence the importance of teaching your dog to go to nothing. If you have a straight but narrow passage or alleyway, use it for practice, as this will help you and your Shepherd to achieve a straight Sendaway.

The completion of an Obedience Sendaway is a Test A Recall, with you walking up to the dog, doing an about-turn, and then following the steward's commands while walking away. The judge can use any Heelwork pattern he/she likes, the only condition being that, as in a Test A Recall you must be walking away from your dog when instructed to call him.

WORKING TRIALS SENDAWAY

The chief differences between this and the Obedience Sendaway are the distance the dog is sent, which is much greater, and the fact that the dog is never sent to a square. You can be asked to send your Shepherd to a definite object, or to nothing, so we must train our Shepherd to go out in a straight line for an indefinite distance with no particular object in view. A daunting task indeed, and one which, unless your Shepherd has been taught correctly, could create a very muddled and insecure dog. The method we have found successful uses either food or a toy as an incentive, whichever your Shepherd likes most, or, of course, you can use a combination of both. The Instant Down is not used, as with the Obedience Sendaway, until we are certain our Shepherd understands the exercise, and goes out fast and straight to wherever we choose to send him. When teaching a Sendaway, never put either food or a toy on the ground at the base of your marker. Doing so could cause confusion in the dog's mind, and create possible problems in the Search and Retrieve exercises.

When using food as your incentive, you need two pieces of equipment. Get a two-metre length of broomstick, put a nail in the bottom for sticking it in the ground, and fix cup-hooks about 15cm apart all the way up it. On the hooks, you hang a soup-ladle, in which you place your titbits. Make certain that the ladle, when hanging on the lowest hook, is well above ground level. Put your Shepherd in a Sit or Down-Stay, provided he does a reliable Stay, and let him watch while you hang the ladle, in which you have placed his favourite titbits, on the lowest hook. If your dog is not yet reliable in his Stays, take him up to the post, show him the ladle with the titbits, and then take it back to the position from which you intend to send him. As with the Obedience Sendaway, make certain your Shepherd is sitting or standing straight, put your hands on either side of his head to form blinkers, and when you are sure he is looking straight at the post, send him. Follow, and praise him while he is eating. Repeat two or three times. Gradually increase the height of the ladle so that, ultimately, your Shepherd will not be able to get his reward and will have to wait until you arrive. This broomstick and ladle idea was given to us by one of the UK's top Working Trial Instructors and we have found it most successful.

Now you can start increasing the distance by moving back, but only by about two metres at a time. If your dog becomes hesitant or starts to veer, go back to the shorter distances. When your Shepherd is confidently running out a distance of 30-40 metres, move your pole to different places, but at this stage, always put it against a barrier of some sort. Stay at each new place for about a week, but occasionally return to one of the old locations to see if your Shepherd will go out without any preparation from you. If he goes out, give titbits and lavish praise plus a game. You are really getting somewhere now!

After a few days you will find your Shepherd will run straight to the pole, so you can dispense with the ladle, but always make certain you have a titbit in your pocket to give him on arrival. You can now start sending him to different objects such as a traffic cone, an upturned bucket or whatever else you can think of. Keep the distance short to start with, and always begin by putting titbits or a toy on the top of whatever object you are using – some form of container is useful for this – and remember never to put anything down at the base.

When your Shepherd is happy and confident going out to whatever object you have chosen, the time has come to send him to what, in your dog's eyes, is to nothing at all. If you are lucky enough to live near the brow of a hill, put your marker over the top so that it is not visible from the starting point of the Sendaway but only when the dog gets fairly close. A gap in a hedge or a gateway can also be used, the object being that your dog cannot see the marker until he is almost there. As before, follow him up and give a titbit, then a game and lots of praise. If you live in flat country, as we do, with very few hedges and none with gaps in them, you will have to adopt a different technique. By now, you should have perfected your Stays and your Instant Downs because, to be successful, you need both. Put your dog down about four metres away from a hedge, and let him see you hide your food-container in a suitable place. Go back to your Shepherd, send him, follow him up, show him where the food-container is, and give him his titbits. As you increase the distance, you will probably find it is impossible to get to your food-container at the same time as the dog, so you must put in the command "Down" as soon as he gets to the hedge. Perhaps now you will understand why it is so important to have achieved that Instant Down. Without it, your

Shepherd will either start coming back to you or wander along the hedge looking for his titbits, and so ruining his Sendaway.

At the beginning of each training session, start with a short Sendaway and then increase the distance. This is most important when using a new location. Do not do more than three or four at each training session for, although most dogs enjoy doing Sendaways, they can very easily get bored, which is fatal with this exercise. Do not always send your dog away to nothing, but every now and again go back to using a marker. You will find this will help to give your Shepherd confidence. Sometimes, try putting a marker in the middle of a field and sending your dog to that. Whatever Sendaway you try, always start with a short distance and see that the exercise is done correctly. Be patient and progress slowly, making certain that each new situation is properly understood before progressing to the next. The Sendaway is a difficult exercise and to achieve perfection, it needs practising every day.

When you are confident that your Shepherd understands what you require, try this. When taking your dog out for his walk, let him see you putting the food-container in a certain place, and then continue with your walk. When you get to a place opposite your marker, set your dog up and send him. Do not be too ambitious about distance to start with. The important thing is that your Shepherd is running straight to the place your food-container has been hidden, and waiting there until you arrive with a titbit. When using a toy, the procedure is exactly the same. However, you do not need a soup ladle, or a stake with hooks. Just place the toy on top of your marker. Whether using food or a toy, it is important that your Shepherd understands that, when being sent to a hedge, fence or whatever, there is always something there for him, even though the dog cannot see it. Once this is understood, you should have no difficulty with your Sendaways.

When competing in Working Trials, you are usually asked to recall your dog which, unless the judge has told you otherwise, is not marked. The completion of the Sendaway is your dog waiting at the marker in whatever position you choose.

SCHUTZHUND SENDAWAY

In this Sendaway, your Shepherd is walking to heel, under control, until such time as you give him your chosen command, where upon he must go, at a fast pace and in a straight line, until you give the command "Down". Your dog must respond immediately and stay in that position until the handler is told to join him. The dog should be facing the direction in which he is going, and not facing you.

Here we are dealing with three different exercises: Heelwork, leaving you, and the Instant Down. Leaving you is taught in the same way as we have already described for Working Trials – to a marker with a toy or titbit on top of it. Possible problems encountered with this Sendaway are anticipation when Heeling, and the dog turning round and facing you before going Down. When practising the Instant Down at your side, make certain your Shepherd does not turn round before going down. A helping hand can be given by pressing on the withers with your left hand, when commanding your dog "Down". You will soon find that, as you move your hand, your dog will immediately drop. If he is doing a good Schutzhund Recall, your Instant Down should be no problem when at your side. Practise your Downs when out on your daily walk. When your Shepherd is a certain distance away from you – not too far to start with – give your command. If not instantly obeyed, get to your dog quickly and enforce the command. Remember, never call him back to you, always go up to him, praise him and then release him.

Now include this in your Sendaway. Set the dog up (still to a marker), send him and when he is two or three metres away from you, command him to go Down. Go up to your dog, give praise and a titbit, set him up again and this time send him to your marker. We find that by doing this we maintain a fast Sendaway. Your Shepherd soon realises that he will ultimately reach the marker (with titbits or toy) even though he might have to go Down sometimes on the way. No titbit or praise is given if the Down is slow, or if the dog has turned round. Try again but with a shorter distance, and if the Down is still incorrect, go back to doing it at your side. This method also helps to keep the dog straight when in the Down position.

If your Shepherd is inclined to anticipate when Heeling, here are two suggestions. As soon as you see the slightest sign of the dog wanting to leave, do a smart-about turn and continue back the way you came. Do this several times until there is no sign of anticipation. Then give much praise and a game. Alternatively, command the dog to go Down and walk on without him.

Set up your marker as if you were going to do a Sendaway, and then practise your Heelwork along that line instead. If your Shepherd never knows whether he is going to be sent or not, you will soon correct any hint of anticipation. Increase the distance your Shepherd goes before dropping him, but remember, do it gradually. Otherwise, progress in the same way as we have described for the other Sendaways.

REDIRECTION

On completion of his Sendaway, your Shepherd is required to redirect either to the right or to the left, to a point decided by the judge, which could be as much as 100 metres away. Your Shepherd must go straight, without hesitation or veering to the right or left, until this point is reached. Redirection is required in Working Trials, but only in the two top Stakes, TD and PD. This exercise is not needed in Obedience, but is required in the Schutzhund Protection phase, in order to direct your dog from one hide to another.

Before starting Redirection, your Shepherd must be doing a really good Sendaway of about 50 or 60 metres, going out to nothing in a straight line, fast, and with confidence. Once you have achieved this, you can start Redirection. Teach Redirection as a separate exercise, and do not include it with your Sendaway training until you need it for Competition.

Put your Sendaway post up against a hedge or some sort of barrier (do not forget to put your toy or titbit on it), and position your Shepherd up against the barrier, about six or seven metres to the right of your marker. Stand one metre in front of your dog, give the command "Left", reinforced by raising your left arm pointing to the marker. When your Shepherd reaches the post, go up and praise, give him his toy or titbit and have a good game. Repeat three or four times in any one session. Having seen you place the marker, and received his reward, your Shepherd should have no hesitation in going. If there is some, give plenty of encouragement, even to the extent of going up to the marker and showing the dog the reward. Gradually move further away from your dog, until he will redirect happily and fast to the left with you standing 30 or 40 metres away from him. Now you can start moving your marker further away until that too is 30 or 40 metres away. When you are confident your Shepherd knows what he is doing, start all over again, Redirecting your dog to the right.

Your Shepherd now understands your left and right Redirectional commands, so now let us see whether we can put the two together. Sit your dog in between two posts, about six or seven metres from each, and put your titbit or toy on only one of the markers. Move back ten metres from your dog, and give him the appropriate command to go to the marker on which you have placed your reward. As soon as your Shepherd moves in the correct direction, praise him and when he reaches the marker have the usual game and praise him. If your dog goes to the wrong post, do not say anything, but when he reaches the marker go up to it and show that there is nothing there. Start again, moving a bit closer to your Shepherd before you give your command.

It is a good idea to wear something white so that your left and right arm signals are clearly visible to your Shepherd. When competing, you might be in a situation where your dog is 100 metres away from you, with the wind blowing in the wrong direction, making it impossible to hear verbal commands. In such a scenario, arm signals come in very handy. When this stage has been accomplished and your Shepherd is redirecting with confidence, start dispensing with your markers as you did with the Sendaway.

SPEAK ON COMMAND

Not required in Obedience, but used in both Working Trials and Schutzhund, this is an exercise which might also be useful for a companion dog. Imagine a situation where, when you are out exercising your dog, and you put a foot in a rabbit hole and break a leg or ankle. If you have taught your dog to speak, his continuous barking could attract somebody's attention and hopefully bring help.

When teaching this exercise, study your Shepherd carefully and find out what makes him bark. Let us give you an example. We had a puppy who was on his own, and in the morning when we approached the kennel door, he would start barking. We then gave him the command "Speak", opened the door and gave him his breakfast. When this had been successfully learned, the next stage was to open the door first, then give the "Speak" command, and when the dog started barking, we gave him his breakfast. In a very short time all we had to do was to give the command "Speak" and Jason, the dog in question, would immediately start to bark.

We then changed breakfast for a titbit. Jason was commanded to "Speak" in as many different situations as we could think of, including his daily walk. When he started barking he was rewarded with a toy or titbit. We also taught him a hand signal, shaking our fist at him, and once he was barking continuously, we would then command him "Stop", at the same time putting a hand in front of his face. Having got so far, we gave him his reward when he stopped barking and not when he started. This worked well with Jason, and he soon learnt to "Speak" and "Stop" in whatever situation we placed him.

Another good way of making a dog bark is as follows. Tie your Shepherd up to a gate or post, and start walking away, waving his favourite toy. As soon as your dog starts barking, give him the command "Speak". If he continues barking, go back to him, praise him and then give a command to stop barking such as "Stop", "Cease", "Quiet". As soon as he ceases, give much praise and let your dog have the toy. With a greedy dog, use food instead of a toy. Some Shepherds are difficult to get to speak, and with the above method you might find that all you get is one pathetic little bark. Be content with this, go back to your dog, praise him, have a game and then try again. Be patient, it might take a long time but you will win in the end. When you have succeeded in making your Shepherd bark continuously until you tell him "Stop", try the same exercise off the lead and then with you out of sight. In Working Trials you never know when or where you will be asked to tell your dog to Speak. It could be during Heelwork, with you out of sight, or it has even been known for your Shepherd to be required to sit on a roof for the "Speak" exercise, so be prepared.

THE ADVANCED STAND, SIT AND DOWN

This exercise is not required in Working Trials, and only for Test C in Obedience. In Schutzhund there is a variation of it, which we have already discussed. If you have followed our instructions, you will already have a Shepherd proficient in executing these positions. When training in this exercise, keep it apart from your Heelwork practice, otherwise you could muddle your Shepherd into thinking that every few paces you are going to stop, and put him in one position or another. Lagging in Heelwork could be the result, so keep the two separate. Practise each position independently, and do not start another until you are confident your Shepherd understands what is required.

We have discussed methods of teaching the various positions in previous chapters. Apply these for this exercise. Start by walking two or three paces forward with your dog at your side. Put your

Shepherd in your chosen position, circle him, go back to his side, give the command of "Heel", take three or four paces forward, halt and then give praise and a game.

When your Shepherd is confidently doing this and immediately taking up the required position, walk two or three paces forward and then circle. Increase the distance you walk away until you have gone about twelve to fifteen paces forward. Now about-turn, pass your dog, if necessary giving a Stay command as you pass, walk another few paces, about-turn and go back to his side. When returning, do not always give the "Heel" command, but walk round the dog again, or else just praise him, give a release command and have a game. This will stop any tendency towards anticipation.

Gradually, reduce the time you stop when putting your Shepherd in a certain position, until you merely falter at his side before walking on. When you can rely on your dog taking up any position on one command, quickly and without hesitation, keep walking without faltering. You can, simultaneously with your verbal command, put your left hand in front of your Shepherd's nose, to keep him from moving forward. Another trick worth trying to stop your dog moving forward is this. Hold a thin stick, bamboo or dowelling, in your right hand and hidden from your Shepherd when you first start Heeling. As you give your position command, bring the stick out and put it across the dog's chest, thereby stopping him from moving forward. This is not suitable for the Down position.

DISTANT CONTROL

This is only required in Test C Obedience. In this exercise, your Shepherd is required to take up the three positions – Stand, Sit and Down – without moving forward. You must be at least ten paces away giving the commands. Your dog has already learnt the various positions, but up till now he has been at your side. Now he must learn to take up these positions with you some way away from him, and must remain in the same place without moving forward or to the side. This is the difficult part. The tone of your voice when giving the commands plays an important part, so think about it and practise making them sound different. For instance, a long-drawn-out "St-a-and", a sharp "Sit" and the use of a low tone for the "Down". When teaching this exercise, you can use hand signals as well as verbal commands, but in competition it must be one or the other, and not both.

Let us start with the Sit to the Stand. Begin with your dog at your side in the Sit position. Put your right hand on his forechest (to stop forward movement), and with your left hand underneath his belly, give your "Stand" command. At the same time, lift his hind legs into the Stand position. The dog's front legs must remain stationary, while his hind legs take a step backwards. Do not let him move sideways. Give much praise, have a game and then try again. When your Shepherd is proficient in this position, the time has come to teach him to go Down from the Stand.

Keep your right hand on his chest, and put your left hand on his withers. Give your "Down" command, simultaneously pressing downwards with your left hand and backwards with your right. You will find your Shepherd will drop down on his haunches, without moving his front legs. To teach the Down to the Sit, put your left hand on your dog's collar and, as you give the command, gently pull him upwards and backwards, thus making him move his front legs a step backwards, while keeping his hindquarters stationary. The other position you must practise is the Down to the Stand. For this, use your left hand underneath the dog's belly and your right hand on his chest. Give your command, and stop your dog from moving forward by pressure upwards and backwards with both hands.

Teach each position separately, and do not start training another until you are certain your Shepherd understands what is required, and is taking up the relative position without moving his front legs forward or receiving any help from you. Leaving the dog stationary, you now take two paces forward, stand in front of him and repeat the positions. If your dog shows any tendency to move his front legs forward, go back to his side again. When your Shepherd is proficient in all positions, find a step – the top of the stairs or some form of platform – and put your dog on it. Stand in front of him, and give commands for the different positions. This is an excellent way of ensuring your dog takes up the positions correctly, without moving forward. When first doing this exercise outside, put a pole or something similar in front of your Shepherd. This will deter him from moving forward.

As your dog becomes proficient in all positions, executing them swiftly and without any forward movement, you can gradually start moving back until you are about twenty paces away. If there is any sign of forward movement, return to your dog and gently push him back into his original position. You have obviously been progressing too fast, so go back to the early stages again.

It goes without saying that throughout the entire training of this exercise, you must indulge in plenty of praise and games. Without this, your Shepherd will find this exercise very boring, and will hate every minute of his training which is the last thing we want. This particular exercise can take a long time to get the desired result. But if you make certain that your Shepherd understands what you require at every stage, you will eventually have a dog which will perform excellent Distant Control.

Chapter Twelve

NOSEWORK, TRACKING, SEARCH AND SCENT

Tracking is a fascinating, but very complex, subject which would require a whole book to deal with adequately. To become proficient in the art of tracking, we must learn about such things as wind direction, different terrains, and moisture, not to mention the really difficult skills like line-handling, reading your dog, and track-laying. Lack of space means we can write about this subject only briefly.

Tracking is required for both Schutzhund and Working Trials and although basically the same in both, in as much as the dog has to follow a path of human scent, the application is somewhat different. Firstly, let us see how they differ. The main difference is that, whereas in Working Trials you never know where your track goes, how many legs there are or how many corners must be negotiated, in Schutzhund there is little difference from one Stake to another.

SCHUTZHUND

Schutzhund I: Consists of a track 350 paces long, three legs with two left/right angle corners, twenty minutes old, and two articles, one of which is at the end, laid by the handler.

Schutzhund II: The pattern is the same but longer – 600 paces, thirty minutes old, and laid by a stranger, and two articles for Schutzhund I.

Schutzhund III: A track 800 paces long, consisting of five legs, four right (or left) handed corners, three articles, two on the track and one at the end, laid by a stranger and at least one hour old.

The FH, or Advanced, Tracking Stake: This has to be between 1000 and 1400 paces long, three hours old and requires four articles to be located. It also has a cross-track, laid half an hour after the original track by another person, which crosses it in three different places.

Whatever and whenever you are competing in a Schutzhund Stake, the formula is always the same as described above, so you know exactly what to expect.

WORKING TRIALS

UD: This the first tracking stake in Working Trials and is usually 250-300 metres long, half an hour old, and with one article at the end. In this Stake, a second post is put 10 metres from the starting post, so that you know the direction in which your track goes.

WD: The second tracking stake, is ninety minutes old, has only a starting pole, which means that the track could go in any direction, and there are two articles to find.

The PD track is two hours old, with two articles to find, and TD, the hardest stake of all, is three hours old with three articles to find. All have an end article, and, from UD onwards, they get progressively harder in terms of the number of legs to negotiate and, of course, the resulting amount of corners. There is no limit either way.

The other big difference is the way in which your Shepherd must work. Schutzhund requires a 'deep nose', which means that, right from the start, the Shepherd must have his nose on the ground the whole time. There must be no casting at corners, or very little, and the dog must work at a steady pace with no help from the handler, who must always be the full length of a 10-metre tracking line behind. The tracking line must be kept slack at all times. When finding an article, the dog must remain stationary in any position (handler's choice) without a command from the handler, who then collects the article and tells the dog to continue. The Shepherd does not have to wear a tracking harness and can be worked on a leather collar, or free if so desired.

In Working Trials, your Shepherd must be worked on a tracking harness. The dog usually works on a shorter line, which does not have to be slack. If your dog casts on corners, the line can be let out or taken in as required. There is also a time limit as to how long your dog is allowed to complete a track, and, if he over-runs the allotted time, you will be 'blown off', and no marks will be given. In Working Trials, the dog is required to track faster than for Schutzhund tracking. There are additional minor differences, but those mentioned above are the important ones.

PRINCIPLES OF TRACKING

Whatever their shape, size or colour, all dogs can track. Some are better than others and in some working breeds, such as GSDs, Dobermanns, and Border Collies, this instinct has been carefully preserved and channelled into work which will benefit humans. But just watch your dog, or any dog who is out for his walk, and see how he uses his nose. What he is smelling, and how, is a mystery to us. All we know is that he is scenting something. Long before the dog became domesticated, he had to search for his food to survive. First he would follow a ground scent (tracking) and as he came nearer to his prey, his nose would go up and he would start wind-scenting until he got close enough for the eyes to take over. His next meal was then well on his way.

What we must do is channel our Shepherd's natural instincts into doing what we want him to do, namely to follow a track laid by a human and find different articles, all of which carry human scent. For success in tracking, it is vitally important that your Shepherd is mad about toys and titbits. This applies whichever discipline you intend to work in, either Schutzhund or Working Trials.

SCHUTZHUND TRACKING

For Schutzhund, it is essential that the dog tracks steadily, never raising his nose except when he has found an article. So work with this in mind right from his very first lesson. Find out which titbit your Shepherd goes really mad for, something which carries plenty of scent such as liver, raw tripe or cheese, and go out with a plentiful supply of your chosen titbit. You will also require three poles and three articles, not too big, so you can put one at the end of each track.

The best terrain on which to start a dog tracking is damp grass, about 15-20 cm high, on which no humans or animals have recently crossed. If you cannot find any, damp earth is the next best thing. Do not choose a very windy day as this does make things difficult. A light breeze or a still day is ideal. Laying the track is most important, and you must know exactly where it has gone. Many a handler has pulled his or her dog off the track instead of trusting him, only to find that the dog was right and they were wrong.

Line up two objects on the horizon such as a tree, telegraph pole, or house, and walk towards them, making certain you keep them in line the whole time you are laying your track. Face into the wind, place your pole in the ground on your left hand-side, and trample an area of about 40cm square, on which you place three or four titbits. Trench the track with your feet, putting down a titbit in your footstep every 30cm. Continue for about five metres and then put down one of your articles, under which you have placed a titbit. Walk on, taking normal footsteps, for about three metres, and then come back, being careful to keep well to one side of the track you have just laid. Lay two more tracks, as above, about ten metres apart.

Now go and fetch your Shepherd who should be wearing a leather collar – never track in a check chain – with a two-metre leather lead attached to it. When first starting tracking, there is no need to use a tracking harness and line. Leave this until your dog has learned to work an easy track with confidence. Take your dog up to the pole, give the command "Track", at the same time pointing to the titbits you have placed on the square. When your Shepherd has found all of them near the pole, unless he starts moving down the track, encourage him to do so by pointing down to the next titbit. Once your dog has started tracking, do not say anything, but let him work things out for himself. Of course, if he goes badly wrong, you must intervene by pointing down to the track and encouraging him to move forward again. When he finds the article, give much praise and have a game.

After a few minutes, go back and repeat with your second and then your third track. You will probably find that when working the third track, your Shepherd will be starting to know what to do. However, if your dog is still uncertain what to do even after completing the third track, you can try this. Get a piece of sponge, tie a string round it, and soak it in something like tripe juice, gravy, or even milk. Still using the titbits, drag your soaked sponge behind you so that there is a continuous trail of strong scent as well as titbits. Once your Shepherd understands what is required, you can go back to using titbits only.

The reason we start with three short tracks, such as we have described, is that tracking requires a lot of concentration on the part of your Shepherd. Working this way gives your dog a chance to relax for a few minutes in between each track. Gradually increase the length of your tracks but remember, always start with a short one. You will soon find that you can reduce your titbits to one every metre, but still keep two or three on your starting pad, so that your Shepherd continues to get a good scent to start with. Make certain that your dog keeps his nose down the whole time, and tracks at a steady pace. Keep putting down titbits every few metres until your Shepherd is tracking for 25 metres at a steady pace without raising his head.

You can now start on corners. Shorten the length of your first leg, and lay your second leg into the wind. Start by putting down titbits every 30cm after the corner, and keep this leg short. Once your Shepherd is negotiating a corner confidently and without hesitation, you can gradually increase the length of the second leg and, as before, start increasing the distance in between titbits. Practise left and right turns in the same manner. You will find that your Shepherd will soon be so intent on finding the track, that he will go over the titbits without noticing them. Now you can stop using them except after a corner, or just put one down now and again to help build up your Shepherd's confidence.

Stop putting titbits under the end article but when you get there, command your dog to stay in your chosen position, Stand, Sit or Down, whichever you prefer, then go up to him, give him a titbit, and have a game with the end article, which he has just found. Gradually increase the time between your laying the track and working it, and if you intend to use a tracking harness, get your Shepherd used to wearing it in his home environment before attempting to track with it on. If you are using a harness, do not put it on your dog until you are just about to start tracking, and take it off as soon as your Shepherd has found the article. Doing this will soon make your dog realise that the harness means tracking, and so he will know what he is about to do.

The method we have described will result in a Shepherd who will work a track in a very methodical and steady way, never raising his head until he has found an article. This is exactly what is required for Schutzhund.

WORKING TRIALS TRACKING

In Working Trials we need a dog who, as in Schutzhund, tracks with precision, but moves at a faster pace. We have found the following method has been successful in achieving this.

Track laying and terrain are the same as those already described. Take your Shepherd, tie him to a convenient hedge or fence, and tease him with his favourite toy. Put a pole in the ground, mark an area at the side of it, and proceed to lay your track as before but this time with *no* titbits. Proceed for about seven metres, every so often showing your dog his toy and rubbing it on the ground. Do not wave the toy in the air, as in your dog's mind, this could easily be mistaken for a Sendaway. Having reached the end of the track, show your Shepherd the article once more, put it down, and return to your dog, walking back along the same track. This is called double-laying .

For the first few tracks, work your Shepherd in a collar and lead and when he is tracking with confidence, change to a harness and line, having previously introduced them at home. Take your dog up to the post, point down to the ground and give the command "Track". A dog with a strong Retrieve instinct will very soon get the idea, and start tracking. If he pulls you along, let him. When your dog finds the end article, take off the harness and line, give lots of praise and let him play with his toy. Repeat two or three times, which will be sufficient for one tracking session.

After the first few times, there will be no need to double-lay your track. If your Shepherd is tracking with his head held high, lay your next track with your back to the wind, which will help to keep his nose down. If he has any tendency to move off the track, even only a foot or two, say "No", stand still, and when he is back on the track, praise and then move forward again. By now, your Shepherd should be tracking in a harness with the line attached. Whatever you do, do not ever try to pull your dog back on to the track by his harness. Remember, when tracking, your dog is in control and telling you where to go, not the other way round. Gradually increase the length of your tracks until your Shepherd is confidently working one about 30 metres long.

Now start on corners. To start with, triple-lay them for about three metres either side of the actual turn, which should be into the wind. When the dog reaches the corner, stand still, and do not speak, but let him work out for himself which direction to take. If, however, he is just casting around with no idea of what to do, go up to him, point to the ground and encourage him to track again. Practise right and left turns in the same way. If your Shepherd is tracking too fast, lean back on the line to slow him down, or try putting some articles on the track, at intervals of about three metres, for him to find. In Working Trials you are not required to have a slack line, nor need you be at the end of it. We usually let the line run out to its full length when starting or after a corner. As soon as we feel the definite pull on the line, which tells us that our Shepherd is on the correct track, we run up the line until we are about five metres behind the dog. If, at any time, your Shepherd shows signs of indecision as to where the track has gone, stand still and see whether he will sort things out for himself. Having laid the track yourself, you should know exactly where it has gone, and so if your dog does seem to be lost, you can help him. But do not be too quick to give help, otherwise you might find the dog will tend to rely on you when he gets into difficulties. Once you are confident that your Shepherd knows what he is doing, both on a straight leg and on corners, you can increase the length of your track and add another corner. Also, increase the time between laying and working the track.

READING YOUR DOG AND LINE HANDLING

Both of these two skills can be learned only by experience and not from a book, although we can give you some guidelines. Study your Shepherd carefully when you know he is tracking. Does he hold his tail up or down, or does he wave it in the air? What does the dog do when he loses the track? Does he alter the position of his tail, or does he suddenly start moving faster? Is the pull on the tracking line different? These are just a few pointers which will tell you whether the dog is tracking or not, so you can act accordingly. It is up to you to observe your Shepherd to find the answers.

Line handling comes into much the same category. There are two schools of thought as to whether you should let the line drag behind you, or keep it coiled. Coiling the line is useful if your tracking ground is heather, bracken or scrubland, but you will have to learn to both coil and uncoil it quickly, so that you can do so when your Shepherd is casting. You do not want a whole lot of slack line in which your Shepherd could easily get tangled. Practise coiling without a dog on the end of the tracking line.

Letting the line drag behind has an advantage if your dog over-shoots a corner, you will know which direction you have come from and can back up the line until you get back to where you think the corner might be. However, letting the line drag will make it become very wet and muddy, and it could become caught up when tracking on heather or similar terrain. There are advantages and disadvantages to both aproaches, and it is perhaps best to learn both ways. But whichever method you use, you must be able to take the line in and let it out without allowing any slack between you and your dog. Hold the line high to prevent it getting tangled in the dog's back legs. The golden rule with line handling is: always keep 'in touch' with your Shepherd.

GENERAL REMARKS
It is a wonderful and thrilling experience to work a TD track with a Shepherd who knows what to do, and who confidently negotiates corners of different angles, long and short legs, and locates the articles, however small. To us, it is the ultimate in dog training. To achieve it, however, takes time, patience and a lot of hard work. To start with, try and track your Shepherd three times a week and make certain he always enjoys his work. If he becomes bored you are achieving nothing, in fact, you are probably doing more harm than good. You have been progressing too fast and making the tracks too hard for your dog to manage, so go back to easier, shorter tracks.

Shepherds vary considerably in their aptitude for tracking, with some knowing what to do right from the first track, and others needing a lot of persuasion before getting the message. Dogs that are natural trackers are also the ones we are most likely to push too hard, so be warned. Always consolidate each stage, making certain that your Shepherd is confident in what he is doing before moving on to the next. Regular work, making steady progress from one week to another, will produce a Shepherd who will track with confidence and precision at any level.

As you progress, take somebody out with you, preferably somebody experienced in tracking, who will lay tracks for you. However, make certain that whoever is helping you knows how to lay a track, and can tell you exactly where the track has gone, should your Shepherd lose his way. This is of vital importance. Nothing will undermine a dog's confidence more quickly than the handler trying to make him start again on a track which is not actually there because the track layer is not absolutely certain where it was laid!

Get your Shepherd used to working on different terrain, such as ploughed land, stubble, heather, winter crops or whatever else you can find. Even if you have to travel some way to find suitable land, it is well worth the trouble. You never know what sort of land you might have to track on when competing in a Trial. Always start with an easy track when first using a type of terrain your Shepherd is unused to. Always ask permission before using a piece of land, and please treat it with respect. Do not leave rubbish about or a gate open, and never let your Shepherd chase any stock which might be about. If you can establish a pleasant relationship with your local farmer, you will have no problem in finding suitable land, but you will have to prove to the farmer concerned that you are a responsible person and will not abuse his privileges. One last point. Be prepared to work your Shepherd in variable weather conditions. Do not be put off by a shower of rain; go out and work your Shepherd regardless.

SEARCH
This is only required in Working Trials. The Scent replaces the Search in Obedience, and we will

deal with this later. Neither is required for Schutzhund. All Working Trial Stakes require a Search. In CD, it is an area 15 metres square, marked by a post at each corner into which three articles have been placed by a stranger, unseen by either the dog or the handler. The articles can be anything, a sparking plug, a six-inch nail, a clothes peg, a piece of string etc. Your Shepherd must find all three, and present them to you within four minutes. In all other Stakes, the area is 25 metres square with four articles to find within five minutes. The articles usually get smaller as you progress from one stake to another.

For a Shepherd to Search well, he must have a good Retrieve. Hopefully, as mentioned in an earlier chapter, you have already been throwing articles into long grass and encouraging your dog to find them, as well as getting him used to retrieving all sorts of different articles, bringing them to you and presenting them without dropping or mouthing them. If your Shepherd can perform the above, keenly and happily, you are well on the way to a good Search. As with tracking, grass about 15 cm high is the best terrain on which to start your Shepherd in Search. Up to now, it has been fun, with you throwing things into long grass for the dog to find. Now, although still a game, the Search must become more formal,with your dog systematically searching an area 25 metres square, in which articles carrying human scent have been placed.

Mark out an area 25 metres square with a pole at each corner. With your Shepherd sitting beside you, facing into the wind, throw in two articles to land simultaneously fairly close to each other. Give your dog a command, such as "Find it", and let him go in to retrieve one. Having successfully found an article, give much praise, a titbit, and send him in again to find the second. If the dog hesitates, pretend to throw in another object, and encourage your Shepherd to go into the square again. Once your Shepherd is easily finding and bringing to hand the two articles he has seen you throw, try doing two about-turns on the spot before sending him in. Your dog will know roughly where the articles have landed, but will have to use his nose to find them.

When first starting a Search, use articles which are not big enough to be visible, but, equally, not so small that your Shepherd has a job to find them. Make certain that the dog is presenting them to you without either mouthing or dropping them. If he fails to do so, do not chastise, but go back to doing more practice on your Retrieve. It does not have to be a formal Present, as he does in a Retrieve or Recall, but the articles must be held by the dog until you choose to take them. When your Shepherd finds an article and either runs off or tries to chew it, it means you need a better Recall, so go back to practising this in all sorts of different situations. You can also put your dog on a long line when first working on a Search square to stop him running off, and also to keep him in the square.

Having successfully achieved the above, enlist the help of a friend, and get him/her to place eight or ten different articles on the side of the square. Let your Shepherd see them being placed. Now send your dog, and when he finds an article, give much praise, call him to you, take the article, give him a titbit and send him out again. Let him find four or five articles, and then stop. If your Shepherd starts getting bored after having found only two or three, stop, throw his favourite toy into the square, and finish for the day. Once your Shepherd is doing the above quickly and keenly, stop him from seeing your helper put the articles down. The next stage is to throw in the articles at random, then use smaller objects so that the dog cannot see them and must rely on his nose. Remember, always send your Shepherd either into or across the wind so that the scent of the articles is being blown towards him.

If your Shepherd goes out of the square, give a sharp command of "No" and call him back in, praising when he does so. Get your dog used to finding articles which have been put just inside a pole. Encourage him to search the whole square, not just part of it. You can move around the square but restrict your movements to the downwind, so that your body scent is not being blown across the square. Talk as little as possible, only speaking when you think your Shepherd has found an article. Too many commands will break his concentration. If your Shepherd starts to lose interest, you have been progressing too fast and using articles which are too small. So go back to larger articles and let the dog see you throw them in.

At the slightest sign of lack of enthusiasm, stop. As with tracking, you want a Shepherd who thoroughly enjoys using his nose and is keen to do so. Put ten or twelve articles, which are easy to find, into the square and let your dog bring out four or five. This will usually improve his enthusiasm. Preferably, use articles carrying somebody else's scent, not yours. When competing, your dog will never have to find articles carrying your scent. We use a 25 metre square when first starting the Search, so that our Shepherd gets used to working the full size. If he does a good Search in a 25 metre square, he will have no difficulty with the 15 metre CD square.

SCENT IN OBEDIENCE

The first Obedience Class to carry Scent Discrimination is Test A, which consists of a total of six cloths set out in a straight line, five of which are sterile and one which carries the handler's scent. In Test B there is a minimum of six and a maximum of ten cloths, one of which carries the handler's scent and another is a decoy, usually carrying the steward's scent. The rest are sterile. In Test C the judge's scent is on the cloth your Shepherd has to find, not yours. Two or more decoys are usually included among the sterile cloths. In all classes, scent-cloths must be minimum of 15cm by 15cm, and a maximum of 25cm by 25cm.

As with the Search, you must have a Shepherd who is a reliable retriever. Before starting this exercise, make certain your dog will retrieve a scent-cloth and bring it to hand without dropping or mouthing it. Having ascertained this, you can now proceed by letting your dog take hold of the scent-cloth, which you have previously held in your hand, so that it is also carrying your scent. Put down one sterile cloth and then the one you and your dog have both handled. With your Shepherd on the lead, give the command "Find" or "Scent", then take him up to the first cloth and let him smell that cloth. If he tries to pick it up, quietly say "No" and take him on to the next cloth. When he picks up the correct cloth, praise him, and with the dog still holding the cloth, take him back to where you started and finish as with a formal Retrieve. Let your Shepherd play with the cloth and try again, but this time put the cloths in the reverse order. Make certain he smells the sterile cloth before picking up yours. That is enough for one day.

Next day, put down two sterile cloths plus your scented one, which should be at the end of the line. Repeat as before. After two or three days, dispense with letting the dog scent the cloth – just put your own scent on it. Let the dog get your scent from the cloth by holding it 5-6cm from his nose for two or three seconds. Then get a helper to put the scented cloth into the line using tongs to do so. This avoids contaminating the cloth with any other scent. Do not let your dog see in what position the scented cloth has been put down, and do not make a big thing about getting your dog to take scent. He has been sitting close to you and walking with you, so by now he should know what you smell like!

In Test A and Test B, once you have scented the cloth it is taken away from you by a steward and put somewhere into the line of sterile cloths – neither you nor your dog know where. Give your Shepherd scent by using your hand, in the same way as you did the cloth. Now proceed. With the dog still on the lead, make certain he scents every cloth, and if he shows any sign of picking up the wrong one, give a firm command of "No". When you are certain your dog knows what to do, try off lead.

Once your Shepherd is finding the right cloth every time, regardless of where it is in the line, you can start using decoys. Get your helper to put his or her scent on another cloth and then put that into the line. Use tongs, so the same person can then put your scented cloth into the line, but not next to the decoy. Put your Shepherd back on the lead and, as before, walk down the line of cloths, making certain he smells every one. When he comes to the decoy, if he tries to pick it up, give a firm command of "No" and go on to the next cloth. When your dog finds the right cloth, continue as you did before.

In Test C there will be two or more decoys scented by different people, and it is the judge's scent on the cloth your Shepherd has to find, not yours. Before trying this, ensure your dog will find the right cloth (your scented one) in spite of two or more decoys among the line of sterile cloths. Try putting the scent cloths in a circle, or two lines at right angles to each other, or any other way you can think of. By changing the pattern you can check that your Shepherd really understands what to do.

When you start training for Test C Scent, be patient and progress slowly. Your Shepherd must now realise that your scented cloth is no longer there, but he must still locate a certain cloth – the one you have given him scent from – and not any of the decoys. Hold the scented cloth by the corner (being careful not to get any of your scent on it) in front of your dog's nose for a few seconds, and then let your helper put it into the line of sterile cloths. To start with, do not put down any decoys. Your Shepherd will soon get the idea, especially as there is nothing there with your scent on it. Before putting decoys down again, try to get as many different people as possible to scent a cloth, so that your Shepherd learns that the one from which you give him scent is the one he must locate.

SUMMARY

In all forms of Nosework, we have no idea exactly what our Shepherd is smelling. On a track there must be many other scents, such as rabbits or foxes, but we must train our dogs to ignore all these and keep to the track laid by one particular person, even though somebody else might have crossed the track. In a Working Trials Search, your Shepherd has to bring out, in a certain time, all articles carrying human scent. You will be surprised what they will sometimes bring you!

The wind plays an important part in all Nosework. In an Obedience Scent, the wind will sometimes blow your scent on to some of the other cloths. Your Shepherd might then bring out the first cloth carrying your scent, even though it might be only a whiff, so you must train the dog to ignore those and only bring out the one heavily impregnated with your scent. Practise in windy conditions, so your dog knows what to do. Whatever type of Nosework you are doing, progress slowly and carefully, making certain that your Shepherd knows exactly what is required before progressing to the next stage. We cannot stress this point enough.

Throughout this book, we have described a system by which you can train your Shepherd using titbits and toys as well as verbal praise. The emphasis is always on fun training and making everything a game. But we must be absolutely honest and admit there are times when all dogs, however well-trained, need reprimanding. We believe that the occasional good shaking or slap on the backside will not come amiss, provided – and this is most important – that you are absolutely certain your dog is really playing you up, and not doing something because he does not really understand what is required.

Let us give you an example: Clarissa was working a dog in UD who had just completed a full mark track and was going really well. He always did a good Search, so Clarissa was confident he would not fail her today. How wrong can you be! He went into the Search square with great enthusiasm, located all four articles, then stood in the middle, wagging his tail and looking at Clarissa as if to say: "I know where they all are, but I am not going to bring them out and you cannot do a thing about it!" Minutes ticked by and despite encouragement and commands, he stood there just grinning at her and doing nothing.

So Clarissa said to the judge: "Can I go in and teach him a lesson? I know I will be sacrificing all my marks, but I do not want this to become a habit." The judge agreed and Clarissa went into the square, gave her Shepherd a good shaking, brought him out, told him to get on with it in no uncertain terms, and sent him in again. He brought all four articles out in next to no time, looking very confident and pleased with himself. Clarissa could have quite cheerfully killed him, but all she did was to give lots of praise and tell him what a good and clever boy he was! He never did it again, so it was worth sacrificing all the Search marks in order to safeguard the future.

NOSEWORK TESTS OVERSEAS

The Working Trials and Obedience we have described in this book are currently used in the UK but not necessarily in other countries. Each country has its own particular Tests and although the basics, such as Heelwork, Recalls, Retrieves, Stays etc. are the same, there are variations so it is best to get details of these Tests from the Kennel Club of whichever country you live in so that you know exactly what is required from you and your Shepherd. Let us give you an example.

In Norway the Tests are a mixture between our Working Trials and Schutzhund. However, no Protection work is allowed in any Test unless performed by police or army dogs. For instance the Track in the first Test (B) is 300m. long, an hour old and you have twelve minutes in which to complete and it is usually laid in a wood. In the second Test (A), the track is 3,500m long and 6 hours old with 25-30 articles on it. You are allowed 1 1/2 hours to get round and presumably to find all the articles.

The Search is similar to ours for the first Test. A 20m x 20m square in which 4 articles have, unlike our Working Trials, been placed an hour previous to you working it. You are allowed 8 mins in which to find the articles. The harder Test (A) has a Search similar to that in our PD Stake in as much as you have a much larger area to cover and have 5 articles to find, one of which is a person. The other articles are large such as a rain jacket or rucksack. The time allowed is 11/2 hours. In our PD Stake you have a person to find but no articles. For the other exercises some are like those in Schutzhund and some like UK Working Trials.

We give you details of the above so as to give you some idea as to how exercises can differ from one country to another. So your best plan is to contact the Kennel Club of your country, your premier GSD Breed Club and also your country's Schutzhund Club for all details. For the UK, get from the Kennel Club their current year book which will give you all details of Working Trials and Obedience. All details of Schutzhund Stakes are given in the WUSV International Working Dog Evaluation Regulations, obtainable from the Secretary of the BSA (British Schutzhund Association).

Chapter Thirteen

PROTECTION WORK

BY ERIC ROBERTS

From an early age Eric Roberts has been interested in dog training, working his first two dogs very quickly up to Ch. Test C Class in Obedience. After a spell in Germany, where he had some contact with the German training system, he returned to the UK and started working a GSD bitch, Amanda of Wallbank, who soon qualified Ch. Test C. In the mid-sixties Eric turned his hand to Working Trials where Amanda quickly qualified TD Ex. His next dog, Callan, took him to Working Trials PD Stake. From then on he went from strength to strength making up WT Ch. Callan's Son of Callanway, who won many working awards.

In 1989 Eric became interested in Schutzhund and is now the National Training Advisor to the British Schutzhund Association (BSA). His dog, Flute, became the first dog to qualify Sch.III and was also the first to gain a World Union title. Eric is the first British qualified Schutzhund Judge.

He is a professional trainer, a behaviour consultant and runs the Callanway Dog Training Centre, near Dumfries. He is married, has three young sons and a married daughter.

WHAT IS PROTECTION WORK?

Training the German Shepherd in obedience and other aspects of practical work is covered in the preceding chapters of this book, but it is in the role of a 'Protection dog' that the German Shepherd really comes into his own. The armed forces, police, security and private sector all over the world select the German Shepherd above any other breed for advanced training in protection work. No one can seriously dispute the fact that this breed has no equal in the canine world as a companion dog who can be relied upon, through correct training and understanding, to protect in a safe and reliable manner; to show courage and yet great powers of controlability.

Protection work must not, however, be mistaken for guard dog duties. There are many breeds who can equal and even better the role of guard dog than the German Shepherd. The term 'guard dog' often conjures up images of severe aggression and ferocity – a dog that is not to be trusted. This kind of dog receives little or no training at all, and is selected purely for the reasons given. A true protection dog is a dog trained in the correct way to react in certain situations or to certain stimuli, and because of this training, to be responsive to commands and under full control. By far the most common product of correct selection and training in protection work is the operational police dog. The ideal police dog is one of sound temperament, character and trainability. When trained in the correct techniques, this dog becomes an ideal companion and asset to the police dog-handler and his family. He is confident and friendly, but when required, is capable of performing protection duties with efficiency and control. It must be remembered that the off-duty police dog spends his leisure time at the home of his dog-handler, and in many cases doubling as a family pet.

DEVELOPING SCHUTZHUND

Modern day police dog work is relatively recent although hounds had been used for tracking, and other breeds, such as the Airedale, had been used for attack work. It was from the continent that the police dog, as we know it, came into being. The founder of the German Shepherd breed, Max von Stephanitz, chose the attributes of the German Shepherd for working ability as well as shape and beauty – in fact, he put more emphasis on the former. It was therefore in Germany that the modern-day police and service dog was born.

At the turn of the century, the German Shepherd was already making a name for himself on the continent as an extraordinary dog of great intelligence and trainability. But it was from the First World War that the British really became aware of this great animal, and from the dogs imported to the UK after the war, enthusiasts started to emulate what they had witnessed overseas. Great pioneers of the breed, such as Lt. Col. J.Y Baldwin of the famous early Picardy kennel, began to make visits to Germany to study not only their breeding techniques but also the working ability and training methods.

Apart from the German Shepherd being a great asset to the armed forces on the continent, a civilian sport or pastime was beginning to take off with great fervour. This sport became known as Schutzhund, which when translated simply means 'protection dog'. This sport became extremely popular, and was also necessary for the selection of correct, trainable types of German Shepherd. Over the decades that followed, Schutzhund became almost Germany's second national sport, and remains so today. Likewise in Britain, the sport of Working Trials was born, with the top class for protection work being called the 'Police Dog Stakes' In the late eighties this was renamed 'Patrol Dog Stakes', but more commonly referred to as the PD Stake – a term that I will use for the remainder of this chapter.

It is sometimes hard to comprehend that this sport was happening in the 1920s, yet it took over twenty years before the British police forces started to take notice. They realised what was happening on the continent, and by the fact that the British armed forces were very involved with the German Shepherd Dog and its training. They also witnessed the progress being made by the British enthusiasts, some of whom were policemen, in the Kennel Club Working Trials sport. Wheels were put into motion, and serious police dog training in Britain was started in the late 1940s, and with more fervour in the 1950s.

TRAINING FOR PROTECTION WORK
As this book has been written for the German Shepherd enthusiast and would-be enthusiast, the remainder of this chapter will be devoted to the training of the German Shepherd for the sports of protection work, i.e Schutzhund and Working Trials Patrol Dog Stakes, thus incorporating some police training exercises.

Although both these sports have other phases of work in their schedule, such as tracking, agility and obedience or control, the main differences lie in the protection work. In the Kennel Club PD Stake, protection work only appears in the top class, whereas in the Schutzhund sport, protection work is included much earlier, thus giving the dog an elementary level before progressing into more advanced work. In the British version of the sport, the tests take the form of a more practical police situation – with all the excitement of not knowing in what order or what form the plot will evolve. Whereas in Schutzhund, the sport is as much for spectator-appeal as for competitors, therefore the tests tend to be more stabilised to give consistency and uniformity.

Before training can commence in the protection phase for these sports, or for any other reason, it must be understood that control must be the most important consideration. There are many techniques and methods used to train a dog for protection work, and differences of opinion as to what is the right age, and the right stage to start training. For example, on the continent it is quite common to train the dog in protection work first, and aim for control later. My own opinion, after many years of involvement in both these sports is to aim for a high standard of control, and at the same time create a very playful attitude to the game of pulling or tug-of-war. The control training must never be over-compulsive, so as to stop the dog from being allowed to pursue his natural motivation to play and pull – referred to in some training circles as the 'prey drive'. In fact, we need to consider and understand certain drives in the dog before we take our training seriously.

PREY DRIVE

This is the dog's natural desire to show interest in or to chase anything that moves. In the wild it would, of course, have been his way of catching his food and surviving, or, at leisure, romping, grabbing and wrestling with his litter or packmates. In the domestic dog, the desire is still present by instinct, and for protection work it is a great asset to the trainer. The 'prey' is replaced by a sack or a purpose-made hessian bite-bar (see Chapter Nine: Choosing A Discipline), so that the dog can focus his interest and attention on this object. Through training, the dog's drive for the object becomes stronger, and if he is allowed to win the object as a prize, then his desire to continue in this play game grows. Later, the bite-roll is replaced by the protection sleeve and the transition is usually automatic.

DEFENCE DRIVE

This is the dog's natural instinct to show something or someone that all is not well with their presence or their attitude. This drive takes many different forms, depending on the natural courage or confidence within the dog. Alternatively, the dog could be lacking in confidence or be of nervous disposition. Although an ideal asset to the guard dog, care must be taken when using this drive in protection training. In the past, particularly with service dogs, it was by taking advantage of the defence drive that protection work was achieved, and to a large extent this is still the case. However, with the strong relationship between civilian and police training fraternity, both in Britain and on the continent, there is a tendency to change and the Prey Drive technique is generally regarded as the best way to start the dog in protection work training.

Later, as the dog progresses, the individual must decide on the amount of defence drive to be introduced. In the sport of Working Trials or Schutzhund, however, I have found time and time again that a very strong prey drive, with just a little defence, to be the ideal compromise for a high standard of efficiency and, most important, control. Generally speaking, the higher the defence drive in the dog, the harder he is to control.

'LEAVE' ON COMMAND

Having created a strong prey drive in the dog, and when the dog will willingly take a firm hold of the bite-bar or protection sleeve, consideration must then be given to teaching the dog to leave go of the sleeve on command. This is referred to as the 'Leave' or 'Out' Again, several methods exist for the training of this part of the exercise, and it usually depends on the way in which the bite was taught in the first place. Severe compulsive methods can be avoided if the dog is high in prey drive and an alternative reward is given when the dog leaves go of the sleeve. The 'Out' becomes more difficult if the dog is strong in defence drive – another good reason for the drives within the dog being of correct balance. When the dog is taking a firm bite and leaving on command (although the winning of the sleeve as a prize must never be totally taken out of the training), the person wearing the sleeve can become more physical and more assertive with the dog by moving quickly into and away from the dog with noise and threatening gestures. The dog is only called Out when this person stands still. In the PD Stake and in police dog training circles, this person is referred to as the 'criminal' and in the Schutzhund sport he is referred to as the 'helper'. As the latter indicates that the handler and the dog are being helped by this person in the training of the dog, then this is the term I shall use for the remainder of this chapter.

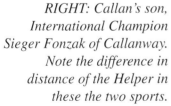

ABOVE: Working Trials Champion Callans Son of Callanway containing a suspect.

RIGHT: Callan's son, International Champion Sieger Fonzak of Callanway. Note the difference in distance of the Helper in these the two sports.

BARKING ON COMMAND

Having taught the dog to take a firm hold of the protection sleeve and possibly to leave on command, we now need to consider teaching the dog to bark at the helper. Sometimes you may have a little luck and find that the dog automatically barks when the helper teases the dog a little, and, in fact, the barking can come naturally this way. However, on occasions some dogs take a little longer before a good bark at the helper is achieved. Once again, several methods and techniques are used to incite the dog to bark, and again, one chapter is not enough to go into great detail for all methods.

However, if the helper runs away a few paces and begins to throw the sleeve from side to side, the dog will usually get excited enough to give a bark. As soon as this happens, the dog must be rewarded by a bite on the sleeve, thus impressing the dog that the bark gave him victory. Alternatively, the helper can run out of sight from the dog but when coming into sight, tease the dog with the sleeve and disappear again. This can cause frustration in the dog, and thereby result in a bark from the dog. Should this be the case, the dog is rewarded as in the previous method. Whatever method is decided upon, I would personally try to avoid a defence method, particularly with a young dog.

LOCATING A HIDDEN PERSON

Having taught the bark, we are now ready to start the locating of a hidden person. Let us start with Schutzhund, as this is a relatively easy exercise to achieve. The event or test takes place in an area about the size of a football field or slightly less. Six purpose-made 'hides' are used for this exercise, three being along one side of the arena and three along the other side. The dog must check the hides by running to and around them, finally ending up at the one containing the helper. On doing so, the dog must bark until the arrival of the handler, who has been walking down the centre of the field, directing his dog from one hide to the next.

In the PD Stake and in practical police dog work, the exercise becomes a little more difficult. The Judge may require the helper to be hidden up a tree, concealed in a vehicle, in a ditch, or anything that simulates a practical situation. Whatever the discipline, the dog is taught by watching the helper go to the hiding place and then being released. On locating and barking, the dog is given his reward. A different hide is used and the exercise repeated. After several different hides on the one field are used, then the dog is taken away while the helper goes into his elected hiding place. The dog is then sent to check the other hides first, then redirected to the successful hide, and again receiving his reward. Rewards tend to be used more in the Schutzhund sport than the PD sport, consequently, I think it fair to say that the location is, generally speaking, more impressive from the Schutzhund-trained dog. However, the PD trained dog is trained in a more practical way and is more capable of a true search for a hidden person.

In theory at least, we have now got a dog that will search for a hidden person, bark on finding the person, chase and detain should the person try to escape, and defend the handler should an attack be imminent. Let us now consider exercises that separate the two sports, or, in fact, separate the sports from the police dog training schedule.

RECALL FROM RUNNING PERSON

This is when a person running away is challenged by the dog handler; the dog is released to give chase, and when the dog is at least equidistant between handler and escaping person, the handler will be required to stop the dog and recall it back. This is applicable to the PD Stake only, and is one of the hardest exercises to teach in any of the sports. Over-teaching of this exercise can easily result in lack of drive within the dog to chase and detain. Dogs have been known to be sent after a running person, only to turn round and return without a command. It is therefore essential to maintain the correct balance, as constantly demonstrated by the top handlers in this sport.

THE 'STAND OFF'

A person running away is again challenged by the dog handler. The dog is then released to detain the person, who, as the dog closes in, will turn to face the dog and stand still. The dog is then required to circle and bark at the detained person until the arrival of the dog handler. This exercise is only applicable to the Police Dog training schedule, but at the time of writing this chapter, I believe it is being discussed by the Schutzhund sport as an alternative to the courage test.

Having compared the two sports in the field of protection work, let us now take a look at the separate schedules for comparison, remembering again that there are other phases of work for the dog to undergo as well as protection work. e.g. nosework, agility and obedience.

THE KENNEL CLUB PATROL DOG STAKE

QUARTERING THE GROUND (for 45 points): The missing person should be protected to the minimum extent consistent with safety. He should remain motionless and out of sight of the handler, but should be accessible on investigation to a dog which has winded him. The Judge should satisfy himself that the dog has found the person, and has given warning spontaneously and emphatically without being directed by the handler. Once the person has been detected and the dog has given voice, he may offer meat or other food, which should be refused by the dog. If the dog ignores the food it may be thrown to the ground in front of the dog. A dog which bites the person or criminal must be severely penalised.

TEST OF COURAGE (for 20 points): This is a test of courage rather than of control. Dogs will not be heavily penalised in this test for lack of control. Handlers must be prepared to have the dog tested when on the lead by an unprotected Judge or steward and/or off-lead by a protected steward. The method of testing will be at the discretion of the Judge.

SEARCH AND ESCORT (for 25 points): The criminal will be searched by the Handler with the dog off-lead at the Sit, Stand or Down. The Judge will assess whether the dog is well-placed tactically and ready to defend if called to do so. The handler will then be told to escort the prisoner or prisoners at least thirty yards in a certain direction. He will give at least one turn on the direction of the Judge. During this exercise, the criminal will turn and attempt to overcome the handler. The dog may defend spontaneously or on command, and must release the criminal at once when he stands still or when the handler calls him off. The handler should be questioned as to his tactics in positioning the dog in both the search and escort.

RECALL FROM RUNNING CRIMINAL (for 30 points): The criminal, protected to the minimum extent consistent with safety, will be introduced to the handler whose dog will be free at heel. After an unheated conversation, the criminal will run away. At a reasonable distance, the handler will be ordered to send his dog. When the dog is approximately halfway between the handler and the criminal, he will be ordered to be recalled. The Recall may be by whistle or voice. The criminal should continue running until he returns or closes. It the dog continues to run alongside the criminal, the criminal should run a further ten or so paces to indicate this.

PURSUIT AND DETENTION OF A CRIMINAL (for 30 points): The criminal (a different one for choice) and handler should be introduced as above and the dog sent forward under the same

A PD Attack by Working Trials Champion Callan's Son of Callanway.

A Schutzhund Courage Test by International Champion Sieger Fonzak of Callenway. Note the difference in protective clothing.

conditions. The criminal must continue to attempt to escape and, if possible, should do so through some exit or in a vehicle once the dog has had a chance to catch up with him. The dog must be rewarded as having succeeded if he clearly prevents the criminal from continuing his line of flight, either by holding him by the arm. knocking him over, or close-circling him until he becomes giddy. If the dog fails to make a convincing attempt to detain the criminal, he should lose any marks that he may have been obtained in the Recall exercise.

TOTAL POINTS 150

In Schutzhund there are three grades of efficiency; for comparison to the PD Stake we will consider the highest.

SCHUTZHUND III

SEARCH FOR HELPER (for 5 points): The helper is placed into a designated hiding place while the handler and dog are out of sight. The helper must be placed in such a manner that it is possible for the dog to search five or six times to the side. The handler is to walk down an imaginary centre-line of the field during the Search exercise. The dog should quickly move away from the handler upon receiving voice and hand signals, and deeply and extensively search the area. When the dog completes a side Search, the handler may call the dog to return, and with a new command, direct the dog in a different direction. Occasional searches to the rear are not faulty.

HOLD AND BARK (for 10 points): As soon as the dog has reached the helper, the handler must stop. The dog must bark continuously at the helper. At the request of the Judge, the handler proceeds up to four paces from the hiding place, and upon further direction from the Judge recalls the dog. The handler now orders the helper from the hiding place and commands the dog into a Down position in front of the helper. The handler searches the helper and then moves into the hiding place to search for any discarded objects.

ESCAPE AND DEFENCE (for 35 points): At the request of the Judge, the helper now attempts to escape by running swiftly away. The dog must stop the escape by a firm grip and holds on the helper immediately and with spellbound attention. When the helper ceases the escape and stands quietly, the dog must release the grip. Upon direction from the Judge, the helper attacks the dog using the flexible stick as a defence weapon, but not striking the dog at first. The dog must immediately move into the attack by firmly gripping, and must stop the helper from further aggression. When the dog has firmly gripped, two hits are permitted. The helper now stands still and the dog releases his grip. The handler steps to the dog and the helper is asked to step back.

TRANSPORT (for 5 points): A back transport of the helper for approximately 40 paces is now performed. The handler orders the dog to heel and directs the helper to move forward. The handler and dog follow at a distance of about five paces.

ATTACK (for 10 points): After the transport, an attack by the helper on the handler occurs. The dog must stop the attack with an energetic grip. The helper is now disarmed, and a side transport to the Judge is performed. The handler leaves the field with the free-heeling dog.

PURSUIT (for 10 points): The Judge now directs another helper into a hiding place at a distance of about 100 paces. The handler and free-heeling dog are instructed to move to a designated spot from which the pursuit of the fleeing helper will take place. When instructed by the Judge, the helper leaves the hiding place and after being ordered to stop, attempts to flee. The helper will not react to the orders to stop. The handler will now command the dog to pursue. When the dog is approaching the helper, he will turn and try to intimidate the dog with harsh, threatening motions. Without being influenced by the helper, the dog holds the helper with a firm grip. Now the helper stops the aggression and stands quietly. The dog must let go.

COURAGE TEST (for 25 points): Upon direction from the Judge, the helper again attacks the dog using the flexible stick as a defence weapon. When the dog has firmly gripped, two stick hits are permitted. The dog maintains his grip until the helper stops his aggression, then the dog must let go. The handler will remain for about thirty seconds without influencing the dog. He will then proceed to the dog and disarm the helper. A side transport to the Judge concludes the exercise and the handler leaves the field with a free heeling dog.

SUMMARY

As mentioned earlier, one chapter on protection work is not enough to go into great detail in every method for every exercise. The purpose of this chapter has been to give an insight into the history of the modern-day 'Protection Dog', and to give some basic facts and methods of training for the competition dog. Although not every German Shepherd owner will rise to the heights of competition and probably may never get involved in Protection training, this chapter will help the German Shepherd enthusiast to understand their dog and its potential. Most of all, it is to remind them that the German Shepherd Dog is a working dog, and every Shepherd not worked in some way is a Shepherd wasted.

In the UK all details of Schutzhund Stakes are given in the WUSV International Working Dog Evaluation Regulations, obtainable from the Secretary of the BSA (British Schutzhund Association).

Chapter Fourteen

THE BREED STANDARD

This is a blueprint of what a perfect Shepherd should look like. It is far more explicit than that of many other breeds as it specifies proportions and angles, giving very detailed descriptions of characteristics and movement. It always surprises us that this Standard, with all its details and guidelines, can be so freely interpreted by some judges. The Standard we are using for interpretation is the authentic WUSV (World Union of German Shepherd Dog Clubs), which is the one used throughout most of the world.

World Sieger and Double Sieger Fanto von Hirschel: Many people throughout the world consider this dog to be the best at this time.

SKELETON OF THE GERMAN SHEPHERD.

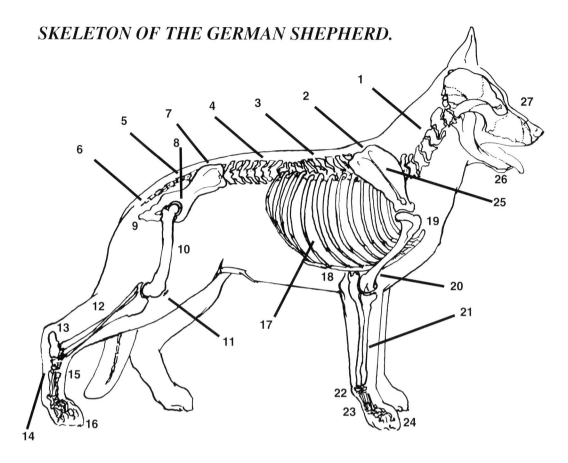

KEY

1. CERVICAL (NECK) VERTEBRAE (7)
2. DORSAL (WITHER) VERTEBRAE (13)
3. DORSAL (BACK) VERTEBRAE (13)
4. LUMBAR (LOIN) VERTEBRAE (7)
5. SACRUM (CROUP) VERTEBRAE (3 FUSED)
6. COCCYGEAL (TAIL) VERTEBRAE (16-22)
7. ILIUM (PIN BONE)
8. PELVIC BONE
9. ISCHIUM (SITTING BONE)
10. FEMUR (UPPER THIGH)
11. PATELLA (KNEE JOINT)
12. TIBIA AND FIBULA (LOWER THIGH)
13. OSCALSIS (POINT OF HOCK)
14. TARSUS (HOCK JOINT, 7 BONES)
15. METATARSUS (HOCK, 5 BONES)
16. PHALANGES (TOES, 12 BONES)
17. RIB BONES (13 PAIRS)
18. STERNUM (BREAST BONE)
19. PROSTERNUM (POINT OF BREAST BONE)
20. HUMERUS (UPPER ARM)
21. ULNA AND RADIUS (FOREARM)
22. CARPUS (PASTERN JOINT, 7 BONES)
23. METACARPALS (PASTERN, 5 BONES)
24. PHALANGES (TOES, 14 BONES)
25. SCAPULA (SHOULDER BLADE)
26. MANDIBLE (LOWER JAW)
27. NASAL BONE

THE WORLD UNION STANDARD OF THE GERMAN SHEPHERD DOG

The Verein fuer Deutsche Schaeferhunde (SV or German Shepherd Dog Club), with its business seat in Augsburg, Germany, and a member of the 'Verband fuer das Deutsche Hundewesen' (German Kennel Club), is, as the country/club of origin of the breed, responsible for the Breed Standard of the German Shepherd Dog. This Standard was originally developed at the first membership meeting of the club in Frankfurt/Main, Germany, on September 20th 1899, based on proposals made by A. Meyer and von Stephanitz. Amendments were made to the Standard during the VI membership meeting on July 28th 1901; also at the XXIII membership meeting in Cologne/Rhine, Germany, on September 17th 1909; the Board of Directors' meeting in Wiesbaden, Germany, on September 5th 1930; and the Breed Committee and Board of Directors' meeting on March 25th 1961. The Standard was revised by the Welt-Union der Vereine fuer Deutsche Schaeferhunde (World Union of German Shepherd Dog Clubs – the WUSV) and approved during its meeting on August 30th 1976.

The German Shepherd Dog, whose planned breeding was started after the founding of the Club in 1899, was first bred out of dogs which originated from Central and South German stock of herding dogs, with the final aim of creating and breeding a dog highly suitable for the most demanding utility work. Based on this, the Standard of the German Shepherd Dog was designed to emphasise correct physical structure, and particularly a sound temperament and a strong character.

Study the skeleton carefully and get thoroughly conversant with the various points of the Shepherd and where they are situated. Now read the Standard.

1. GENERAL APPEARANCE

The German Shepherd Dog is a medium-sized dog. His height is measured by taking a perpendicular line from the withers – with the coat parted or pushed down – to the ground, touching the elbow. The ideal height is 62.5 cm for males and 57.5 cm for females. A deviation of 2.5 cm above or below the ideal height is permissible. Both over-size or under-size diminish the working and breeding value of the dog.

The German Shepherd Dog is slightly long in body, strong and well-muscled. His bones are dry and their texture is dense. The proportion of the height to the length of the body, and the angulation of the fore- and hindquarters, must be in such a relationship as to assure a far-reaching, enduring trot. He has a weather-resistant coat. A harmonious appearance is desirable; however, the workability and overall use of the German Shepherd Dog are of primary importance. The secondary sex characteristics are strongly marked, and every animal should exhibit a definite expression of masculinity or femininity according to sex.

To an observer, the first impression of a German Shepherd Dog, according to the Breed Standard, presents a picture of great strength, intelligence, and agility, well-proportioned and balanced in every respect. It must be clearly evident, by the way in which he moves and reacts, that a sound mind lives in a sound body, thus meeting the physical and mental prerequisites of the extreme endurance of a dog always ready to perform his duties as an all-round working dog.

Only the trained specialist is able to determine the presence of the characteristics in the German Shepherd Dog required for a good working dog. Therefore, only Specialty judges should judge this breed at shows, and they must test the exhibited dogs regarding temperament and gun-shyness. The rating of 'Excellent' should only be awarded if the German Shepherd Dog has a recognized working title (i.e. Schultzhund Title).

Exhibiting an exuberant temperament, he should be easy to handle, easily adapting to each situation, and always willing and able to joyfully carry out his assigned tasks. He must show

Odin v. Tannenmeise, Sch III, FH, VA showing correct topline and overall proportions.

courage and strength of character, when it becomes necessary to defend his master or his master's property. He also must be willing to attack if his master so commands. However, on the other hand, he must be an attentive and pleasant house companion, friendly toward the family and family surroundings, especially towards children and other animals, and at ease in the presence of strangers. The ideal dog is stamped with a look of quality, nobility and respect demanding self-assurance.

2. ANGULATION AND GAIT

The German Shepherd is a trotting dog. His gait, the movement of his front and rear legs, is in diagonal sequence, which means that he has two diagonally opposite feet on the ground while the other two diagonally opposite feet are off the ground. Therefore, his forequarters and hindquarters must be angulated in such a way to allow him to propel himself forward by a long step of the hindleg, compensating for this stride by a long step of the foreleg. While trotting, the back should appear steady and smooth and should not indicate any movement. The correct proportion of length of height and respective length of the bones permit a far-reaching gait, travelling, seemingly effortlessly, close to the ground with the head stretched forward, the tail slightly raised, and showing a soft curved line from the tip of the ear over the neck and back to the tip of the tail.

3. TEMPERAMENT, CHARACTERISTICS AND DISPOSITION

Good, sound nerves; attentiveness, self-confidence, trainability, willingness to guard, faithfulness, an incorruptible character as well as courage, willingness to attack if so commanded, and vigour are the most pronounced characteristics of the pure-bred German Shepherd Dog. He is fit and willing to serve in any capacity as companion, utility dog, guard dog, sentry dog, leader of the blind and herding dog.

His sense of smell, in combination with the body structure of a trotting dog, make it possible for him to track steadily and surely, with the nose close to the ground and without physical exertion. This makes him highly suitable for various tracking and search dog purposes.

4. HEAD

The size of the head should be in porportion to the body (the length being approximately 40 per cent of the body's height at the withers); it should not appear to be too broad, nor too fine or too pointed. It should be dry and of moderate width between the ears.

FOREHEAD: Viewed from the side and front, moderately arched without, or with just a slight, centre indentation.

CHEEKS: The cheeks are slightly rounded and are not protruding.

SKULL: (Approximately 50 per cent of the length of the head.) The upper part of the head, viewed from above, gradually tapers from the ears to the tip of the nose into the wedge-shaped, long muzzle (with a strongly developed upper and lower jaw). The stop is gradual. The width of the skull should be about as broad as its length, although it is acceptable if this measurement exceeds slightly in a male and is slightly less in the female.

MUZZLE: The muzzle is strong, the flews are tight and firmly fitted. The nasal ridge runs parallel to the imaginary extended line of the forehead.

5. TEETH

With complete dentition, the teeth must be healthy and strong (42 teeth, 20 in the upper jaw and 22 in the lower jaw). The German Shepherd Dog has a scissor bite, i.e. the upper incisors fit closely over the lower incisors. Overshot or undershot are faults, as are larger spaces between the teeth. An even, level, or pincer bite is also faulty, i.e. the meeting of front teeth at the edges, with no overlap of upper or lower teeth. The jaws must be strongly developed, and the teeth deeply imbedded into the jaws.

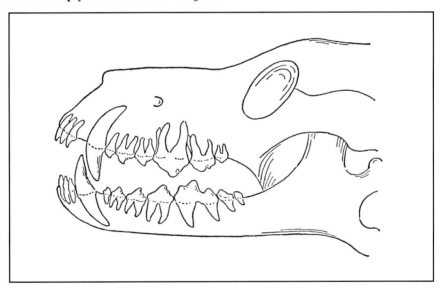

Permanent teeth: The upper jaw contains six incisors, two canine, eight premolars and four molars. The lower jaw contains six incisors, two canines, eight premolars and six molars. a total of forty-two teeth.

DENTITION: The four bites that can be found in a German Shepherd. Undershot mouths are rare but occasionally seen.

Level bite: The incisors striking edge to edge.

Scissors bite: The upper incisors striking just along the the front face of the lower ones.

Overshot: The top incisors extended out beyond the lower incisors.

Undershot: The lower incisors extending beyond the upper incisors.

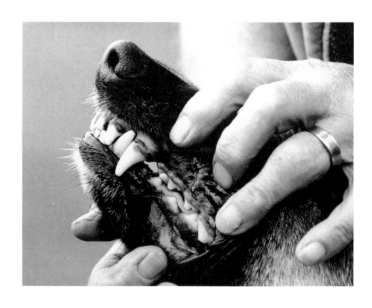

Correct scissor bite.

6. EARS
Of medium size, broad at the base, high set, carried erect (not bent toward the centre of the head), they are pointed and the ear shell is directed forward. Tipped ears, cropped ears and hanging ears are disqualifying. Ears bent towards the centre of the head excessively affect the image of the breed. Up to the age of six months, sometimes longer, and during teething, puppies occasionally have hanging or inward-bent ears. While moving or while lying down, many dogs fold the ears. This is not a fault.

7. EYES
Of medium size, almond-shaped, slightly oblique, and not protruding. Colour according to the coat colour of the dog, as dark as possible, with a lively, intelligent, self-assured expression.

8. NECK
Strong and muscular with well-developed muscles, without dewlap. Carried horizontally, at a 45 degree angle. When excited carried higher, while trotting carried lower.

9. BODY
The length of the body should exceed the height at the withers. It should be 110 per cent to 117 per cent the height at the withers. Dogs which are short in overall length, square, and high on the legs are undesirable.
CHEST: Deep (approximately 45-48 per cent of height at the withers), however not too broad. Lower chest and brisket as long as possible and well-developed.
RIBS: Well-developed and long, neither barrel-shaped nor too flat, the sternum reaching to the elbows. A correctly formed ribcage permits free movement of the elbows while the dog is trotting. An excessively round ribcage causes the elbows to be too tight. The ribcage reaches far back, and the loins are proportionately short.
BELLY: Moderately tucked up.
BACK: Including loins, straight and strongly-developed. Not too long between the withers and croup. The withers must be long and sufficiently high, well-pronounced and, in contrast to the back, gradually sloping into the back without an interruption of the topline, slightly sloping towards the rear.
LOINS: Broad, strong and well-muscled.
CROUP: Long, slightly sloping (approximately 23 degrees). The pelvis bone forms the foundation. Steep or straight croups are undesirable.

11. TAIL
Bushy-haired, reaching at least to the hock joint, not extending beyond the centre of the hock. Even though undesirable, occasionally it forms a slight, sideward-bent hook at the end. When in repose it forms a slight curve; when excited, and when in motion, the tail is raised. However, it should not be raised beyond a horizontal line. Therefore, the tail should not be carried straight up or rolled over the back. Artificially-cut tails are a disqualification.

12. FOREQUARTERS

SHOULDER BLADE: Long, diagonal (approximately at a 45 degree angle) and lying flat. The upper arm connects at an approximately right angle to the shoulder blade. Just like the shoulders, it must be strong and well-muscled.

FORELEG: The foreleg is straight when viewed from all sides. The bones of the upper arm and foreleg are more oval than round.

PASTERN: Strong, but not too steep and not too soft, forming approximately a 20 degree angle.

ELBOWS: Neither turned in, nor out. The length of the foreleg should extend beyond the lowest point of the brisket (approximately 55 per cent).

13. HINDQUARTERS

UPPER THIGHS: Broad with strong muscles. Viewed from the side, the upper thighs are diagonal to the lower thighs, which connect at an angle of approximately 120 degrees. The angulation approximates that of the forequarters, without being over-angulated.

HOCK JOINTS: Strong and firm. The metatarsus is strong and, with the lower thigh, forms a strong hock joint. The hindquarters in general must be strong and well-muscled in order to be able to effortlessly drive the body forward while gaiting.

14. FEET

A German Shepherd Dog's feet should be round, short, compact and arched.

PADS: Very hard, however, not brittle.

NAILS: Short and strong, dark in colour.

DEWCLAWS: Occasionally a puppy is born with dewclaws on the hindlegs, which should be removed within the first few days after birth.

15. COLOUR

Black with evenly-distributed brown, yellow to light-grey markings, also with a black saddle, sable (indication of black with a grey or light brown base with respective lighter markings), black, grey, unicoloured or with lighter or brown markings. Small white marking at the chest or very light inside of legs is permissible, but not desirable. The nose must always be black. (Dogs with a light or missing mask, with yellow eyes or piercing light eyes, light marking at the chest and inner side of the legs, as well as light nails and a red tip at the tail, or washed-out, soft colours are considered to be lacking in pigmentation). The undercoat is, except on black dogs, always light grey. The final colour of puppies can only be determined after the outer coat has fully developed.

16. HAIR

a. THE STOCKHAARIGE (DENSE, HARSH COAT) GERMAN SHEPHERD DOG

The outer coat is dense. The individual hair is straight, firm, and lies flat. The hair is short on the head of the dog, including the inner part of the ear, front of the legs, feet and toes; it is longer and denser at the neck. On the hindquarters, the hair is longer down to the hocks, forming 'trousers' on the upper thighs. The length of the coat differs in the various dogs, and, because of the different lengths of hair, different types of coat may be found. A short, gopher-like coat is faulty.

b. THE LONG-STOCKHAARIGE (LONG, DENSE, HARSH COAT) GERMAN SHEPHERD DOG

The individual hair is longer, not always straight, and is not lying flat against the body. In particular, the hair is longer at the inside of the ear, behind the ears, at the rear side of the foreleg and usually in the loin area, occasionally forming tufts at the ears and feathering from the elbow to the pastern. The 'trousers' at the upper thighs are long and dense, the tail is bushy with feathering on the lower side. Due to the fact that this type of coat is not as weather-resistant as the normal coat, it is not desirable. However, with sufficient undercoat, dogs with this type of coat may still be used for breeding, if the breeding regulations of the respective country permit it.

c. THE LONG-HAIRED GERMAN SHEPHERD DOG
The hair is considerably longer than that of the Long-Stockhaar (see paragraph b above) and usually parts on the back. An undercoat is only found in the area of the loins, or is completely non-existent. The long-haired German Shepherd Dogs are usually narrow-chested and have extremely pointed muzzles. The coat of the long-haired German Shepherd Dog is not weather-resistant and the use of the dog for utility work is highly diminished. Therefore, long hair is undesirable.

17. FAULTS
All faults reducing the use, endurance and working capability. Missing or weak sex characteristics (i.e. bitchy dogs or doggy bitches). Temperament faults contrary to the desired Shepherd Dog characteristics; lackadaisical, highly-excitable, shy dogs, those lacking trainability and vitality; monorchids, chryptorchids (disqualifications for showing and breeding), or a very small penis; weak or flabby constitution, deficiency of bone or body substance and lack of firmness. Washed-out colours, bluish colour, albinos (without any pigmentation and red nose), as well as white dogs (i.e. almost white to completely white dogs with black nose). Furthermore, over- or under-size dogs, badly-structured or proportioned dogs, dogs which are higher than long, too light or too heavy in body structure, soft back, lack of angulation, as well as all faults negatively influencing the desired far-reaching trot and endurance; overly short, weak, pointed, or long muzzle; over- or undershot, and other dentition faults, especially weak, discoloured teeth. Finally overly soft coat, too short or too long without undercoat; hanging or continuously badly-carried ears, cropped ears; curled or ring tail, badly carried tail, docked tail, as well as dogs with genetically inherited short or stumpy tails.

INTERPRETATION
There are some countries, the UK and USA being two, which have made certain alterations to suit their particular needs. In the World Union Standard the proportions desired are 9 in height to 10 in length, in the British Standard it is 8.5 or 9 to 10, and in the USA it is 8.5 to 10, which seems to mean that the Americans favour a longer dog than that desired by the WUSV Standard. You will also find differences in the wording of the section dealing with temperament according to which country you live in, but the overall interpretation remains roughly the same.

We must mention two more interesting points which come into the first section: 'General Appearance'. In the World Union Standard it is stated that only 'Specialty' judges should judge the breed, which automatically rules out the non-specialist in GSDs, even though the judges concerned might be specialists in many other breeds. You will find that in some Standards, including the British, this is left out.

The WUSV Standard also states that no Shepherd should be given the grading of 'Excellent' unless it has a working degree, i.e. Schutzhund I. In countries where they do not have Schutzhund, the above is obviously impossible. But we notice that visiting German SV judges still give the grading 'Excellent' in spite of no dogs having working qualifications.

In March 1989, the American Kennel Club reformatted its Standard and, although the meaning is fundamentally the same, there are a few differences such as the two we have already mentioned.

We have found that it is sometimes difficult to visualize a Shepherd only from the written word so we have illustrated, as far as possible, various sections with photographs and some line drawings. With very few exceptions, the pictures are of top-winning dogs in the UK and abroad, as are the line drawings. Study the skeleton carefully and get thoroughly conversant with the various points of the Shepherd and where they are situated.

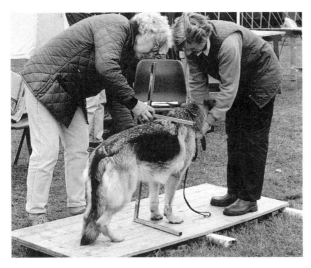

Measuring a dog with a WUST measuring stick. The dog must be standing on a level surface

HEIGHT

The WUSV Standard states that the ideal height of the GSD should be 62.5cm (dogs) and 57.5cm (bitches), with a deviation in both sexes of 2.5cm either way. The height is measured by taking a perpendicular line from the withers touching the elbow, down to the ground. The British Standard is the same, but the USA Standard states 24-26ins for males and 22-24ins for bitches measured – notice the difference – from the highest point of the shoulder blade.

TOPLINES

Too long, too deep, soft in back.

Too short, run-up in loin, roach back.

Moving with a level back. Head held a bit high, although this might be due to the tight lead and check-chain up behind the ears.

An excellent moving bitch. Note she has only one foot on the ground at this moment of suspension.

GAIT

There would appear to be a divergence between the World Union Standard, the British and USA. The difference is with regard to the backline. The World Standard says: "close to the ground with head stretched forward, the tail slightly raised, showing *a soft curved line* from the tip of the ears over the neck and back to the tip of the tail". The British Standard is similar, but says: "displays a *flowing line* running from the tips of its ears." The USA goes into far greater detail than either of the others regarding step sequence and gait, but their description of the back in movement is as

Head held too high; dip over withers, which would indicate a soft back.

follows: "At full trot the back must remain *firm and level* without sway, whip or roach."

Study the line drawings and the three photos of Shepherds when moving, and decide which you think is correct. All are first prize Championship Show winners, and two of them are Champions.

TEMPERAMENT

All three Standards mean more or less the same, though expressed in different wording. For instance in the World Union Standard under 'General Appearance' it states: "must be willing to *attack* if his master so desires".

In the British Standard it states: "must have the courage to *defend* himself or his master." Here the emphasis is on "defend" rather than on "attack". The American Standard discusses Temperament in general, but without any particular reference to either attack or defence.

HEAD

All Standards require good sex characteristics. The photogaphs show this, so study them carefully.

ABOVE: A lovely masculine head showing good sex characteristics and correct ears.

TOP RIGHT: A typical feminine head – there is no mistaking this for a male.

RIGHT: A rather strong head, but still feminine.

Narrow head, lacking stop, rather a long muzzle.

TEETH

All three Standards mention the number of teeth required, but not much is said about missing teeth, other than that a complete set is desired. The American Standard, however, states that anything other than the first premolar missing is considered a serious fault. Incorrect bites are mentioned in all three Standards. In view of how seriously SV judges, when judging in this country, penalise missing teeth, it surprises us that not more is said about this fault in the WUSV Standard. In the section 'Faults' it merely mentions "other dentition faults", but does not say what they are. The SV gives judges guidelines on dental faults, with which they must comply when issuing gradings. In Germany, no Shepherd can be awarded the Grade VA (Excellent Select) or a V (Excellent) unless it has a correct bite and a full set of teeth. Now and again you will find a Shepherd with an extra tooth, usually one of the small premolars. Although a fault, this is not considered as serious as a missing tooth.

EARS

Without good ear carriage, a Shepherd just does not look like a Shepherd. By six months, when it has completed teething, your puppy should have its ears up. There are varying degrees of soft ears and often if not too soft, they will firm with age.

LEFT: The ears are firm, but they are splayed and therefore do not stand straight up.

RIGHT: Soft ears.

BODY

All three Standards give the proportions height to length as previously mentioned, but only the WUSV and British Standards give the depth of body and length of front legs in measurement. The American Standard states: "an impression of depth to solidity without bulkiness". The Standards differ with regard to backs, with the American Standard desiring that "the withers should slope into a *level* but straight back." The WUSV requires a back, including loins, to be "straight and strongly-developed." The British Standard asks for the same. It is interesting to note that all three Standards require a straight back with the American asking for it to be level. Please note, a straight back is not necessarily level!

All three Standards require a croup which is long and gentle-sloping; the WUSV and the British give an angle of approx. 23 degrees. They then go on to discuss forehand and hindquarter construction, all of which are roughly the same. It is interesting to note that the British Standard is the only one which requires, on the hindquarters, a slightly longer lower thigh than upper thigh.

With regards to pasterns, the three standards differ slightly. The USA requires a pastern at an angle of 25 degrees, the British quotes 20-23 degrees,and the WUSV is 20 degrees. All three Standards require "the forelegs viewed from all sides to be straight". This also applies to the hock joint.

BODY INCLUDING FOREHAND AND HINDQUARTER ANGULATION

A very well-constructed dog of correct proportions.

Steep in front, steep in pasterns and upper arm. Good topline (perhaps a little exaggerated slope), croup of correct angle, but short. The hind angulation would appear better if the dog was not over-stretched by his handler.

This dog is over-loaded in front, with a level topline and a very short, flat croup. Lacks width and length of lower thigh.

A young dog of the correct proportions – height to length, and depth of body to length of front legs. However, he flattens over the withers, has a slight peak in his back and a very steep, dropaway croup. He lacks width and and length of lower thigh and has a short, steep upper arm.

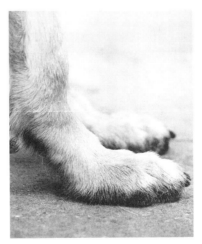

The feet turn out, though only slightly in this case.

Slack pasterns and flat feet.

Cow hocks.

COLOUR
All Standards agree on this.

COAT
All Standards agree on this, and go into quite lengthy details describing the various types of coat with their advantages and disadvantages. There are, however, listed in the WUSV and British Standards, three different categories of coats.

LEFT: An all-white German Shepherd, rejected by the Standard.

BELOW: A long coat. Notice the abundance of feathering on the front legs and the bushy tail.

Notice the difference between the dog (pictured right) with the correct coat, and the long-coated dog with fringes round the ears and down the chest.

CONCLUSION

Although the Standards are similar, it amazes us how such a wide divergence of type can have occurred. In the UK, where we have two different types, the Standard is the same. Who is to blame, breeders or judges? We would say a combination of both because, after all, the breeders in most cases are also judges and thus dictate the way the breed should go.

During the thirty or so years we have been involved with the breed we have seen vast changes. The dogs that are winning today in our show rings, or at least where pro SV Judges are officiating, would certainly have not won in the sixties. Over the years some excellent German dogs have been imported into Great Britain which have done wonders in improving type and temperament. Through careful selection by conscientious breeders who have abided by the Standard, you can now visit a show where SV style Judges are officiating and you will see dogs and bitches who correspond very closely to the WUSV Standard. In this Chapter, we illustrate the two types which currently prevail in Great Britain. Having studied both word and picture, and comparing them with the WUSV Standard, you must decide which you think is correct and corresponds more closely to the Standard.

Chapter Fifteen

BREED TRAINING

The big difference between showing in the Breed ring and competing in any form of Working event is that when Working your Shepherd, it is entirely up to you and your dog to show what you can do, whereas in Breed it is the judge's opinion of the character, anatomy and movement of your Shepherd in comparison with the rest of the class which decides where you are placed. In a class consisting of exactly the same dogs, you could come first on one occasion and last the next, depending on the type of dog the judge prefers – Alsatian or GSD. It is all a matter of how the judge on the day interprets the Standard, and in a country such as the UK, where there is a split in the Breed, this can happen all too often. It should not, but alas, it does.

There are those who favour the more Germanic type of dog, in other words, a harder, shorter dog, and those who prefer what we refer to as the UK type (Alsatian), the longer, level-backed dog, who tends to have exaggerated fore and hindquarter angles and is not so muscular as its German relation. In this chapter, we will refer to them as UK judges or SV-style judges, depending on which type of dog they favour. Study the chapter on the Breed Standard and decide which type of dog you consider corresponds most closely to yours.

AWARDS
Different countries have different systems by which your Shepherd can become a Champion. In Germany, under the SV system and in other countries abiding by the same judging rules, there is no title of Champion. They use a Grading system, which grades every dog from the first to the last. (The grading system is explained more fully in another chapter.) There are two types of German shows, Ortsgruppen and Landesgruppen. The latter is the more prestigious and the Grading 'V' (Excellent), obtained at one of these shows, is very highly regarded. The Classes are divided into age Groups, 12 months-18 months, 18 months-24 months, and over 2 years old. This system is used throughout Europe as well as in many other countries around the world, at shows where only Shepherds are being exhibited.

However, there are also All Breed Shows in Europe, at which a system similar to the one used in the UK is employed. The Best Dog and Best Bitch are each awarded a CACIB, which is the equivalent of the British Challenge Certificate. Three of these have to be won, in different countries, for the dog to become an Int. Ch. (International Champion). In the UK we have four different types of shows: Sanction, Limited, Open and Championship. If your dog has won more than a certain amount of awards, you cannot enter in Limited or Sanction Shows.

Open and Championships can consist of All Breeds, or just one Breed in which there are no restrictions on entry. Although we have Age Classes, we also have several Classes which, for entry, depend on how much your Shepherd has won. To become a Champion, your dog must win three Challenge Certificates under three different judges. To win a CC your Shepherd has to be either Best Dog or Best Bitch at a Championship Show, which is the only Show where CCs are on offer. You can find full details of Shows held in the UK in the *Kennel Club Year Book*.

Some countries, such as Southern Ireland and the USA, work on a point system. Your Shepherd has to win 15 points before it can become a Champion. The number of Shepherds entered at any one Show decides how many points – three, four, or five – your dog will be awarded. If there is a small entry, only three points will be given. A bigger entry awards more points. As in the UK, your Shepherd has to be unbeaten in its respective sex to obtain top awards. In Ireland these are called Green Stars.

For full details of shows, check with the Kennel Club or Breed Club of the country in which you live. Classes and qualifications can vary quite considerably from one country to another.

OUTSIDE ATTRACTION
This is just what the name implies – a means of getting your Shepherd's attention when he is having his individual examination and when gaiting, thus making him show himself to better advantage. It is done by one or more persons, who are positioned somewhere outside the ring, and with some Shepherds it makes all the difference.

When we first became interested in showing, at the end of the 1950s, the outside attraction was minimal, a discreet cough, a jangling of keys and such like, but during the seventies, when more people were visiting the Sieger Show (Germany) and more German dogs and judges were arriving in the UK, it started to increase. People started copying what was done in Germany, running round the outside of the ring, shouting, blowing whistles, and doing whatever else they could think of to attract their Shepherd's attention. Some exhibitors would take three or four helpers to a show who would be placed at strategic positions round the ring in order to attract their dogs.

When Outside Attraction took place at All Breed Shows, Championship or Open, it caused immense confusion, and, needless to say, exhibitors of other breeds started to complain to the Kennel Club. There were some quite nasty incidents between show officials and Shepherd exhibitors who, when asked to refrain from Outside Attraction, refused and used foul language in doing so. This incensed the Kennel Club, which now bans any form of Outside Attraction. If someone using it is caught by an official, it can result in the Shepherd's awards being revoked, or in extreme cases, the person concerned being suspended from attending any shows, either as judge, exhibitor or spectator, for as long as ten years. To a certain extent, Outside Attraction still goes on. But if a lot takes place at a Breed Championship Show, and is not controlled by show officials, the Kennel Club can, and do, withdraw the right to award Challenge Certificates from the society involved. In some countries Outside Attraction takes place to a limited degree, but in others, it is completely banned, and not even a cough or something similar is allowed.

BREED TRAINING
As with Working disciplines, start training your puppy when he is young. As soon as a puppy will accept a collar and lead you can start. Careful thought needs to go into Breed training, so as not to get your GSD puppy confused between this and Control. In earlier chapters we have stressed the importance of getting your puppy's attention with toys and titbits, and persuading him to walk at your side looking up at you. Now your GSD puppy must learn the complete opposite! He must now walk out in front, looking straight ahead and ignoring his handler.

How can we achieve this? As well as using different commands, we have got to make our puppy differentiate between the two disciplines, Breed and Obedience. To start with in Breed training, your Shepherd is worked on a dead check-chain (the lead put on the ring so that it cannot tighten) and at a later stage a pulling collar (half-leather, half-chain) is used. Your puppy will soon realise that when such a collar or check-chain is put on, it will be training for Breed.

Whoever is going to train the puppy in any of the Working disciplines takes on a different role for Breed training. In the following, we describe the person who is training the puppy in any of the

Ch. Quant vom Kirschental showing off his excellent side-gait. This illustrates the legs moving in a diagonal pattern. Notice the 'dead' check-chain and loose lead.

Working disciplines as the trainer. The helper is literally somebody you have asked to help you.

Let the helper take the lead while the trainer walks ahead showing the puppy his favourite toy or a titbit. As soon as the puppy moves forward, the helper gives the command "Walk on". Continue like this, with the trainer walking about ten paces ahead of the puppy for about 20 or 30 paces. The trainer then stops and lets the puppy catch up, praising him with a toy or titbit when he does. There is no reason why the trainer cannot continue with Heelwork practice both on and off lead, although preferably not on the same day. Training for the Breed ring in the way we have described in no way muddles your puppy, because it is the trainer who is giving praise, not the helper. The helper is merely somebody at the end of the lead, the puppy's attention is on his trainer as it is with other Working disciplines.

Continue as above, gradually increasing the distance before stopping. When your puppy is walking twice round an area the size of a Breed ring, out in front on the end of the lead without either hesitating or looking round at the handler, increase the pace so that your Shepherd is gaiting. It is important to give the command "Walk on" and, when asked to gait, "Trot on", so that your dog learns the meaning of the respective commands. At this stage it is a good idea to make a ring by putting a post at each corner of an area of ground and attach a piece of rope to it. This will make your puppy learn what a ring is, and make him realise that he must stay within the roped-off area.

Be careful when changing from walking to gaiting, that your Shepherd does not start to amble. Ambling is a movement in which the two legs on the same side move together instead of, as when gaiting, the legs are moving in a diagonal pattern e.g. left fore leg and right hind leg moving together. If your puppy starts ambling, stop, and try again. If he persists, by use of the lead, lift the forehand off the ground to break your Shepherd's stride. Ambling is a bad habit which can be quite hard to correct, especially in the older dog, so do not let it happen in the first place. Your Shepherd puppy must learn to move smoothly from walking to gaiting without breaking into an amble or galloping. This can sometimes take quite a lot of practice.

When you feel that your puppy knows the meaning of the commands, try this. Stand in one corner, tell your helper to give the appropriate command, and see whether your Shepherd will go round the ring as before, but without you – the trainer – in front. If successful, give your dog praise and a titbit, and have a game. The next step is to move to different corners, calling the puppy's name now and again to keep his attention. You can now try the same exercise gaiting, and as before, gradually increase the distance until the puppy is gaiting round the ring four or five times. Whatever you do, do not let your Shepherd become over-tired or bored. This is as dangerous when training for Breed, as it is when training for any of the Working disciplines.

When going round corners, hold the lead in the left hand moving it away from you as you go round, using it rather like a rein with which to guide the puppy. When your puppy is almost five months old and is proficient in both walking and gaiting round a ring on command, take him to a Breed Training Class, so that he can get used to moving with other dogs both in front and behind him. We have found this method successful in training our Shepherds to move in the Breed ring, and we continue it into their adult lives and all through their Show careers.

SHOW PROCEDURE

Before we continue with Breed training, here is an outline of what is required in the show ring.

When your class is called, you proceed into the ring where you are given your number as per catalogue. When all the class have been given their respective numbers, the steward will ask you to line up in numerical order and then stand your dogs. You will then be asked to move them round. The length of time you do this for depends very much on the judge, and also whether the dogs are walking or gaiting.

With an SV-style judge, you will be asked to walk, sometimes for quite some considerable time, while the judge assesses the quality and type he/she has to examine and place. If, on the other hand, the judge is pro-UK, you will be asked to gait, and twice round the ring will probably be all that is required. When this stage has been completed, you are called into the centre, still in numerical order, for the judge's individual examination. You will be asked your Shepherd's age and, in mixed classes, its sex. You will then stand your dog, and again, depending on the type of judge, you will either stand your Shepherd naturally, or pose him. The examination of teeth comes next. The bite is checked, and the rest of the mouth is examined to see whether there are any teeth missing or badly placed.

If you have a UK judge, there can be quite a lot of laying-on of hands, such things as feeling the forehand construction, running a hand down the back and croup, flicking the tail, feeling the depth of chest or lifting a front leg. The SV-style judge will walk past the Shepherd, who will be standing on a loose lead, watching the dog carefully to see his reactions. If the dog shows any sign of fear, he might well be put at the end of the line, depending on how strict the judge is on temperament. Notes will then be taken on your Shepherd's anatomical construction, and when this is finished, you will be asked to move your dog away and back, so the judge can check on how sound the dog is in front and behind. You will then gait round the ring to assess the side gait, firmness of back, wither height and lay of croup.

When all dogs have been seen, a UK judge will ask you to stand in numerical order and he/she will pick out a certain number of dogs, depending on the size of the class and how many prizes there are to be awarded. Having pulled out the required number, the rest will be asked to leave the ring. The remaining few will then be asked to gait round the ring, the judge will place them in order of merit, and prize cards will be given out.

Under an SV-style judge, the procedure is quite different. While doing individual examinations, the judge will make a provisional list of the order in which the dogs are to be placed. The steward will then call out the numbers. The dogs will be placed in order of merit from first to last. The class will now start walking, and the judge might make slight alterations in the placings. The class will then be asked to gait, and again, slight alterations might be made. After this, the dogs will be asked to stand. If you live in a country where there is grading, this will now take place.

The difference between UK and SV-style judging is that with grading, if the quality is sufficiently high, even though your Shepherd is standing near the end, you could still get a grading of 'Excellent', so that at least you know what the judge thinks of your dog. With the UK judge, once the chosen few have been selected, your Shepherd is, as we used to say, "out with the rubbish". You have no idea whether it is a good, bad or indifferent specimen.

SHOWING THE TEETH

If, when grooming, you have accustomed your Shepherd to having his ears and teeth looked at, you should have no difficulty when it comes to showing your dog's mouth to the judge. Get the dog sitting at your left hand-side, and give him the command "Teeth". With your right hand underneath his chin, put your left hand over the top of his muzzle and gently stroke his nose. Continue stroking two or three times then give much praise, release him, have a game and try again. If your Shepherd tries to back away, put your left foot behind his backside or, if that does not work, sit him up against a wall.

When your Shepherd shows no resistance, as you stroke, gently lift up his lips with your fingers on one side and your thumb on the other. Praise as before. As your Shepherd gets used to this, pull the lips further back, so that the whole of the mouth is visible, and at the same time, pull the lower lips down with your right hand. Show the bite in the same manner. If the judge requires you to open your dog's mouth wide – and some SV-style judges do – it can be done quite easily in the way we have described, but do get your Shepherd used to it before having to do it in the ring in front of a judge.

Showing the teeth – note the position of both hands.

The correct way to walk a German Shepherd into a show stance. When the right foreleg has moved forward, this bitch will be standing in correct show stance. Note the lead in the left hand with the right hand under the neck.

Improving hind angulation.

STANDING YOUR SHEPHERD

It is when a Shepherd is standing that a good handler and a well-trained dog can be best seen. The experienced handler will walk a Shepherd into a show stance, with a minimum amount of handling, tell the dog to Stay, and walk to the end of the lead. It all looks so easy! But you often see the first-time handler take hold of the dog, putting one front leg in one place, then fiddling around with the other, yanking the hind legs here, there and everywhere. The end result is a very unsettled Shepherd, who is completely unbalanced and looks like a sack of potatoes.

A correctly-constructed, well-balanced Shepherd will need very little posing. In fact, when looking at our dogs in the kennels, we often see some of them standing in a perfect show stance. First of all, study your Shepherd's construction carefully and note his faults and virtues. In a puppy, this only applies to a certain extent because they can alter so much as they mature. But be honest with yourself. See the dog as he really is, and not as you would like him to be. If you do not acknowledge your dog's faults, how are you going to improve them by careful handling? We will assume that your Shepherd has been taught the command "Stay" because you do need this.

Firstly, stand sideways on to your Shepherd, about level with his shoulders. With your lead in your left hand and with your right hand held fairly high up your Shepherd's neck, walk him slowly forward. When the left hind leg is extended back, just before the dog is about to take another step forward, give the command "Stand", at the same time applying pressure to the neck with your right hand. Now tell your Shepherd to "Stay", and keep him in that position for a few seconds. Praise, have a game, and try again. Your dog will not be standing in a perfect show stance, but what we are doing at the moment is teaching your Shepherd to walk forward and stop with the left leg extended back.

When your Shepherd is happy walking into a stance, and – very important – will stay there, you can go into the finer details. There are several pictures in this book of Shepherds standing in a correct show stance, so try and imitate them. The front legs must stand together, in a straight line down from the top of the shoulder blade, and when viewed from the front should drop straight down from the elbows. If your Shepherd has a tendency to stand with his front legs too close together, or turn his feet out, you can improve this by altering the legs with your left hand.

Likewise with the hindquarters. If your Shepherd lacks hind angulation, try this. Take hold of the left hind leg just above the hock, with your thumb on the inside and your fingers on the outside of the leg, and as you lift the leg up, apply pressure to the tendons which will make the dog bend his leg more. Now place the leg down again, still extended. If your Shepherd is a little long in loin, place the right hind leg a little further forward, which will give the illusion of the dog being shorter. If, on the other hand, your Shepherd is steep in croup, do not pull that right hind leg quite so far forward.

Above are just a few tricks of the trade which might help you. However, handling is an art which can only be learnt by careful observation and experience. A good judge will not be fooled by any of these ploys, for it is when the Shepherd is moving that all is revealed with regard to its construction. But here again, by careful handling, you can improve some things. For instance, if your Shepherd tends to flatten over the withers when moving, try to keep his head up. Discover the speed at which your Shepherd moves best, and when doing your 'Individual', make certain you gait at the pace best suited to your dog.

UK HANDLING

What we have just described in handling techniques is what you will use when exhibiting your Shepherd under SV-type judges. Under a UK judge, the handling methods are somewhat different. To start with, you will very rarely be asked to walk your Shepherd; UK judges are only interested in gaiting. Three or four times round the ring – usually a small ring – is all that is required.

UK handlers normally use a very fine check-chain, held right up behind the dog's ears and sometimes put on so that the chain will not loosen. When standing a Shepherd, they stand in front of him and walk backwards. The result is similar to that already described, except that the dog usually ends up with his head held high, giving it the appearance of being swan-necked.

When gaiting, the Shepherd will remain at the handler's side, and although he might be moving on a loose lead, the fine check-chain will still remain up behind his ears. This will stop the dog from lowering his head – as he should when gaiting – restrict this fore-reach, and in some cases make the dog hackney (throwing his front legs into the air). Holding the head up completely destroys a flowing and correct side gait. If you intend to exhibit under a UK judge, your best bet is to go to a UK Show, and study the methods employed by the handlers.

TEMPERAMENT

So far in this chapter we have mentioned nothing about temperament. The reason is that we do not consider any Shepherd with a nervous or over-aggressive temperament should be shown in the Breed ring.

Having stated this, we must add that there are exceptions. When first taking a puppy into the ring, the youngster can sometimes appear to be nervous when he is really bewildered by all the new sights, sounds, and different breeds of dogs which he has never encountered before. When taking your Shepherd puppy to his first Show, get there early so that you can walk him around and get him used to the unusual surroundings. In the ring, especially when in the centre having the individual examination, a puppy can get completely overawed, and possibly you feel nervous too, so keep very calm and remember all you have taught your dog at home. Whatever happens, try and make this first appearance in the show ring a happy one.

CONCLUSION

However well or badly you have done at a show, try and enjoy yourself and learn something. If you have come last, do not go around saying how crooked the judging has been, but go up afterwards and politely ask the judge for a constructive critique of your Shepherd. This way you will learn something. We all have to start at the bottom. It is those who are prepared to take the rough with the smooth who will ultimately get to the top – and we hope you are one of those.

Chapter Sixteen

GENETICS AND THE GERMAN SHEPHERD DOG

By Dr Malcolm B Willis
Senior Lecturer in Animal Breeding & Genetics, University of Newcastle-upon-Tyne.

ORIGINS AND CHROMOSOME NUMBERS

It is now widely accepted that the domestic dog (*Canis familiaris*) is descended from some version of the wolf (*Canis lupus*). Domestication first occurred some 10,000 years ago, but the basic genetic structure of the dog is still compatible with that of the wolf, golden jackal and coyote. All these species have 78 chromosomes within each of the millions of cells making up an individual. It is therefore quite feasible to mate dogs with wolves, coyotes or jackals and obtain viable offspring. Man has created innumerable breeds of dog ranging in size from a Chihuahua, which could fit into a man's pocket, through to the St Bernard, which would outweigh most men. Despite this enormous variability, more pronounced in this species than any other, all breeds of dog could be interbred, albeit with some difficulty in practical terms.

Although, superficially, the German Shepherd Dog might appear to resemble a wolf, there are many quite obvious differences. The GSD has a wider muzzle relative to length, larger ears, a more pronounced stop, considerably smaller teeth, a longer tail and, although often missing in the GSD, the presence of a hind dewclaw. The GSD will have, on average, a larger litter size than the wolf, it will reach sexual maturity earlier than will a wolf, and it will breed twice per year instead of just once. Despite these differences, brought about by human selection, the behaviours of the dog and the wolf still show many similarities. Perhaps the greatest difference is that wolves are Type III hunters, in that they will co-operate to kill prey. Dogs, like jackals and coyotes, are Type II hunters. In a feral state they will hunt alone or in pairs, and will not normally hunt as a team or group to bring down large prey. The descent of the dog is important, in that understanding canine behaviour is enhanced with some knowledge of wolf behaviour.

The GSD has been selected as such only for some 110 years, but many of the features seen in the breed, and certainly many of the defects known to occur, will trace back much further than do pedigrees of the breed. Most of the features we see today have been brought about by deliberate selection, which has led to different gene frequencies in the modern dog to those seen in the original GSD of the 1890s. Different gene frequencies are not the only changes that have occurred. There have also been changes in nutrition and in veterinary knowledge, which have helped to influence the physical expression of those genes.

Chromosomes are the thread-like structures on which the genes are to be found. Genes are themselves proteins, largely made up of deoxyribonucleic acid (DNA). The animal breeder need not become too involved in the nature of the gene, since he is more concerned with its transmission and its action upon the animal than with its chemical nature.

CHROMOSOME TRANSMISSION AND THE INHERITANCE OF SEX

The number of chromosomes is constant within a species, and the 78 of the dog are actually made up of 39 pairs. These pairs vary in size, but they can be matched for size and shape within the pair. However, one pair is slightly different from the others. In females, this pair is a matching set of relatively large chromosomes, whereas in males, only one of the pair resembles that seen in females, while the partnering chromosome is quite small. This pair is termed the sex chromosome pair, and it is common practice to call these X and Y chromosomes. The remaining 38 pairs are termed autosomes. Thus, a female is XX + 38 autosomal pairs, while a male is XY + 38 autosomal pairs.

Genetic material (the gene) is transmitted from generation to generation, essentially without change, and it is important to understand this concept in order to understand animal breeding. Normal growth occurs by cells duplicating their chromosome numbers, and then dividing to form two identical cells where one existed previously, but each cell has the 78 chromosomes unchanged by this somatic growth. When it comes to sexual reproduction, a different process is needed. Germ cells (sperm and ova) contain only half the number of chromosomes i.e. they have only 39 chromosomes. This follows a reduction division during sperm/ova production. The 39 chromosomes are not a random sample, but represent one member of each chromosome pair. In any given sperm or ovum, one chromosome from each pair will be found, but it may be a chromosome derived from either parent. Thus, by chance, a particular sperm or ovum may carry more chromosomes from that dog's father (or mother) than usual.

A sperm has only 39 chromosomes and an ovum has the same number, when sperm and ovum meet in fertilization, so the resulting embryo carries the 78 chromosomes, or 39 pairs, normal in the species. Thus, every dog inherits half its chromosomes (and thus, half its genes) from its mother, and half from its father. The half from one parent may be a better or worse half than that from the other parent, but each parent contributes equally in terms of numbers.

Because females are XX their ova carry only one X chromosome, while in males sperm may be either X or Y. In theory, there should be as many X-bearing sperm as Y-bearing, but in reality the Y-bearing sperm are more effective at reaching the ovum. Thus, more embryos are XY (male) than XX (female), but males suffer slightly greater mortality so that, at birth, there are about 51 males and 49 females in every hundred puppies. At very rare intervals, chromosomal anomalies may exist, creating embryos that are XXY or XXX, or even XYY. These anomalies are not usually viable, but at times they can be, though they are usually infertile if they survive. Often such abnormal sex chromosome numbers are associated with physical anomalies. They are, however, relatively rare events.

SIMPLE MENDELIAN INHERITANCE

Chromosomes are paired, and in any given pair, a specific gene will always be found at the same location (locus) on the chromosome. The location of genes on chromosomes has been studied in several species, but is only now being examined in the dog, in a study called the Canine Genome Project. Eventually, several years from now, we will know where specific genes are found on which chromosomes, but at present we have to be content with identification of genes through the animal's appearance.

Genes are usually given letters of the alphabet, and some genes may be found in more than one version. Versions of a gene are termed alleles, and a specific gene might have half-a-dozen alleles or versions. However, because that gene is always found at a specific locus on a specific chromosome, and the dog has only two versions of that chromosome, it can only have two versions of any gene. If a dog has the same version on both chromosomes, it is termed homozygous. If it has different versions, it is said to be heterozygous.

As an example, let us take the issue of coat length. Most GSD are relatively short-coated with a thick undercoat. However, there are some (around 10 per cent of all puppies born) which have a long coat, often without the undercoat. This coat length feature is controlled genetically by a single gene which has two versions. One version, designated L, is the normal coat, while the alternative is l or long coat. The L allele is more powerful than the l, since it will express itself in the animal even if present on only one of the chromosomes. In contrast, a dog must carry l in duplicate (i.e. on both chromosomes) if it is to have a long coat. We therefore call L a dominant allele and l a recessive allele.

The feature you can see (or measure) is termed the phenotype, and in connection with coat length, there are two phenotypes: normal (short-coated) and long-coated. The underlying genetic structure is called the genotype, and in this case we have three genotypes: LL, Ll and ll. The first two of these will be short-coated, because L expresses itself in a single or double dose. In contrast, ll will be long-coated. We can call LL homozygous normal, Ll heterozygous normal and ll homozygous long. The type of coats found in any mating will depend upon the genetic make-up (genotype) of the parents and upon the laws of chance.

Suppose we mate two normal-coated dogs which (unbeknown to us) are of the genotype Ll i.e. they carry long-coat. Then the male will produce sperm which carry either L or l and the female will also produce ova which are either L or l. To determine the resultant progen, we can construct a square system.

		Sperm will be	L　or　l	
			LL	Ll
		L	normal	normal
Ova will be		or		
			Ll	ll
		l	normal	long

The body of the table shows all the combinations which will result from the various sperm and ova. In this mating, we would obtain a ratio of three normal-coated animals to every one long coat. However, the real ratio is 1:2:1 i.e. one homozygous normal, two heterozygous normal and one long coat.

There are actually six different kinds of mating that can be made with respect to coat length, and these are shown in Table 1. In this table, the parents are given by genotype (LL/Ll/ll) and by phenotype (long or normal) and it does not matter which way the mating is done, i.e. which is the father and which the mother.

Mating 1 involves two parents which are both homozygous dominants, and thus they can only produce their own kind in respect of coat type. Matings 2 and 3 involve one parent carrying long coat, but no long coats can result because the other parent is free of long coat (i.e. is LL). Matings 4, 5 and 6 can all result in long coats, but only because *both* parents carry the long coat allele (l) at least once.

This is an important principle: recessive traits, like long coat, can only come to the surface and be seen when *both* parents carry the recessive allele. If, in any mating, a recessive trait appears in the progeny, you can be certain that both parents *must* carry the recessive trait. Sometimes you will see a dog referred to as producing a lot of long coats, and this is quite misleading. A dog can only ever produce long coats if that dog is either Ll, or is actually long-coated ll. Even then, it needs the other parent to also carry l for long coats to result. These are matings 4, 5 and 6. If a specific sire (or dam) seems to give a high number of long coats, it is either through the laws of chance, or because that animal has mated more than its share of Ll and ll animals.

Within each of matings 1, 3 and 6, the progeny are all the same in genotype and phenotype, but in all the other matings the ratios of 50/50 of 25/50/25 will only apply over large numbers. Thus, if you mate Ll to Ll you ought to get 25 per cent long coats but in a litter of three, 25 per cent is an impossible figure, and even in a litter of eight there is no guarantee that two will be long-coated. By chance, you may get more or less than the expected ratio, but if you made a large number of Ll x Ll matings, the ratios would work out more and more exactly, the larger the numbers of puppies accumulated.

MATINGS INVOLVING A SIMPLE MENDELIAN GENE (COAT TYPE)

PARENTS	PROGENY
1. LL x LL Normal Normal	100% LL All Normal
2. LL x Ll Normal Normal	50% LL 50% Ll All Normal
3. LL x ll Normal Long	100% Ll All Normal
4. Ll x Ll Normal Normal	25% LL 50% Ll 25% ll Normal Normal Long
5. Ll x ll Normal Long	50% Ll 50% ll Normal Long
6. ll x ll Long Long	100% ll All Long

MENDELIAN INHERITANCE WITH TWO GENES

Long coats are not the only Mendelian trait. There are several within the breed. Let us consider the B/b gene, where B is the allele allowing black pigment to form, and b is the allele preventing black pigment, and thus giving rise to liver (or chocolate or brown) coloration instead of black. Again B is dominant to b, so we have three genotypes BB, Bb and bb, but two phenotypes black or liver (brown).

Note that a BB or Bb dog is not necessarily all-black, but it will carry black pigment. In contrast, the bb dog cannot form black pigment, and where it would otherwise have been black it will be liver-coloured. Thus, an all-black carrying bb would be all-liver, a black-and-tan bb would be liver-and-tan, and a white carrying bb would be white but with a liver nose. The bb combination not only removes black from the coat but it causes the nose leather to be brown or pink, and the eye colour to be lighter than normal. We can substitute B for L, b for l, Black for Normal and Liver for Long in Table 1, to see that B/b operates exactly like L/l in terms of genetic ratios. However, what if we combine L/l and B/b? L/l and B/b are quite independent of each other, and will segregate separately. Let us look therefore at just one combination.

Suppose we mate LLBB (normal-coated carrying black) to llbb (long-coated liver), then we will produce progeny all of which are LlBb, and thus, normal-coated carrying black. Now let us mate two of these together, so that we are mating LlBb with LlBb. Sperm and ova must contain one of each series, i.e. an L or l, and a B or b, and sperm and ova will thus be of four kinds, as shown in Table 2.

MENDELIAN RATIOS INVOLVING TWO GENES

Sperm will be

		LB	Lb	lB	lb
	LB	LLBB Black Normal	LLBb Black Normal	LlBB Black Normal	llBb Black Normal
	Lb	LLBb Black Normal	LLbb Liver Normal	LlBb Black Normal	Llbb Liver Normal
Ova will be	lB	LlBB Black Normal	LlBb Black Normal	llBB Black Long	llBb Black Long
	lb	LlBb Black Normal	Llbb Liver Normal	llBb Black Long	llbb Liver Long

Again, the body of the table shows the combinations to be found. In this case, there are 16 different combinations to be found in terms of genotypes resulting from this mating, but, in terms of phenotypes, the ratio found will be as follows:

9 will show both dominant traits (i.e. Black/Normal).

3 will show one dominant and one recessive trait (i.e. Black/Long).

3 will show the reverse dominant/recessive combination (i.e. Liver/Normal).

1 will show both recessive traits (Liver/Long).

Obviously, you are unlikely to get 16 puppies in a litter, and even if you did, they will not usually work out exactly according to expectation, but over large numbers, the 9:3:3:1 ratio will apply. Note that in the above table, Black refers to the presence of black pigment, not to an all-black coat. The actual coat colour will depend upon which of the agouti series is present as well as other colour genes.

MULTIPLE ALLELES

Some genes have more than two options, and one such is the agouti coat-colour series, the principle colour gene in the GSD. There are, as far as the GSD is concerned, five versions (alleles) of this gene. These are:

A^Y   golden sable

a^w   grey sable

a^s   saddle marked black-and-tan

a^t   black with tan points (termed bicolour)

a   all-black

These alleles are listed in descending order of dominance, such that golden sable is dominant to grey, which is dominant to saddle, and so on. Every GSD will have two of these alleles, and these may be two the same or two different ones, but it cannot have three because there is only a locus on one pair of chromosomes where these are found. If you have a golden sable carrying grey, then it could not give rise to any colours other than these, no matter what it was mated to, whereas an all-black dog would have to be aa, and it could give rise to other colours of progeny depending upon the genes carried by its mate. To obtain an all-black GSD, both parents must carry at least one a allele.

SEX LINKED, SEX LIMITED AND SEX CONTROLLED
SEX-LINKED

Because dogs carry two sex chromosomes, any genes carried on these two are termed sex-linked characters. In the GSD, haemophilia A is one such trait. This is a moderate bleeding disease which can cause death, and is known to have stemmed principally from Canto vd Wienerau (1968-72), though he may not be the only source of the problem. Haemophilia A is a recessive trait caused by the allele h, but it is found on the X chromosome. Because males have only one X chromosome, and because the Y chromosome is largely inert, we have two kinds of male but three kinds of female. In the following explanation, H or h indicate the X chromosome and O indicates the Y chromosome.

Males   HO normal or hO haemophiliac
Females   HH normal, Hh carrier or hh haemophiliac

Most haemophiliacs are males, and result from mating a normal (HO) male to a carrier (Hh) female. Such a mating would result in 50 per cent normal (HO) males and 50 per cent haemophiliac (hO) males. All females would appear to be normal, but half would be HH (normal) and half Hh (carriers). These percentages apply over large numbers and not in any specific litter. If a haemophiliac male (hO) is used for breeding, his sons are all normal (HO), but his daughters are all Hh, and thus carriers. Haemophiliac females are rarely seen because they would usually have to stem from a mating of carrier female (Hh) to an affected (hO) male, and such matings would be exceedingly rarely undertaken.

SEX LIMITED

A sex limited trait is not carried on the X/Y chromosome, but is autosomal. However, it is seen in only one sex. Cryptorchidism (failure of testicles to descend) can obviously only be seen in males, and is therefore sex limited but it can be carried by females. In contrast, milk production or litter size are sex limited traits seen in females. These sex limited traits may not be simple Mendelian features. It is important to realise that because a trait is seen only in one sex (i.e. sex limited) it does not mean that it is transmitted *only* by that sex. It can be transmitted by either sex.

SEX CONTROLLED

A sex controlled trait is one seen more often in one sex than the other, but is not confined to one sex. Spina bifida in man is more often seen in females, as is hip dysplasia. There is some evidence that in the dog, hip dysplasia is more often seen in females or seen to a higher degree such that females, as a group, tend to score or grade higher on this trait.

INHERITED AND CONGENITAL

An inherited trait is one controlled by genes, rather than one that is acquired, as is disease through infection. Inherited traits may be simple Mendelian traits 100 per cent controlled by genes, or they may be more complex in their inheritance and may have some element of environmental influence. Congenital traits are those seen at birth or immediately afterwards, and they may or may not be inherited. In dogs, hip dysplasia is inherited but not congenital because it is not seen at birth. Some defects are inherited and congenital, like certain cataracts, while other defects can be congenital but not inherited, such as manufacturing defects caused by drugs or trauma during the bitch's pregnancy. A list of some relatively simple traits seen in the GSD appears in Table 3.

SOME MENDELIAN TRAITS OF THE GSD

TRAIT	GENES SEEN
<u>Coat colour</u>	
Agouti series	A^Y a^w a^s a^t a (see text)
B series	B b (see text)
C series	C (coloured) c^{ch} (fading of tan)
E series	E^m (mask) E (no mask) e (fading of black pigment except on nose)
S series breed	S (self coloured) other alleles exist but not in the
W series	Wh (coloured) wh (white)
<u>Coat type</u>	L (normal length) l (long coat)
<u>Dew claws</u>	D (presence on rear leg) d (absence) Many GSD are dd and have no rear dewclaws

Ehlers-Danlos syndrome	Believed recessive trait
Giant Axonal Neuropathy	GAN (normal) gan (neuropathy)
Juvenile cataract	CT (normal sight) ct (cataract in puppyhood)
Pituitary dwarfism	DW (normal growth) dw (dwarf growth)
Retinal dysplasia	Believed recessive trait
Von Willebrands Disease	VWD (blood disease) vwd (normal)
	The combination VWD VWD is usually lethal.

POLYGENIC FEATURES

Some traits are not inherited in a simple Mendelian way but are quite complex in their mode of inheritance because several genes combine to influence the trait. With Mendelian traits we are dealing with fairly distinct or discrete traits, often called qualitative traits.

In coat type, for example, although dogs may vary from ultra-short to long, they are basically classifiable as normal (short) or long. Similarly, coat colour may come in various forms but there are clearly defined groups. In contrast, wither height in GSD ranges, in imperceptible gradations, from below 55cm to over 66cm, and it is difficult to put animals into clearly defined groupings. Height itself is affected by sex, with males tending to be taller than females. These sort of traits are termed polygenic traits, and they are usually determined by a number of genes termed polygenes, hence the description polygenic traits. Another name for such traits is quantitative traits.

There is a further complication, in that such traits may not be totally influenced genetically, but may have an element of environmental influence. The colour of a dog is not much influenced by its diet, whereas the height of a dog depends not only on its genes for height, but also on its sex, the way it was reared, and especially its diet. Even with identical genetic make-up for wither height, a male would be taller than a female because sex itself, through hormones, influences the expression of height.

Although it is not always the case, most polygenic traits can often be seen to follow what is termed a normal curve. That is, they range from small numbers at the extremes, to a larger number of cases in the centre. Normal curves have clearly defined mathematical properties, and this allows scientists to assess the extent to which such traits are inherited. Most polygenic traits show variation, and this total or phenotypic variation is made up of several components.

Phenotypic variation =
additive genetic influence + non-additive genetic influence + environmental influence.

The most important of these features, from a breeder's point of view, is the additive influence. If, for example, this was 40 per cent of the variation, then it would mean that 40 per cent of any superiority among parents, relative to the population from which they were selected, would be transmitted to the offspring. This feature is termed the heritability, and the higher the heritability, the easier it will be to select for advances in the next and future generations.

Unfortunately, heritability studies on dogs are not common, but some have been undertaken in the GSD and in other breeds. In Table 4, some heritabilities for specific measurements and traits are shown. These values are rounded estimates, and not necessarily applicable to every situation or population, but they are presented merely as a rough guide to values. High heritability traits will respond to selection quite well, both in terms of increasing or decreasing the trait, but low heritability traits will not respond the same way and will be more difficult to change by direct selection.

HERITABILITIES OF SOME GSD TRAITS (ESTIMATES)

TRAIT	HERITABILITY %
Character traits	
Fear	50
Fetch (chasing a ball at 8 weeks)	75
Retrieve (retrieving a ball at 8 weeks)	20
Diseases	
Hip dysplasia (BVA/KC score)	40
(OFA grade)	25
Osteochondritis Dissecans (OCD)	25
Panosteitis	15
Physical measurements	
Body length	45
Body weight	40
Chest depth	55
Chest width	80
Head width	35
Rear pastern length	50
Wither height	65
Reproductive traits	
Cryptorchidism	15
Litter size	<20

Selection for polygenic traits is possibly the most important aspect of dog breeding. Physical measurements are clearly important in dogs bred to conform to a standard, while mental traits are vital for the well-being of the dog, as are health traits. Several measurements appear to be quite highly inherited, suggesting that attempts to change the shape of the breed will meet with reasonable success, even if that attempt is not in the ideal direction. In contrast, seeking to improve reproductive performance would prove much harder to achieve.

THRESHOLD TRAITS

Although most polygenic traits follow the normal curve pattern, this is not always the case. Some traits are seen as all-or-nothing features, yet are controlled by many genes rather than by a single Mendelian factor. Some heart defects are of this kind, such as Patent Ductus Arteriosus (PDA) and Persistent Right Aortic Arch. These are congenital defects, and they usually exist in only two versions, Normal and Affected, though sometimes, as in PDA, two forms of affected exist.

Despite the simple expression into a Normal and one or two affected versions, the traits tend to be controlled by many genes. They present problems for breeders, in that there is a kind of threshold number of genes which, if this point is reached, results in affected as opposed to normal dogs. Thus, it is fairly easy to identify affected stock, since they are beyond this threshold point and exhibit the problems of the disease. However, normal animals can vary from those which are very far from the threshold point, to those on the borders of this line. All will appear normal, but those close to the threshold are clearly more dangerous to breed from than those well-removed from it. At present, no tests exist other than pedigree analysis. Breeders must thus take care with animals which, while normal, show close familial relationship to known affected cases.

SELECTION

When seeking to select breeding stock, Mendelian traits are fairly easy to deal with. In some cases, pedigree data can identify known carriers. Therefore, all daughters of a haemophilia A case male must carry the condition, though in themselves they will seem normal. Similarly, all offspring of an all-black will carry all-black, even if they are a totally different colour from black. Such dogs will, however, only give rise to black offspring when mated to a known black carrier or to an all-black mate.

Mendelian recessives can lie hidden for generations and their eradication is very difficult if not impossible at present, but once the genetic make-up of a dog is known, further pedigree study and progeny data do not add to your knowledge. If, for example, your dog is Ll (i.e. normal-coated, but a known carrier of long coat) then his genotype is known exactly for this trait, and no information can be added by further pedigree study or by examination of progeny. With polygenic traits, this may not be the case. If a trait has a high heritability, then there will be a greater tendency for features seen in the parents to appear in the offspring.

Suppose we were mating a 66cm dog to a 60cm bitch, then we are mating at the higher end of the height scale. If the sire was from a population averaging 64cm and the bitch from one averaging 57cm, then the dog is 2cm over the mean and the bitch 3cm over the mean. Together they average 2.5cm above the mean, but only 65 per cent of this is inherited (see Table 4). Thus, only 65 per cent of 2.5 will be passed on, which is 1.625cm. Thus this mating should give rise to males that are 64 + 1.625 = 65.625cm and to females that are 57+1.625 = 58.625cm. Clearly, these are average figures and will not apply to every dog born, nor will the average values work in small numbers, but in rather over-simplified terms they illustrate selection for a polygenic trait.

In general, the higher the heritability, the greater the chances of success. Progress will depend upon how high the heritability of the character is, and what superiority was selected. The phenotype of a dog will give a guide to that dog's potential as a breeding animal, but once the dog has progeny they will be an indication of what he is producing, and thus be more valuable in prediction terms. Dogs which seem to have the virtues that you seek are the ones to consider for breeding. However, those which have the virtues, but which do not appear to transmit them to their progeny, should be discarded from the breeding programme.

MATING POLICY

Having decided which animals demonstrate the virtues you are trying to obtain, your next choice is how to mate them together. This is not intended to mean the physical process of mating, but in pedigree terms. As a breeder of pure-bred GSD, cross-breeding is not an option. Your options are to mate unrelated animals together (out-breeding), to mate related animals (in-breeding or line-breeding), to mate animals which resemble each other (like-to-like matings) or to mate animals which are not alike, but which excel where the mate fails (compensatory mating). Most breeders will indulge in like-to-like matings, and this is going to show some degree of success. Offspring resemble their parents because they have common genes. If those parents resembled each other, then there is an even greater chance of the offspring looking like their parents. However, this may not result in offspring capable of stamping their type upon their progeny in due course, unless the like-to-like policy is continued. That is, it will not increase prepotency.

Compensatory mating is widely practised if a line has defects. If your bitch fails in length of upper arm, she is best mated to a dog excelling in this feature, who is known to come from a pedigree of good upper arm length. Ideally, you use a dog known to produce good upper arm length. In-breeding is the mating of animals showing a fairly close degree of relationship. It is a policy known to be potentially dangerous, if carried to extremes. In-breeding can bring to the surface hidden recessives that are deleterious, and were possibly hitherto unknown but it does not create these recessives, only exposes them. More seriously, inbreeding can lead to a worsening of traits that are of low heritability. Thus, in-breeding can adversely affect fertility, litter size, general viability and the like. For this reason, in-breeding must be undertaken with caution and the breed should avoid excess emphasis upon specific animals. In history, there has been excess emphasis upon such animals as Avon Prince of Alumvale (UK), Lance of Fran-Jo (USA) and Palme v Wildsteiger Land (Europe). Such bottlenecks usually lead to problems of a longterm nature, and should be avoided if at all feasible.

Chapter Seventeen

BREEDING GERMAN SHEPHERD DOGS

BREEDING RESPONSIBILITIES

If you decide you want to breed from your bitch or use your dog at stud, there are certain things that you must do before progressing any further. First of all, your Shepherd must be X-rayed for hip dysplasia. In Germany, and most other EC countries, the dog or bitch must obtain an 'A' stamp (HD), have a working degree, and pass a Breed Survey, before being bred from. Failure to obtain any of these means that the progeny cannot be registered. In the UK this is not essential, which we feel is a great pity. However, the Breed Council does recommend that no dog with a higher score than 20 or a bitch who scores higher than 25 should be bred from, unless there are special circumstances, and only after consultation with the GSD Breed Geneticist, Dr Malcolm Willis. Different countries throughout the world have different rulings on this subject, so it is wise to check on the requirements of whatever country you live in.

Except in America, all Shepherds can be X-rayed and scored at 12 months of age and over. In the USA, however, dogs are X-rayed at two years of age and over. If your Shepherd's hips are not up to scratch, forget about breeding from it. It is hard luck, but if you go ahead, knowing that the dog has bad hips, you are doing a grave disservice to this lovely breed, as well as creating a rod for your own back. At a later stage, young animals will be returned to you by distraught owners, complaining about bad hips, and possibly demanding their money back. You will then realise how foolish it was to ignore high hip scores.

THE STUD DOG
Unless your male is an outstanding example of the breed, or an excellent worker, you are very unlikely to be asked for a stud card. But if you feel you want a puppy by your own dog, and you have or know of a suitable bitch to mate him to, then go ahead. But do not be tempted unless the dog fulfils the following conditions:
1. The dog has a good temperament.
2 The dog is entire.
3. The dog has all his teeth.
4. The dog is a good specimen of the breed.
5. Nowadays, with the danger of haemophilia, it is also wise to have your dog blood-tested.

THE BROOD BITCH
Before you consider mating your bitch, make certain you have a suitable place for her to whelp. (This is discussed in the next chapter.) You could have a litter of more than ten puppies, so not only do you need suitable accommodation, but you will also have to find suitable homes for them. Breeding can become a very expensive business if you do not have a ready market for your puppies at eight weeks. Do not be taken in by friends who tell you how much they want a puppy

from you. But when the crunch comes and it is money up-front, you would be amazed at the excuses some people make. You will be left – literally – holding the babies, and a very expensive luxury this can be, especially when they start to grow and need more food. Then comes the time for inoculations and so it goes on. The pups grow larger and larger, eat more and more, and still nobody buys them. You get desperate, and finally you have to decide either to put them all down, sell to a dealer at a greatly reduced price (which means they may go into unsuitable homes) or put them all into Rescue.

HEALTH
No Shepherd should be bred from unless it is in peak condition – not too fat, and certainly not too thin. Our definition of good condition is that you should be able to feel the ribs and pin bones, but not see them. The coat should be clean and free from any vermin such as fleas, ticks, or lice etc. In some Mediterranean islands, fleas and ticks are endemic, and it is practically impossible to get rid of them. Hot countries have other parasite problems, and if these conditions apply you will will know how to deal with them, or you can seek veterinary advice. A Shepherd carrying a lot of parasites, or one suffering from a skin condition, is not a fit animal and should certainly not be used for breeding purposes. There are many excellent products on the market to cope with these problems, so it should not present too hard a task to cure them. Before embarking on a litter or using your dog at stud make certain that you, with the help of your vet if necessary, have a Shepherd free from all skin complaints and parasites.

Not only have we external parasites to cope with but also internal ones. All Shepherds should be regularly wormed about once a year. A badly-infested dog is not in good condition, and should be dosed accordingly. There are several different types of worms, not all found in all countries. To find out which particular variety your dog is carrying, the only reliable way is to take a sample of faeces and get your vet to diagnose the worm or worms your dog is carrying. A dog can carry more than one species at a time, but with a sample, your vet will know what medication to give you. A worm-free stud dog is important, but with a bitch it is vital, because those worms are sapping her system of vitamins and trace elements which are essential if she is to produce a healthy, strong litter.

CARING FOR A STUD DOG

DIET
Unless your stud dog is being used regularly, say three, four times a month, or even more, a maintenance diet is sufficient. The odd stud or two will do him no harm. But if you are lucky enough to own a popular stud, which can be very lucrative, he must have a higher protein diet, and if a complete food is being used, make certain that it contains the vital vitamins and trace elements which your stud dog needs to keep his fertility up to a high level. If you are feeding a meat, tripe and biscuit meal diet, increase his red meat and add a good vitamin supplement, otherwise you could invite trouble with both his condition and fertility. An extra teaspoonful of Vitamin E in oil form, or two pills, according to their strength, will not come amiss in his daily diet to keep up his level of fertility.

BOOKINGS
A stud dog should have regular exercise, and if he is a trials or Schutzhund dog, cut down on the work the day he has a booking. If you are working your stud dog in competition, turn away the stud work for at least two days before he is due to work. Yes, you will lose out on stud fees, but you will have a fresh dog who will enjoy his work and do well for you, rather than one who is

tired and plods around like a broken-down old carthorse. Personally, we think that apart from exceptional cases, no dog should be used more than three or four times a week on a regular basis. Unfortunately, bitches tend to come into season together, and you usually get a whole lot menstruating at one time – hence a run on your stud dog – then for several months, just the odd booking. Never use a dog more than once a day. Some dogs will refuse to mate a second time, but others will, although the result is either a very small litter or the bitch misses. If you have taken a stud fee, the bitch will have to come back later for a free mating.

CONDITIONS AND STUD FEES

When a bitch is booked to your stud dog, make up your mind what your conditions are. How much are you charging as a stud fee, and will you take a puppy or two in lieu of a fee? Are you prepared to give more than one mating, and if the bitch misses, or has a small or dead litter, will you give a free mating on her next season? Are you prepared to give a mating free and then collect the stud fee when the puppies are born? Are you going to accept bitches who have not been X-rayed, are unregistered, have faulty temperaments or missing teeth, long coats, incorrect colours such as whites, blues, browns or brindles? All these questions have to be answered, and a clear policy outlined.

Our advice is to think very carefully before accepting a bitch with any of these faults, possibly excepting a long coat. Accept only approved bitches, which means those you have seen and consider good enough for your dog. This is a wise precaution, because you can be sure that, if anything goes wrong with the resulting progeny, your dog is likely to get all the blame! Do not forget, good bitches are needed to establish the reputation of your stud dog. So think carefully before you allow your dog to be used.

Stud fees depend on the popularity of your dog – how much he has won in the show ring etc. – and the current rate of fees in your particular country. Unless the bitch is of our breeding, or comes from a bloodline that we particularly want, we will not take a puppy in lieu of a stud fee. We are prepared to give as many matings as required, provided our stud dog is free to offer his services and has no other bitches booked during the desired period. We will give a free mating if the bitch misses, has dead puppies, or produces a small litter of one or two. We do stipulate, however, that it must be on her next season, and in all cases we suggest the vet takes a swab from her to discover the reason for the previous disappointing result. If the bitch cannot be mated again, for a particular reason, we are prepared to accept another bitch, provided that it is within a year of the original mating. To help our customers, we are prepared to wait for the stud fee until the puppies have been born, provided that we know and trust the people concerned.

In the UK, at the time of mating, you sign a document issued by the Kennel Club, which includes date of mating, name of dog and name of bitch, plus their breeding, which has to be sent up to the Kennel Club before the puppies can be registered. We withhold this document until the stud fee has been received, and cleared by the bank in the case of a cheque. This acts as a safeguard, as the puppies cannot be registered without the KC document. Other countries have different rules and regulations, and the national Kennel Club will provide all the necessary information.

THE BROOD BITCH

CHOOSING A STUD DOG

When you have decided that you can afford a litter and have suitable premises, take a careful look at your bitch. Temperament is of paramount importance. If your bitch is not 100 per cent in this respect, do not mate her. However good the stud dog's temperament, some of the litter will display

Shootersway Gundi: A well-constructed bitch who should make an ideal brood. She has a hip score of 10, is very well-bred and has an excellent temperament.

Eros v. Hambachtal ScH III: A lovely dog who fulfils all the qualities which make him an excellent stud dog.

These two German Shepherds are very similar in type and so complement each other. Mated together they should produce an outstanding litter.

your bitch's shortcomings in this respect. Do not be fooled by people who say it will improve the bitch's temperament to have a litter. It might, but what about the poor people who buy the puppies? The stud dog you choose must have an impeccable temperament and come from a line which produces the same. Whatever dog you decide on, make temperament your number one priority.

Your bitch has been X-rayed, has acceptable hips and a reliable temperament. Now look at her faults. Read the Standard carefully, and try to assess her structural qualities. Is she of correct proportions, is she a good colour and not too pale, has she a good topline with no roach or dip behind the withers, and so on? Jot down all her faults and virtues, then try and find a dog who will consolidate her virtues and correct her faults. Always remember, when planning a litter you are aiming to improve on what you have. It is just as expensive to rear a bad litter as a good one, so go for the best possible for your bitch. Now comes the difficult task of choosing a suitable dog. Take time and have a good look around before going ahead. Do not use the dog down the road just because he is near and cheap. The odds are that he will be totally unsuitable for your bitch, and the resulting litter could be disastrous. On the other hand, he could be a fine GSD specimen and exactly what your bitch requires. The lesson is, do your homework on the stud dog, and do not choose him merely because he belongs to a friend or happens to live close by.

Having decided on what you want, visit some breeders, see their stud dogs, and, if possible, see what they are producing. Make certain the stud dogs are X-rayed, have good hips and are also registered with your country's Kennel Club. Allow yourself plenty of time to visit several kennels before your bitch comes into season so you are quite certain you know which dog you want to use when the time comes. Discuss your bitch with the breeders and ask for their opinion as to which dog is most suitable. Most breeders are pleased to give advice and if they are any good at all, they should know what is most suitable for your bitch. Another important point is the matter of pedigrees. Some bloodlines are not suitable to mix with others, while it is a good thing to double up on certain lines. When visiting breeders, take your bitch's pedigree and discuss it with them to determine whether they think their stud dog would suit your bitch.

WHEN TO MATE YOUR BITCH
The season before you intend to mate your bitch, study her carefully. Find out how long she remains in season, and try to work out which is the most suitable day on which to mate her. One of our bitches had finished her season by Day 12 and always had to be mated on Day 6 or 7. We have also had some bitches who would not stand until Day 17 or 18, so be aware of this wide variation. Ask the stud dog's owners which day they would like you to bring the bitch, but let them know about any signs you have noticed regarding the correct day for mating.

Your bitch should be in good, hard condition – not too fat or too thin. She should also be free from all parasites, both external and internal. Some breeders will tell you not to mate your bitch until her third season. We feel a better guide is to wait until she is over two years of age, and for a first litter, we would not mate a bitch over four years of age. In Germany and, in fact all SV countries, you are not allowed to use a dog or bitch for breeding until they are over two years and have passed their Breed Surveys, hip X-rays and Working Tests. We feel this is an excellent idea and would like to see it adopted in this country. Some breeders mate their bitches every season, but we do not agree with this, unless the bitch has had a small litter, say one or two, which will not put too much strain on her. Then it will do her no harm to have litters in two consecutive seasons.

In some countries, bitches are mated on every season, but are only allowed to rear six puppies. Any surplus pups are either reared by a foster mother, or put down. As soon as the bitch has whelped, the local Breed Warden has to be contacted, who will come and inspect the puppies, take details, and more or less tell you what you can keep. Any faulty colour or other abnormality means the puppy must immediately be put down. These countries have an excellent foster mother scheme so that if your bitch has whelped too many puppies, it is not difficult to find an alternative bitch to rear them.

THE MATING
Many people think that stud work is just a question of bringing a bitch in season to the dog and then letting them get on with it. If only it were that easy! We have had bitches throwing themselves on to the ground, attacking the dog, turning on us or their owner, and all sorts of other things. Usually, this is due to the bitch being brought on the wrong day of her season. We suggest that the bitch be brought on her twelfth day, which appears to suit the majority of bitches, but by no means all. Some will have finished their season by then, and others will not be ready until the

Day 18 or 20. We suggest to owners that they study the bitch very carefully during the season before they intend to mate her. Make a note of when she starts showing colour and the length of time this continues. You will find that her vagina will start to swell and become soft. Some say that the time to mate is when she stops bleeding, but we have found that with some of our bitches, if we did this we would never get them mated! They appear to bleed the whole way through their seasons. If you have another dog, try to note your bitch's reaction to him. When the bitch is standing with her tail to one side, and her interest is obvious, this is the time to take her to the stud dog.

For your dog's first mating, try to find a bitch who has had a litter or two previously, even if it means giving a free service for your stud dog's first mating. The bitch will know what it is all about, and this will help the dog enormously. Always have a muzzle handy for a difficult bitch, and a jar of Vaseline for lubricating the bitch's vagina if it appears rather tight. It is desirable, when dog and bitch are first introduced, to let them free in a confined space and allow them to get to know each other. Often the bitch will urinate, the dog will go and inspect the spot, and his teeth will start to chatter. We take this as a sign that the bitch is probably ready. The dog will quickly go and inspect the bitch's rear end and you can then note the bitch's reactions. Some will fly at the dog, others will dance around playing hard to get, and some will stand with their tails on one side waiting for the dog to mount.

If you are lucky, the bitch will stand firm, and after a few probing actions and a padding of his hind feet, the dog will give the final thrust. With this final thrust the dog ejaculates, his sperm is passed into the bitch's ovaries and thus fertilisation takes place. During the probing action, you and the bitch's owner should walk quietly and slowly up to the pair, you to the side and the owner to the bitch's head. You have previously instructed the bitch's owner how to hold her securely, one hand underneath each ear and her head in between the the owner's legs. Try to impress upon the owner not to let go. You must hold the dog on the bitch's back for a minute or two, then gently push one of his front legs over the bitch's side so that they are standing side by side.

If the dog wants to turn, he will try and lift a hind leg over the bitch's back so that they will end up standing back to back. Not all dogs want to turn, but we allow our males to do so if they wish, although to start off we train them to stand at the bitch's side. Dogs are one of the very few species of mammals who 'tie' during a mating, which means that the dog's penis has swollen and become locked in the bitch's vagina. During this period, fluid is passing from the dog into the bitch, helping to wash the sperm well into the bitch's ovaries, which aids fertilisation. The two will not come apart, until this phase has been completed.

It is important not to let the bitch pull away from the dog, because if the tie is broken too soon, serious damage can be inflicted on either dog, bitch, or both. So you have been warned. An average tie lasts between ten and thirty minutes but can be very much longer, so be prepared for a long wait. A tie is not vital to a successful mating, and sometimes the dog will detach himself as soon as he has ejaculated. The bitch can, and in fact often will, conceive without a tie, but we always like to see one and feel success is more likely if it occurs.

What is described above is a normal and straightforward mating with a ready and receptive bitch. Alas, this is not always the case. If the bitch flies at the dog, she is usually not yet ready. Tell the owners to come back a day or two later. If she is as bad the next time, try muzzling her. On no condition allow any bitch to really attack your dog. Not only can she do serious damage, but it can also put off a young stud dog for life. The occasional bitch simply refuses to be mated whatever you do, and we have heard it suggested that the bitch should be sedated. Although we are not completely against this, we feel that if the bitch really will not be mated, it is perhaps nature's way of highlighting a physical reason why the bitch should not have puppies.

If the dog finds it hard to penetrate the bitch, use Vaseline to lubricate both inside and outside the bitch's vagina, and on the next attempt, the dog will slip in without further difficulty. But, if possible, try to get an experienced breeder to help you with your first few matings. When the mating is completed, wash your dog's penis and sheath down with a weak disinfectant, just in case the bitch is carrying some form of infection. A well-used stud dog can pass on an infection from one bitch to another, hence the reason why, in America and some other countries, the stud dog owner's insist on a vet's certificate of clearance before they will accept a bitch for mating.

FEEDING THE IN-WHELP BITCH

Your bitch needs no extra feeding until you can see that she is definitely in whelp, which is usually around the fifth week. After that, put her on a higher protein diet and gradually increase her rations. It is difficult to say just how much she will eat, as this varies from one bitch to another, and according to what kind of diet you are feeding. After about the sixth or seventh week we give our bitches as much as they like. At this time we feed twice daily to start with and then three times as her time draws near.

After about the eighth week we find that our bitches start to go off their food, and have to be tempted to eat. We normally feed a complete food, but to encourage our bitches to eat, even if only a little, we add tripe, raw meat, tinned meat, cheese or whatever they fancy. Some are far more fussy than others. A normal pregnancy is reckoned to be sixty-three days, but this can vary by as much as five or more days either side of the due date of whelping. If too early, the puppies could be termed as premature, and may need very careful management. They might not be strong enough to suck, so must be helped. If your bitch goes over time, do not worry too much, as long as she appears OK.

Keep a careful check on any form of discharge. A clear one is perfectly normal, but if you see a dark-green or brown discharge, get her to the vet quickly. It could mean either a dead puppy or a dead litter which needs to be removed as soon as possible. A Caesarian might be required, which, sad though it is, will at least save the bitch and possibly some of the puppies. Never put your bitch at risk for the sake of the puppies. She can always have another litter. If you are unlucky enough to have a dead litter, or the bitch has missed, it is a wise precaution to have a swab taken to ascertain what has caused the problem. If she has some form of infection, it can be treated and cleared up before you try mating her again.

WHELPING AND REARING

At last the big day has arrived, and you are about to become a breeder. You are probably both excited and a bit worried about what might happen. But try not to be too anxious, as most first-time whelpers seem to know exactly what to do. Whelping a bitch down is a fascinating experience and when it is all over and the puppies are happy and contented, you will experience a sense of supreme happiness at having whelped your first litter. Now is the time to have that stiff drink!

SIGNS OF IMMINENT WHELPING

The question we are often asked is: "How will I know when the puppies are about to be born?" The answer is that we do not know, but there are certain signs which tell us when the birth is imminent. Some bitches go off their food but drink a fair amount of water. Some start to dig holes in the garden, usually under your best shrubs, as if looking around for a place to have their pups. If an outside kennel is being used, we like to put the bitch in there at least ten days before she is due, so that she can get thoroughly used to her whelping pen. If it is to be indoors, decide well in advance where the whelping will take place and get your bitch happy and settled in that area.

Immediately prior to whelping, a bitch will often start to pant and look at her rear end as if waiting to see whether anything is happening. Soon she may start to shiver, and this is usually the sign of the onset of labour. Before long you will notice her straining. Two or three days before the due date of whelping, take the bitch's temperature. This is done by inserting a thermometer, greased with Vaseline, into the bitch's rectum. The normal temperature in a dog is 38.5 degrees C (101.2F). Just before whelping, this will usually drop down to about 37C (98.5F). The drop in temperature is to prepare the puppies for their entry into a cooler world, and it is usually a very reliable guide.

PREPARING THE WHELPING AREA

See that you have plenty of newspaper in the whelping box as your bitch will start to tear it up and dig, as if trying to make a nest for her puppies. If she is in the house she might start to scratch and tear at your carpets, so beware as she may do a lot of damage. As soon as she starts this, take her quickly into her whelping area as the birth could be imminent.

For outside use, we have a whelping box measuring 106cm by 138cm and 76cm high, and we add sides to it measuring 106cm by 138cm and 20cm high. These are easily removed when you have finished with them. The base can then be used as a bed-board, and the sides scrubbed and stored away for future use. Whether outside or indoors, make certain you have adequate heating arrangements. We use an infra-red light over one end of the whelping box, so that if the bitch gets too hot, she can move to the other end of the pen, leaving her puppies warm at the heated end. Obviously, during the summer, a lamp is not required during the day, but have one ready because it can become very cold in the early hours of the morning. One of the commonest causes of death in new-born puppies is hypothermia. The puppy moves away from its mother, gets left out in the cold and the next thing you know you have a dead puppy.

Get everything ready well before the day. Have a plentiful supply of clean newspaper, a good supply of clean towels, some sterile umbilical cord and a sterilised pair of scissors. We have a comfortable chair handy, because one of us always stays with the bitch throughout the entire whelping, whatever the time of day or night. Some breeders let their bitches get on with it and believe in letting nature take its course, but we cannot agree with this. Nine times out of ten you will probably get away with it, but the tenth time you might find that you lose the whole, or some, of the litter and possibly even the bitch. We also find that our bitches like somebody to be with them.

WHELPING

By the time your bitch has started to strain she should be safely in her whelping box. Prior to the whelping, the bitch will probably pass a lot of pale-green liquid which means the sac containing amniotic fluid has burst, but some bitches will strain for a considerable time before this happens. During this period, you will notice the contractions becoming closer and stronger until at last you will see part of a puppy appearing from the bitch's vagina, then with one final push out it comes. The bitch will be busy tugging at something, and to the novice it might look as if she is trying to eat the puppy. What is happening is that she is pulling out the afterbirth and severing the umbilical cord. Most bitches will eat the afterbirth, which sounds and looks pretty awful, but this is perfectly normal, so do not try and take it away from her. The puppy will probably still be in its bag, and only when the bitch has finished with the afterbirth will she turn her attention to it, licking it strongly to stimulate breathing. We are always pleased to hear the puppy cry which means that its lungs are functioning properly.

Sometimes, immediately after birth, a bitch will take no notice of her puppy which is lying in its bag, still attached to the umbilical cord and afterbirth. Wait a few minutes and if there is still no sign of action on the part of the bitch, push her nose down on to the cord to persuade her to sever it. If there is still no reaction, thoroughly wash your hands, then gently ease out the afterbirth and sever the cord about 3-5cm from the puppy's stomach, cutting it at an angle with sterilised scissors. Make certain that all membranes are removed from the puppy's face, enabling it to breathe. If the puppy shows no sign of movement, rub it with a towel and shake it with its head pointing downwards to get rid of any fluid which may be left in the lungs. This will usually succeed in making it cry and it can then be put on to a nipple and encouraged to suck. Some puppies take longer than others to suck, but if the puppies appear strong and active, they will soon begin. If the cord is bleeding excessively, now is the time to use the sterilised umbilical cord. Get somebody else to hold the puppy while you tie the cord in a reef-knot as close as possible to the puppy's stomach. This will soon stop the bleeding and perhaps save the puppy's life.

Some bitches pass a lot of water and constantly need fresh newspaper to mop it all up. Others seem to produce a lot of blood, making the bed look more like a battlefield than a whelping box. Whichever is the case, plenty of newspaper will keep the puppies warm and dry. We always keep a careful time-check on when the puppies are born, and we find that a puppy every two hours is about average. Your bitch might go longer, and then have two or three close together, but if she goes more than about three hours without producing a puppy, call the vet, who will give her an injection to start the contractions again. Within about ten minutes, another puppy will be born. If the injection is not successful, the vet will decide whether to give further injections or proceed with a Caesarian section.

Although puppies can be born head or tail-first, head-first is considered normal. If the puppy is presenting sideways, no amount of straining is going to shift it. Your only answer is to enlist the help of a vet or an experienced breeder who can push the puppy back and turn it, so that it presents itself in the correct manner. Only attempt this if the bitch has been straining hard, almost to the point of exhaustion, and still nothing has happened.

If the bitch has a big litter, she will probably go to sleep half-way through to allow herself to build up strength for the remaining births. During the whelping, we provide a plentiful supply of warm milk and honey, which all bitches seem to appreciate. We also like to give them a chance to relieve themselves, but many bitches will not leave their puppies until whelping is complete. The puppies are not able to relieve themselves without the stimulus of their mother licking them, so you will notice that your bitch will spend a lot of time cleaning her litter.

CAESARIAN SECTION

If, by any chance, a Caesarian is necessary, the bitch will not be able to deal with the puppies until she has recovered from the anaesthetic. As soon as she returns from the vet, we put the puppies straight back with their mother but take care that they are all 'topped and tailed'. Dampen a piece of cotton-wool and gently massage their genitals, and you will soon find they will relieve themselves. Make a point of doing this every hour or so until the bitch is able to take over. While still under the anaesthetic, care must be taken to see that she does not lie on her puppies. We find it best to stay with her until she has recovered sufficiently to deal with the puppies herself.

It is handy to have a cardboard box, containing a hot-water bottle covered with a clean towel, so that when the next puppy is imminent, those already born can be put into the box and kept warm and dry. However, we have found that some bitches resent their puppies being removed even for a short period. They get very agitated and promptly pull them out of the box, so if you try this procedure, you must be sensitive to your bitch's attitude.

POST-WHELPING

How do you know when your bitch has finished? With experience, you can feel when there are no more puppies. When the litter is complete, most bitches will settle down with their puppies,

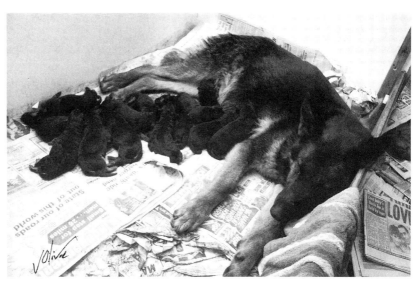

A litter of thirteen puppies just a few hours after whelping. The whole litter was reared successfully.

appear very relaxed and will usually sleep. However, unless you have an experienced breeder with you, ask your vet to call. He will check your bitch and all the puppies to see that nothing is amiss, such as a retained afterbirth. If this is the case, he will probably give an injection to make her expel it, and also an antibiotic in case of infection. Your vet will check the puppies for any deformities such as a cleft palate or a heart problem. If one of the puppies is abnormal in any way, we have it put down. There is no point in trying to rear an abnormal puppy. Nobody will want to buy it, and when a home is finally found, the chances are that the new owner will face enormous vet's bills, so harden your heart and do not try to rear it.

With a normal birth, you can normally wait until the next day to call the vet. Before retiring for a well-earned rest – especially if the whelping has taken place during the night – see that the bed is dry and the puppies all have suckled and appear warm and contented. Give the bitch a drink of milk, sweetened with honey, take her out to relieve herself, then leave her to sleep. We wait until the next morning before changing the entire bed and cleaning her, as she needs a little peace and quiet after all her hard work. Having changed the bedding, wash away the green fluid which will have stained her coat. If left, it can sometimes burn off the hair and leave the poor bitch with an undignified bare bottom!

For the next two or three days, you will find that all your bitch will want in the way of nourishment is some form of milk and porridge diet. We use a porridge made especially for lactating bitches and puppies until she is ready to go on to a solid food. The bitch will still be losing a lot of blood and water, and you will need to constantly change the bedding in order to keep both bitch and puppies clean and dry. This discharge will gradually diminish, and by the end of a week there should be very little. At this stage, put a piece of fleecy synthetic bedding on top of the paper to keep the puppies dry and warm. Any discharge or urine goes through to the papers underneath, leaving the top dry. This also helps the puppies to move around, as their tiny feet can get a much better grip on this surface than on paper.

WHELPING PROBLEMS
The above is a description of a normal whelping, and in most instances this is the case. Whelping is a natural process, and if your bitch is in good condition and healthy, you should have little or no trouble. But, with a maiden bitch, you will sometimes find that she gets very panicky, even to the

extent of killing or badly damaging the new-born puppies. This is why we consider it essential to be present during the whelping. If you are unfortunate enough to have such an experience, take the puppies away from the bitch and only let them suckle when you have somebody with you to hold her head. Usually, after the first two or three births, she will accept the puppies and settle down happily.

If you have to take them away from her, just let her feed them (you will have to clean them), and then take them away again. If she rejects them completely, you will have the job of hand-rearing. In many countries, there is an excellent network of foster mothers. All you have to do is to get in touch with your local GSD club and they will put you in touch with a foster mother, usually a bitch who has either lost all her babies or has a very small litter.

Hand-rearing can be successful, but very hard work. The puppies have to be fed every two hours, day and night, for the first ten days and then every three hours until you start to wean them at about fourteen days. You are taking the mother's place, so make certain that each puppy is cleaned as soon as you have fed it. A premature baby's bottle (you can obtain this from a chemist's shop) is ideal, and the puppies soon learn to suck from it. For milk, use a brand specially made for dogs, which is the same formula as bitch's milk. Mix as per instructions.

Fading Puppy Syndrome is another other hazard you might encounter. Puppies who are born vigorous and healthy gradually refuse to suck, are noisy and develop a high-pitched cry which is most distressing. They become limp and die, and, if this happens, we feel completely helpless and unable to do a thing. It is believed that the problem arises from the mother's milk and one solution is to hand-rear the entire litter. Better still, contact your vet and have the puppies all injected with a broad-spectrum serum, designed specially for this purpose. If a swab is taken from the bitch or a post-mortem done on a puppy, you will find that she is probably carrying some form of Strep, Staph or Ecoli, which is infecting her milk and killing the puppies. If the serum is given within 24 hours of birth, all the puppies can be saved. The bitch will also be given a course of antibiotics. Before mating the bitch again, have her tested and treated so the same thing does not happen again.

In a large litter you will sometimes find there is one small, weak puppy that, whatever you do, just will not suck. We have tried feeding, with an eye-dropper, milk expressed from the bitch but it rarely, if ever, works and a lot of time and trauma can be wasted on it. So, if it will not feed on its own, we let nature take its course and probably within a few hours it will be dead. Sometimes, you will find that the bitch will deliberately push it away and ignore it. We feel this is nature's way of saying there is something wrong with it.

One other problem worth mentioning, although uncommon, is the puppy who when it rolls over on to its back, cannot get back on its feet. Usually they have difficulty feeding and, again, the kindest thing is to have the puppy put down. We have never discovered what causes this condition, or whether it is curable. All vets with whom we have discussed it seem to have no answer or cure, but think it is something to do with balance and could possibly be caused by a difficult birth. The condition is known as Congenital Peripheral Vestibular Disease. However, we recently had a bitch puppy who had a tendency to this condition. However, after a difficult struggle, she could get back on her feet. She was strong and seemed determined to survive. We made a point of always finding her a teat, thus giving her every chance and she seemed to be keeping pace with her brothers and sisters. When her littermates started to stand up and move around, this pup's head was tilted to one side. We had made up our minds to have her put down, but when we started to wean the litter, she made a miraculous recovery and at five weeks of age there was no visible difference between her and the rest. By the time they were ready to go at eight weeks, she was absolutely normal. We think really bad cases are best put down at birth, but when a situation arises like the one we have described, it is worth trying to save the puppy provided – and this is very important – that if it does not show marked improvement over the coming weeks, you have the courage to end its life. It is easy to get very fond of this sort of puppy and therefore very hard to make the decision to put them down. But remember, it is your duty as a GSD breeder to put sound, strong, healthy puppies on to the market. They will cause their future owners a minimum of worry and expense and give them much joy and pleasure.

We have gone into detail about whelping and some of its hazards. Obviously, we cannot cover all aspects but we hope we have given the reader some idea of what can happen when whelping a bitch for the first time. It is a wonderful experience to see the puppies grow from little whelps to maturity, and knowing that the final results are your brainchild is quite fascinating. You will have disappointments, but also successes which will make everything worthwhile.

CARE OF THE LACTATING BITCH AND PUPPIES
Having successfully brought the puppies into the world, your next hurdle is their rearing. A strong, healthy litter, without proper care of the lactating bitch and the weaning of the puppies, could become weedy and undernourished with little chance of growing into strong, healthy German Shepherds. Alas, we have seen it happen all too often. The breeder concerned has no idea of the cost and time involved in rearing a healthy litter, and so tries to rear the pups on the cheap. The outcome is a disaster. Do not embark on breeding unless you are prepared to spend time and money looking after the litter.

After the first two or three days, the bitch will be ready to go back to a solid diet. We feed the bitch four times a day, gradually increasing the amount until she is getting about 1-1.5kg per day of a 36 per cent protein complete food, specially made for the lactating bitch. Some will eat more and some less, depending on how many whelps there are in the litter. For the bitch to rear her pups well, she needs a good diet to produce a plentiful supply of milk. By the time the pups are ready to be weaned, she will be producing quite a lot to satisfy their appetites.

MASTITIS
Check her teats every day for any soreness or hardness. If one of her teats feels hot and hard, she probably has mastitis. An antibiotic from the vet will quickly cure this problem and, within a day or so, she will be back to normal. To prevent her teats getting sore, cut the puppies' claws every ten days or so. For this task, use sharp nail-scissors and just clip the white tips off. Failure to do this will cause a lot of unnecessary suffering to your bitch. Just imagine the damage six or seven pairs of feet, with four sharp claws on each foot, can do to her tender belly!

DISCHARGE
Check the bitch's rear end for any excessive discharge. By the end of the first week, there should be little or no mess on the paper. If your bitch is still losing a lot of bloody, greenish fluid, a visit from the vet is desirable. Sometimes, two or three days after she has whelped, you will suddenly notice her straining again and may think that, in spite of all your precautions, she still has another pup and is going into labour again. She probably has a womb infection, such as metritis. A course of antibiotics will soon cure this problem. In the thirty years we have been breeding, we have only seen this condition once, so we can safely say it is comparatively rare, but nevertheless worth mentioning.

Always make certain your bitch has plenty of clean drinking water. Producing milk is a very thirsty occupation, and she needs plenty of fluid to help her maintain a plentiful supply.

WEANING
If the bitch has six puppies or less, we leave weaning until the pups are three weeks old. With a

bigger litter we start weaning at two weeks. The time to start depends entirely on the amount of milk your bitch is producing. If she has insufficient, you will have to start earlier, but we have found the above a pretty good guideline. You will probably wonder whether the pups are getting sufficient milk. Well-fed puppies are contented puppies, and as soon as they finish feeding they drop off the teat and sleep. When picked up, a puppy will feel solid and heavy, whereas undernourished puppies start to cry and will feel light. Some breeders weigh their puppies every few days right from birth, to be sure they are maintaining a steady weight increase, and this is a good idea for the first-time breeder. The average puppy's weight at birth is between 395 and 510g. But, depending on the size of the litter, this can vary considerably.

At around ten days, the puppies' eyes will start to open and you will notice that they are beginning to be aware of sound. Until now they have been both blind and deaf, and have found their way on to the teat by their acute sense of smell and touch. Now they will be moving about the whelping box quite freely and making their first efforts to get on their feet.

The puppies' first feed consists of milk made up from a milk powder, especially made to the formula of bitch's milk. After two or three days on this, we add a powdered food from the same manufacturers. Each puppy is fed about a tablespoonful of this mixture once a day, and when they are all eating this hungrily we start them on a second meal. At this stage, we feed each puppy individually to make certain all the pups are getting their fair share. We use a saucer which is not too deep, so the pups cannot get their noses into the milk mixture and start to choke.

The puppies now have their eyes open and, although still rather unsteady, are moving around quite a lot. You have increased their rations to two tablespoonsful twice-daily, and it is now time to start on solid food. Their third daily meal can consist of a 32 per cent protein pellet food, which we soak in hot water or milk for about ten minutes prior to feeding. This is a complete food with all the necessary vitamins and trace elements which puppies must have to ensure they are well-boned, strong and healthy, giving them an excellent start in life.

In some countries these complete diets (and there are many excellent brands on the market) are unobtainable, which means a flesh diet with a good quality biscuit meal must be used instead. Whatever diet you feed, and this must inevitably vary from one country to another, make certain that a good vitamin supplement and bone-meal is included to ensure correct growth. As before, we feed individually and start with about 14g of pellets (weighed when dry) per puppy.

WORMING

When the puppies are in between three and four weeks of age, and before they start on a solid diet, they will need worming. There are many brands of worming tablets, powders and fluids, which can be bought from your local pet shop. Some are good and some not so good. We prefer to get tablets from the vet, who will supply a safe and reliable product specially made for worming puppies.

We worm our puppies every ten days until they are ready to leave us at eight weeks of age. We recommend to new owners that the puppy is wormed once a month until about six months, after which once a year is sufficient. Obviously, if the puppy still has worms at six months, which is unlikely in a well-reared animal, the treatment must continue until all worms have been eliminated. Different countries have different worm problems, so it is wise to consult your local vet to find out what treatment is recommended.

INCREASING RATIONS

The puppies are now doing well on three daily meals, two porridge and one solid, so gradually change, a meal at a time, to solid food until, at around five weeks of age, the puppies are on three meals of soaked pellets per day. At this stage we start adding natural, live yoghurt to their solid meal giving one teaspoonful per puppy. This is gradually increased so that at eight weeks each puppy is getting a dessertspoonful. Yogurt is beneficial in preventing digestive problems. Increase the amount given at each meal and feed all the puppies together, but make certain every pup gets a fair share. Feed in two separate bowls, putting the greedy pups at one and the smaller not-so-greedy ones at the other. If you are weighing your puppies, you will soon see whether each puppy is getting its correct ration or not

When the puppies are about four weeks of age, start reducing their mother's food supply, thus cutting down her milk production. At five weeks, we take the bitch away from her puppies during the daytime, and cut out her lunch. It is also the time to start giving the puppies their fourth daily meal, usually last thing at night. At six weeks the bitch is taken away from her puppies. She can discontinue her high-protein diet, and return to her normal maintenance diet fed twice daily.

The puppies are now eating four meals a day consisting of 42.5g of complete food (weighed dry, then soaked) per puppy per meal, giving each puppy a total of 170g per day. Gradually increase their daily rations, until at eight weeks of age, each puppy should be getting 227-283g of food per day. Keep a careful check on their motions. If they seem anything other than firm, you are probably feeding too much, so cut down on the daily ration. It is very easy to over-feed, so be careful. A slightly hungry puppy is far healthier than one which picks at its food, not really wanting to eat. When feeding, always watch carefully to see that all the puppies eat hungrily and clear everything up. If not, take the food away and give them less at their next meal. Never leave food lying around. It will get sour and also encourage vermin, which is the last thing you want.

LOOSE MOTIONS
Always watch your puppies carefully, and if you see a loose motion, try to find out which puppy it belongs to. The puppy concerned will usually be a bit listless, not interested in its food, or even its mother when she is returned for suckling. You will quite often find around six weeks of age, when the puppies are completely weaned, that you might get one or more puppies behaving in the manner described. We keep an antibiotic handy which deals with this type of situation, and the puppies are back to normal within twenty-four hours. However, if the condition persists, call in the vet. It might be nothing, but it is better to be safe than sorry. Sick puppies can be most distressing and they can go downhill very quickly with a considerable loss of weight, which is very difficult to replace.

THE OUTSIDE WORLD
At about four to five weeks of age, the puppies will be moving about quite happily, so we like to get them into an outside run – weather permitting! If this is not possible, make certain the puppies are in a situation where they can see the outside world. If they are in an outside kennel, even if you do not want them to go out, make sure that they can see through the door. An inside door covered with chain-link makes it possible for the puppies to see people, cars and general, everyday life.

If the puppies have been born indoors, you should get them out as soon as possible. Gazing at four blank walls all day is very detrimental to both character and temperament. Sunlight and fresh air are vital to the rearing of a healthy litter. If the puppies were born outside, allow them to follow you into the house so they get used to the sounds of the washing-machine or vacuum cleaner.

All our puppies seem to love these house expeditions, and revel in the toys we leave around. An old sock, leather glove, coffee-jar lid, a piece of wood are all ideal puppy toys. We play with the pups, letting them tug at the sock and throwing the other toys for them to fetch. We also pick up each puppy in turn and give it a good cuddle. We get great pleasure out of these daily sessions and learn a lot about the litter's individual characters.

INOCULATIONS

If the puppies are all fit and healthy and eating well at six weeks of age, we give them a parvovirus inoculation which over-rides the bitch's immunity and protects them from this often fatal disease. Some breeders do a blood test on the dam while she is rearing the puppies to ascertain the level of antibodies. It is thus possible to tell at what stage the immunity she gives to the puppies will decline, and so know when a parvovirus inoculation is required. Of course, this will vary according to which part of the world you live in. Ask local breeders for advice.

TATTOOING

Your puppies are now seven weeks old and it is now time to have them tattooed, before they go to their new homes at eight weeks of age. Now most countries have a tattoo scheme; it is compulsory for all countries under SV jurisdiction. Most breeders in the UK now have their puppies tattooed. It causes little or no pain to the puppies, and is a wonderful method of identification. Many a lost or stolen dog has been returned to its rightful owner because of its tattoo.

LEAVING THE BREEDER

At eight weeks, our puppies leave and are supplied with a pedigree, inoculation certificate, registration card, tattoo number and the all-important diet sheet, plus an insurance cover for the first six weeks after leaving us. The new owners can then decide whether they wish to continue with the insurance or not. We feel that this insurance policy is very important, as things can go wrong when a puppy moves to a new home, and at least the new owners' vet bill will be paid for.

As far as diet is concerned, we suggest that the new owner continues with the same diet as the breeder has fed, gradually increasing the ration so that at six months the puppy will be getting 0.5k to 0.6k per day, fed in two meals. At fourteen weeks we usually phase out the last meal at night, and at sixteen weeks the lunch meal is dropped. If the new owners wish to change to another diet, they must do so gradually so as not to upset the puppy's digestive system. With our own puppies, we continue the special diet until they are about nine months of age, when we change to an adult

Well-reared puppies look bright-eyed and healthy and are interested in everything that is going on around them.

A German Shepherd puppy ready to leave the breeder and go to its new home.

diet. In the complete food range, there are many different diets you can change to, and which one the new owner chooses depends on what the puppy's intended future will be. Is it going to be shown, worked, or will it be a family pet? A working dog needs a far higher protein diet than one which just goes out for its daily walk and stays in the house for the rest of the day. So consider carefully, and ask your local food agent's advice before changing to an adult diet.

So far, we have said nothing about registration. Most reputable breeders will automatically register the litter soon after birth and on selling the puppy will supply the registration certificate along with the rest of its papers. If you are the breeder of the litter, you will have to do this. On paying the fee for your chosen stud dog, you will have been given a form stating the dog's name, registration number and other details. Get the registration forms from your national Kennel Club, fill in particulars of the stud dog and your bitch, decide on names, then send the whole lot, plus the required money, back to the Kennel Club. If you follow the instructions given, your litter will be registered. Unless you have previously acquired an affix, you will not be allowed to use one. Different countries have different rules and regulations, so check on these before the litter is born.

SOCIALISATION

This starts from the day puppies are born. Every day we make a point of stroking each puppy in turn and picking them up, which can be done when changing the paper. Even when only a few days old, the puppies seem conscious of you, and when you run your hand down their backs, they will stretch with pleasure. As their eyes open, you will notice different reactions from each puppy. When you pick them up some will cry, and if you stroke their heads they might flinch, but all these reactions are merely the puppies becoming conscious of the outside world.

Much has been written about the dominant puppy always going for the back teat, so we decided to put the theory to the test. In our last three litters, we marked each puppy and kept a chart on where each one was sucking. We did this twice-daily, morning and evening. The results were quite interesting. In the first litter, the puppies swapped around and were never consistent. It appeared to be a matter of the puppies using the first teats they came to. In the other two litters, the puppies appeared to have favourite teats and went straight to that one, but after a good drink from the teat of their choice, they would all change and move to another. In none of those three litters was there any evidence of the dominant puppy always going for the back teat, although our little test could simply mean there was no dominant puppy in any of the three litters.

As the puppies get older we subject them to loud noises, starting off by tapping a saucepan with a wooden spoon. Watch their reactions, and if they all seem OK, increase the sound. Rattles and whistles can be introduced at an early age, but do not go over the top. Let the puppies learn gradually that there is nothing to fear from these sounds. At a later stage, provided that none of the puppies shies away from the sounds already mentioned, you can introduce them to gunshot. But do be careful to keep well away from the puppies to start with, and gradually move closer only when you are sure that they are all steady. Noises introduced over a period of time, in the way described, will ensure that when the puppies leave you they will be unworried by the majority of loud sounds which they are likely to encounter.

So far, all socialisation has involved the litter as a whole so, at around seven weeks of age, we take out the puppies one at a time and see how they react on an individual basis. This is when you can really see what their characters and temperaments are like. Those that have been correctly socialised should react as they did before, but occasionally you might find one, who when it has no back-up from the rest of the litter, is a bit hesitant to face up to the traumas of everyday life. Make a point of spending a lot of time encouraging the hesitant puppy to boost its confidence.

The above method of socialisation should mean that at eight weeks all your litter will settle into their new homes without any problem. It is up to the new owners to continue with their new puppy's socialisation, and as soon as it has settled in, start introducing elementary play training.

Chapter Eighteen

HEALTH PROBLEMS

The German Shepherd, if correctly bred and reared, should go through life with very few visits to the vet, other than the yearly renewal of its vaccinations. The list of ailments discussed in this chapter might seem long, but although many of them are uncommon, they can all occur. We feel we must mention them all – or at least those we know about!

EYE PROBLEMS: Compared with some breeds, German Shepherds have very few eye complaints.

JUVENILE CATARACT: This is an uncommon hereditary condition. In the UK seven or eight puppies, aged around five or six months, were found to have developed this complaint. They were all sired by the same dog. He was withdrawn from stud, a measure that seems to have successfully controlled the condition in this country. If your Shepherd is found to be suffering from this complaint, an operation can improve its sight, but on no account should it be bred from.

PANNUS: This is an uncommon form of corneal inflammation which affects both eyes and can result in blindness. It is characterised by a pink membrane growing across the cornea.

CONJUNCTIVITIS: Inflammation of the eye which can be caused by a virus or bacteria. It is characterised by a pus-like discharge, and sometimes an inflamed third eyelid. Bathe with cold water or a dilute solution of Boric acid made up for ophthalmic use. If there is no improvement within a day or two, consult your vet.

CLEAR DISCHARGE: This is usually caused by a foreign body in the eye. Treat as for Conjunctivitis.

ENTROPION: This is very rare in German Shepherds and is caused by ingrowing eyelashes. The condition can be corrected by surgery. This is hereditary and the Shepherd should not be bred from.

EARS: These should be examined regularly to make certain they are clean and free from wax. To clean, soak some cotton-wool in calamine lotion. If the wax is dark-red in colour it could indicate an infection. Your vet will give you some ointment which will soon clear the condition. If your Shepherd keeps on rubbing an ear which appears sore and has a pus-like, smelly discharge, it is suffering from otitis (canker). Consult your vet.

MOUTH: Examine your Shepherd's mouth regularly and see that its teeth are kept free from tartar. A raw marrow-bone given once a fortnight will help keep teeth clean, but if they get badly discoloured, take your dog to the vet to have its teeth scaled. Any teeth that are broken or appear to be going rotten, should be shown to your vet, who can advise on whether they should be extracted or not.

FEET

THORNS: An embedded thorn can be very painful and sometimes difficult to remove. Try softening the surrounding area by applying a hot compress and then, if possible, extract with tweezers. Dry carefully and dust with antiseptic powder.

GRASS SEEDS: Treat as above.

INTERDIGITAL CYSTS: These are pus-filled lumps in between the toes which can cause lameness. Try hot fomentations, then dry and apply antiseptic powder. If they continue, consult your vet. Sometimes a change of diet will help this condition.

NAILS: Keep your Shepherd's nails short. Unless the dog is running on a hard surface such as the road or a concrete run, nails will need cutting fairly often. Check the dewclaws on the front legs. If these are not kept short, these can sometimes grow round and into your dog's legs. Watch out for broken nails.

SKIN PROBLEMS: In most cases, a change of diet is indicated. In hot weather, maize or soya-meal based protein can often cause over-heating of the blood which will make your dog scratch. Garlic powder or tablets will help purify the blood. You might also encounter some skin problems while your Shepherd is casting its coat. If you notice the dog scratching or licking, take a careful look and see whether you can see anything.

WET ECZEMA: If the skin appears raw and wet, with what seems like pus around the edges, your dog is probably suffering from this. Quite a large area can appear overnight for no apparent reason. Use a sulphur-based ointment twice daily, but if it does not improve, visit the vet who will probably give your Shepherd an injection.

DRY ECZEMA: This is a similar condition. It usually appears underneath the dog's belly and on the inside of the hind legs. Treat as for Wet Eczema. If, in both conditions, there is no improvement after an injection, your vet will probably take a skin scraping to find out what is causing the problem. Some dogs are allergic to straw, so if you are using this type of bedding, change to something different. Some types of wood-shavings can also cause skin irritation. It could be a flea allergy, so check your Shepherd for unwanted visitors.

CYSTS: As you groom your dog, you might come across a small lump, which when gently squeezed, emits a hard, string-like pus. When empty, dab with a little disinfectant. If the lump when squeezed, does not emit anything, leave it alone but keep a careful eye on it. If it gets larger, consult the vet and have it removed.

RINGWORM: If you notice rapidly-spreading circular bare patches on your dog, it might well be caused by ringworm. It can appear on any part of the body and is caused by a fungus. It is contagious, so isolate your Shepherd, burn all bedding and thoroughly disinfect its kennel. Consult your vet, who will prescribe a suitable ointment and probably some tablets.

MANGE (SARCOPTIC): If roughened bare patches appear on your Shepherd around the eyes, elbows and stifle causing the dog to scratch continually, it might be mange. Consult your vet, who will prescribe a skin shampoo with which to bathe your dog until the condition is cured.

MANGE (DEMODECTIC): Bare patches appear on any part of the dog. They are dark-grey in colour and have a peculiar smell. There is little or no scratching. At one time this was incurable, but with modern drugs – especially if you catch it early – this condition can be cured. If you suspect mange, consult your vet immediately.

ANAL FURUNCULOSIS: This is a horrible complaint. If you notice your Shepherd licking its anus a lot, have a look. In most cases it is nothing, or possibly an indication of worms or full anal glands, but if you see pus-filled holes appearing, you know your dog is suffering from this. Take your dog straight to the vet. If the condition is not too serious, it can be cured by injections, but if several holes have already appeared, skilled surgery is necessary which is not always successful.

ANAL GLANDS: If your Shepherd regularly has a marrow-bone, the anal glands should empty themselves normally. If, however, they are full and your dog is rubbing its bottom along the ground, anal glands might well be the problem. Take your dog to the vet and ask him to show you how to empty them – it is not difficult, just a case of knowing where to squeeze. If the condition occurs again, you will know how to deal with it.

PARASITES: We are including external parasites in this section because they are often the cause of some of the skin conditions we have already mentioned. In a well-run kennel, parasites should not occur. However, fleas and lice can be very easily picked up from hedgehogs and rabbits. If, when grooming your dog, you notice lots of little black things, these are probably flea excrement. The usual sites are the chest, round the ears, and at the root of the tail, although if badly affected, your will find them all over the body. Bathe the dog in shampoo containing an insecticide, then spray your dog every few days with a good flea spray. There are several good brands available from pet shops or from your vet. As fleas breed off the dog, it is advisable to spray its living quarters as well.

TICKS: If you live in the country, especially where there are sheep or deer, sooner or later you are going to find a tick on your dog. Do not pull it off, because if you do the chances are that the head will still remain in the dog's skin and could cause a nasty sore. Cut the tick in half with a sharp pair of scissors, and the head should drop off. Dab the place with a little disinfectant. If you live in a hot country, or anywhere infested with ticks, dip your dog once a week in a tick-killing insecticide, obtainable from the vet. In some places, flies bite around the edge of the dog's ears causing a lot of discomfort. Consult your vet, who will give you a suitable spray to control this.

INTERNAL PARASITES: There are five different varieties of worms, not all of which are found in every country. The presence of hookworm, heartworm and threadworm can be diagnosed by a test on faeces. These three are relatively uncommon in the UK.

ROUNDWORM: These are usually found in puppies. A good breeder will have wormed the puppies three times before they are eight weeks old, and will give you particulars as to when they need worming again.

TAPEWORM: Usually found in the adult dog. If you see what look like grains of rice which are moving in your Shepherd's motions, the dog has tapeworm. As with roundworm, there are many preparations to be found in pet shops. However, we get tablets from the vet. Fleas are the host of tapeworm so if your Shepherd has fleas, take the precaution of worming.

In whatever country you live, check with your vet or your puppy's breeder to find out what varieties of worm your dog is likely to get and how to treat them accordingly. If your Shepherd is thin in spite of having a voracious appetite, or rubs its bottom along the ground, or has a staring coat, suspect worms and treat accordingly.

DIGESTIVE PROBLEMS: It is a common misconception that German Shepherds are more prone to digestive problems than other breeds. If your Shepherd is fed a sensible diet, suitable for the amount of work or exercise it is getting, there is no reason why the dog should suffer from digestive complaints unless it picks up an infection. However, as problems can occur, we list those that you are most likely to come across.

GASTROENTERITIS: This is an inflammation of the intestines and can be caused by an infection. The symptoms are sickness and diarrhoea. If the infection is mild, it will quickly clear up. Starve your Shepherd for two days, giving a drink of honey and water at regular intervals. Do not let your dog drink too much at any one time because this will cause sickness. Give a kaolin-based medication. If your dog vomits or passes blood, and seems off-colour, take its temperature, and go to the vet who will prescribe a broad-spectrum antibiotic.

PANCREAS DEFICIENCY, MALABSORPTION, BACTERIAL OVERGROWTH: Any of the above can be caused by a serious attack of gastroenteritis. If your Shepherd appears to be active, has a voracious appetite but is as thin as a rake and has perpetual diarrhoea, suspect one of these three conditions. Take your dog to the vet, who will collect blood samples to identify which condition it is suffering from. With these three conditions, the digestive system is not absorbing all the food, hence the poor condition. Once the condition has been diagnosed, tablets will be given to help control the situation. If your dog is found to be suffering from one of these conditions, great care must be taken with diet, which must be bland, such as chicken and rice. There are now several food manufacturers who cater especially for these conditions. You might not be able, in all cases, to cure the condition but, with careful feeding and tablets, it can be kept well under control.

BONE CONDITIONS

HIP DYSPLASIA: This is by far the most common of these conditions. The hip is a ball and socket joint with the femur head fitting neatly and deeply into the socket. The severity of the problem depends on the depth of the socket and how well-moulded the femur head is. If your Shepherd puppy shows signs of intermittent lameness on one or both of hind legs, or finds difficulty getting up, consult your vet. It is possible to take X-rays at an early age, but the plates can only be scored if your dog is over twelve months old. But early X-rays can ascertain if the problem is dysplasia and how serious the condition is. In the USA your Shepherd has to be two years old before hip plates can be scored. Each hip is scored individually, 53 points on each side, making a total of 106. The higher the score, the worse the hip.

If you intend to work your Shepherd in Working Trials or Schutzhund, you must have a dog with good hips. However, your dog can live a normal life as a pet with moderately severe HD. As this is a hereditary condition, only breed from Shepherds with good hips. At the moment the average score is 17. The Breed Council of the UK gives guidelines with regard to hips, and states that no dog with a score over 20 and no bitch over 25 should be bred from.

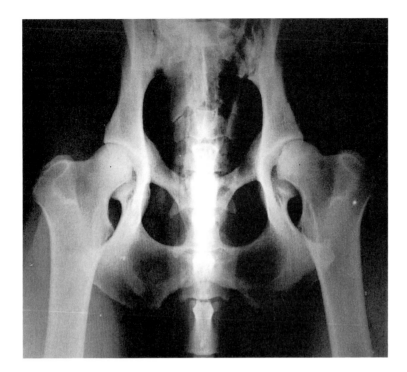

Good hips: Note the well-formed femur head fitting neatly into a deep socket.

Bad hips: Note the shallow sockets and flattened femur head.

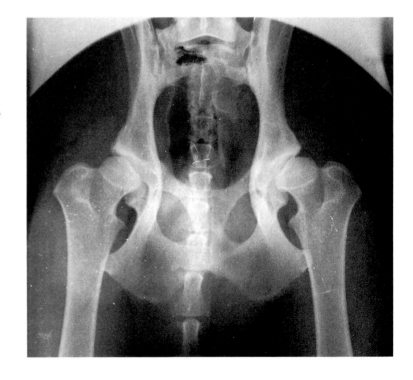

UNUNITED ANCONEAL PROCESS: An uncommon complaint, often referred to as elbow dysplasia or nonfusion of the elbow joint. The condition is caused by a faulty union of the anconeal process (one of the elbow bones) with the ulna. A loose fragment of bone sets up irritation in the elbow joint which will cause intermittent lameness. This complaint usually causes a thickening over the elbow and the Shepherd turns its feet and pasterns outwards. It usually becomes apparent at four to five months of age and can only be diagnosed by X-ray. An operation to remove the loose fragment of bone will correct the condition, but as it is believed to be hereditary, so it would be wise not to breed from affected dogs or bitches.

PANOSTEITIS: Again this condition is uncommon. It is caused by excessive production of bone along the long bones. The cause is unknown and the condition usually affects puppies between five and twelve months of age. It can cause lameness. Nobody knows very much about it and why it occurs, but it usually corrects itself by the time the dog is twenty months old.

CHRONIC DEGENERATIVE RADICULO MYELOPATHY (CDRM): This is a condition usually found in the elderly dog. The first signs are loss of muscle on the hind legs, a situation which gradually deteriorates until the Shepherd finds it difficult to stand up. It is a distressing condition because in every other way the dog is perfectly normal. Finally, you will find that your Shepherd will not be able to stand, and drags its hindquarters along the ground. The dog then becomes incontinent, which is very distressing to most dogs. When your Shepherd gets to the stage of dragging its hind legs along the ground, we think that euthanasia is the kindest solution. There appears to be no pain attached to this condition, which has been little researched and, at present, appears to be incurable.

VIRAL AND BACTERIAL INFECTIONS: All the following are serious infections, but some are covered by yearly inoculations. These are: Distemper (Hard Pad), Leptospirosis, Hepatitis (two types). There are five other serious infections which you should be aware of:

KENNEL COUGH (PARAINFLUENZA): There are several different forms of this, some more serious than others. All are highly contagious. A visit to the vet is indicated for any form of kennel cough, but a good cough mixture can help relieve the dog's sore throat. In most countries inoculations against these are available.

TONSILLITIS: This is a bacterial infection which can also result in a fever. Your vet will prescribe drugs which will soon effect a cure. Keep your Shepherd warm and feed a liquid diet.

PNEUMONIA: This is an inflammation of the lungs which can be caused by a bacterial or virus infection. Your Shepherd's breathing will become laboured and, if you put your ear to its chest, you will hear a bubbling sound. The dog will usually have a high temperature. Your vet will prescribe a broad-spectrum antibiotic. It is essential to keep the dog warm, especially the chest area. Take an old cardigan or pullover, put your dog's front legs down the sleeves and, with safety pins, make it fit snugly around the chest and abdomen. If the dog will allow, feed liquid food such as chicken broth or branded convalescent preparations.

BRUCELLOSIS: This is a bacterial infection which can cause abortion and fading puppies. In some countries, a clearance certificate is required before a bitch will be accepted for mating. Your vet will take a swab from the bitch and, if she is found to be carrying the infection, it can be cured with antibiotics.

NEPHRITIS: This is inflammation of the kidneys, usually caused by some infection. With this condition, your Shepherd will drink a lot and also urinate more than usual. The urine will appear rather thick and dark-yellow in colour. The vet will prescribe antibiotics. We have found barley-water very helpful with this condition. You can make it in two ways. Either boil pearl-barley for half an hour, then cool and strain, or soak flaked barley overnight and then drain.

All these infections require very careful nursing and after-care.

BLEEDING COMPLAINTS

HAEMOPHILIA: Only males are affected, but bitches are the carriers, so any female producing a haemophiliac puppy must be immediately discarded for breeding. Blood tests can be taken in most countries and Shepherds can be tested at an early age, so if your dog comes from a line known to produce haemophilia, have the dog tested.

VON WILLEBRANDS DISEASE: This can occur in either sex. The type of bleeding is different from haemophilia. The USA seems to be the country mainly affected at the moment.

EPILEPSY: Not all convulsions are hereditary. They can be caused by a knock on the head, a brain tumour or the after-effects of distemper. Your Shepherd will suddenly go rigid, shaking its head, champing its jaws, and producing a lot of white, frothy saliva. The dog will then fall over on its side, with the legs making galloping movements, and sometimes the dog will lose control of its bladder. The attack will be over in about two minutes. The Shepherd will then appear dazed for a few minutes before becoming normal again. The only way to ascertain whether this is idiopathic (hereditary) epilepsy or not, is for your vet to give the dog a thorough clinical examination and take a brain reading with an encephalograph. If hereditary, do not breed from your Shepherd. Epilepsy can be controlled with drugs, but if your dog's condition deteriorates, the kindest solution is euthanasia. Epilepsy usually starts between one and three years of age but it can also occur in between eight and nine years.

STOMACH TORSION OR BLOAT: This is a horrible complaint, and unless the dog is rushed to the vet within twenty minutes of the onset, it will be fatal. For no apparent reason, the stomach, turns on its axis, thus blocking gases from being passed at either end. The dog becomes restless, whines and tries unsuccessfully to be sick. If you feel the stomach, it will be as hard as a rock. The vet will operate immediately and return the stomach to its correct position. If caught in time, the operation is usually successful, but it can recur. Many opinions exist as to the reasons for this complaint, but to date, no real explanation has been found. It seems to occur more in larger breeds.

HEATSTROKE: This is an emergency which requires immediate attention. Dogs left in cars during the summer months without suitable ventilation, those tied up in full sun, or left in concrete runs without access to shade are all liable to develop heatstroke. Special care must be taken to ensure your Shepherd always has access to shade if living in a hot country. The first signs are rapid panting, staggering and then falling over. It is imperative to bring the dog's temperature down as quickly as possible. Put the dog in a bath of cold water, hose down with a garden hose, or put ice-packs around the dog. Packets of frozen food make excellent ice-packs. Unless you can bring your Shepherd's temperature down quickly, heatstroke can prove fatal.

PYOMETRA: This condition is similar to metritis, but far more serious. It does not usually occur in a bitch with puppies, but older bitches are more prone to it. If your bitch goes off her food but drinks a lot, has a temperature and a smelly vaginal discharge, take her immediately to the vet, who will operate at once. If ignored, pyometra will prove fatal.

CONDITIONS AFFECTING PUPPIES

PITUITARY DWARFISM: This is caused by a hormone deficiency. An affected puppy looks quite normal at birth but as it gets older you will notice a big difference between the size of it and its littermates. At eight weeks, a dwarf will be about half the size, or even less, and will often appear to have a short muzzle. As dwarfs get older, they usually never change their puppy coats or teeth, and so by twelve months of age their baby teeth are beginning to wear down and they look more like a Mexican Hairless than Shepherd. They do not usually live long, although some have been reared successfully.

A pituitary dwarf. This photo was taken when this puppy was eight weeks old. He weighed 4.5lbs and measured eight inches at the shoulder. Note the short muzzle and rather round protruding eyes, which are typical of a dwarf.

OESOPHAGUS, AORTIC ARCH, PYLORIC STENOSIS: These three conditions are usually not apparent until the puppies are eating solid food. If you notice a puppy, who is promptly sick as soon as it eats a solid meal, then eats it again with the same result, suspect one of the above conditions.

The oesophagus is a bag in front of the stomach, which because of lack of muscle, fails to push solid food into the stomach. The aortic arch is a foetal artery which should automatically close after birth. In some cases it fails to close, but presses on the oesophagus with the result described above. Pyloric stenosis has similar symptoms, but in this case the food is unable to pass from the stomach into the intestines. All of these conditions can only be correctly diagnosed by your vet after certain tests have been made. In all cases euthanasia is the only answer.

INTUSSUSCEPTION: This is a condition in which the bowel telescopes in upon itself. It can occur after an attack of gastroenteritis if there has been excessive sickness and diarrhoea. Unless immediate veterinary attention is sought, which means an operation, the puppy's condition will deteriorate rapidly. The operation is not always successful, and it can occur again.

HERNIA: If your bitch is over-enthusiastic in severing the cord, a lump will sometimes remain which is part of the intestine. Keep an eye on it and if the lump gets larger, take the puppy to the vet, who will push the intestine back and insert a stitch to stop it coming out again. An umbilical hernia can be hereditary.

FIRST-AID SUPPLIES
Adhesive tape
Antihistamine tablets
Aspirin
Different bandages, including a pressure pad
Calamine lotion
Cotton-wool
Cough mixture
Curved scissors
Disinfectant
Eye Ointment (obtained from your vet)
Ear Ointment (obtained from your vet)
Gauze
Honey
Nail-clippers
Liquid paraffin
Soda (washing)
Thermometer
Tweezers
Vaseline
Worm tablets (roundworm, tapeworm, or whatever applies in your country)
Anti-parasite spray
Antiseptic dusting powder
Shampoo or dip (whatever applies in your country)

If your vet knows you are reliable, he may supply a stock of antibiotics, which can be given as soon as you see any signs of bad diarrhoea in your dog. If you are isolated, or living in a hot climate, it is important to discover which remedies you are most likely to need, and get a stock in accordingly.

GENERAL FIRST AID

CUTS: Examine a cut carefully and clean with disinfectant. If the wound is deep or jagged, take your Shepherd to the vet and have it stitched. If there is excessive bleeding, apply a pressure-pad and keep it on for some time after all bleeding has ceased. If it is taken off too soon, the bleeding could start again. If an artery has been severed, the blood will be bright-red and pumping. Apply a tourniquet between the wound and the heart, and get to the vet as soon as possible. Never leave a tourniquet on for longer than twenty minutes. Release for a few minutes to allow blood to get to the limb, then apply again. For small cuts, dust with antiseptic powder.

STINGS: If your dog has been stung by a wasp, bee or anything else, give antihistamine tablets and try to remove the sting. If it is in a tender place, such as the eye, and there is undue swelling, take your dog to the vet.

POISON: The most common posions are Warfarin and slug bait. If you suspect your dog of eating poison, shove a lump of washing soda down the throat to induce sickness. Take the dog to the vet immediately, and if possible give details as to what poison your dog has eaten.

LAMENESS AND BROKEN BONES: If you suspect your Shepherd of having broken a bone it needs immediate veterinary attention.
    Lameness can be caused by a variety of different things, including strained muscles or tendons. Try and rest the dog as much as possible (easier said than done with a Shepherd), and see whether there is any improvement. If, however, there appears to be no improvement after a few days, a visit to the vet is the best answer. If a limb or any part of the body is swollen, apply hot and cold poultices one after the other. We have found a course of Vitamin C tablets has been most beneficial in the case of strained muscles and tendons.

CONSTIPATION: If your Shepherd has failed to pass a motion for two or three days, a dessertspoon of liquid paraffin should do the trick. But if the condition persists, and the dog keeps on straining without passing anything, it possibly has a blockage. Seek your vet's advice.

CONVALESCENCE: This is a most important part of getting your Shepherd fit again, and must be taken very slowly and carefully. When starvation has been necessary, give only boiled water or a saline solution (obtainable from your vet) to start with. A teaspoonful of honey can be added. Start solid food very gradually with natural yoghurt, followed by scrambled eggs, fish and chicken. Take great care to remove all bones. Feed small meals at regular intervals, taking care not to overload the stomach. Use brown, boiled rice when starting on cereals.
    Watch your dog's motions carefully. Any sign of looseness means that you are progressing too fast in getting your dog back to a normal diet. Never mind how thin your Shepherd gets; as soon as recovery is underway the weight will return to normal. Just because your Shepherd appears to want more food, do not give in. If too much food is given at any one time, you could be back to square one. As long as the dog is gaining strength and the motions are normal, you can gradually increase the quantities you are giving.
    Check your dog's temperature every day. Make certain your Shepherd is kept warm and quiet. In all cases, give lots of comfort and assurance. If the problem has been a broken limb, your vet will advise you on how much and what kind of exercise your Shepherd should be getting.

HOMEOPATHY: Many breeders and dog owners think very highly of this form of treatment. Certain vets practise homeopathy with remarkable success. We have tried some of their remedies with a certain amount of success, but we are by no means experts on homeopathic practice, so we feel we are not in a position to give any conclusive comment.
    Dog owners and breeders must make up their own minds, and before either condemning or endorsing homeopathy, study the whole practice carefully and draw your own conclusions.

HERBALISTS: We feel that some herbs can definitely be beneficial. Garlic is one which we have found most helpful in dealing with certain skin complaints. Several UK firms supply herbs, and if you contact them, they will supply you with a booklet giving all the information you need.

CHAMPION LAIOS VAN NOORT Sch H3 FH
TOP MALE GSD U.K. 1992

CHAMPION QUANT VOM KIRSCHENTAL Sch H3 FH
TOP MALE GSD U.K. 1993
ARDENBURG GERMAN SHEPHERD DOGS
WENDY & GRAHAM STEPHENS
ARDEN GRANGE, LONDON ROAD, ALBOURNE, WEST SUSSEX BN6 9BJ.
TEL: 0273 832416   FAX: 0273 833612

THE GERMAN SHEPHERD DOG BREEDERS' DIRECTORY

NORTH WEST: *Lancsman*. Mr and Mrs B.E. & S. Mason. 54 Higher Meadow,
Clayton-le-Woods, Leyland, Lancs. PR5 2RT.
Tel: 0772-454947. Puppies occasionally for sale.

WEST MIDLANDS: *Nikonis*. Nikki Farley. Meadow Cottage Kennels, Middle Bickenhill Lane, Solihull, West Midlands B92 0HJ.
Tel: 0675-443133. Dogs at stud, Puppies occasionally for sale. Boarding facilities available.
Pinedo & Lornstone. Mrs A.E. Roxburgh & Mr L.V. Yates. 30 Ellerslie Road, Billesley, Birmingham B13 0DP.
Tel: 021-604-5695. Dogs at stud. Puppies occasionally for sale.

SOUTH WEST: *Sacuer*. Mrs S. Douglas, The Old School House, West Kwoyle, Warminster, Wilts. BA12 6AE.
Tel: 0747-830752. Puppies occasionally for sale.

EAST ANGLIA: *Doltara*. Barry & Marilyn Pritchard, Blue Tile Cottage, Besthorpe Carr, Attleborough, Norfolk NR17 2LR.
Tel 0953-788523. Dogs at stud. Puppies occasionally for sale.

LONDON & HOME COUNTIES: *Quaesita*. Mrs Jean H. Green, Hazelgrove, Epsom Road, West Horsley, Leatherhead, Surrey KT24 6AP.
Tel: 0483-284467. Dogs at stud. Puppies occasionally for sale. Dog training classes.